JK585 .K45 2010
The road to war :Congress'
historic abdication of responsibility /
33663004778342

DISCARD

D0612851

DATE DUE

APR 2 1 2016	

BRODART, CO.   Cat. No. 23-221

The Road to War

The Road to War

*Congress' Historic Abdication
of Responsibility*

ROBERT KENNEDY

PRAEGER SECURITY INTERNATIONAL

 PRAEGER

AN IMPRINT OF ABC-CLIO, LLC
Santa Barbara, California • Denver, Colorado • Oxford, England

Copyright 2010 by Robert Kennedy

All rights reserved. No part of this publication may be reproduced, stored in a retrieval system, or transmitted, in any form or by any means, electronic, mechanical, photocopying, recording, or otherwise, except for the inclusion of brief quotations in a review, without prior permission in writing from the publisher.

Library of Congress Cataloging-in-Publication Data

Kennedy, Robert, 1939–
    The road to war : Congress' historic abdication of responsibility / Robert Kennedy.
        p.   cm.
    Includes bibliographical references and index.
    ISBN 978-0-313-37235-3 (hard copy : alk. paper) —
ISBN 978-0-313-37236-0 (ebook)   1. Executive power—United States.
2. United States. Congress—Powers and duties.   3. Legislative power—United States.   4. Separation of powers—United States.   5. War and emergency powers—United States.   6. United States—Politics and government.   7. United States—Foreign relations—Law and legislation.
I. Title.
    JK585.K45   2010
    327.73'0746—dc22   2009050882

ISBN: 978-0-313-37235-3
EISBN: 978-0-313-37236-0

14   13   12   11   10   1   2   3   4   5

This book is also available on the World Wide Web as an eBook.
Visit www.abc-clio.com for details.

Praeger
An Imprint of ABC-CLIO, LLC

ABC-CLIO, LLC
130 Cremona Drive, P.O. Box 1911
Santa Barbara, California 93116-1911

This book is printed on acid-free paper ∞
Manufactured in the United States of America

ACC LIBRARY SERVICES AUSTIN, TX

To

Vevonna

Contents

Preface

When the delegates met in Philadelphia in 1787 to amend the Articles of Confederation, they were deeply concerned about the state of the new American union. The ideals proclaimed as the American colonies broke from England were in jeopardy. The articles that had served as the nation's constitution had yielded a government that was largely inadequate to the task of effective governance of the new nation. Congress had little power. There was no executive. Taxes could not be regularly collected. Debts could not be paid. Trade was at the mercy of the whims of the states. A rebellion had already occurred. Indeed, many in England believed that the Americans would soon come crawling back to join the Kingdom of Great Britain, and leading figures in America were growing increasingly concerned that the grand experiment in republican governance upon which the 13 colonies embarked in 1776 was near failure.

Yet convinced of the merits of a republican form of government that tightly constrains the powers of the head of state and imbued with the republican philosophy that the conjoined wisdom of many is superior to that of one or a few, those who met from May to September in Philadelphia were determined to continue on the path that had been set when the United States declared its independence from Britain. Though they had assembled in order to amend the Articles of Confederation, they soon realized the need to craft a new document that would strengthen the national government while preserving the new Union.

The articles had divided power between a national government embodied in a Congress and the 13 individual states. That arrangement was on the brink of failure. The national government would need to be strengthened if the Union was to prosper. As the convention got under way, thoughts immediately focused on the nature of the national government. Well versed in ancient history and the factors that led to the failures of Greek democracy and the Roman republic, equally aware of the triumphs and failures of Englishmen in their efforts to limit the power of kings, and apprehensive of the potential for an insidious slide toward tyranny should powers granted the executive so avail themselves, the delegates quickly focused their attention on creating a mixed government. Power was to be divided among three branches—Congress, an executive, and a judiciary, each possessing its own powers and prerogatives. However, each also was to possess powers that would hold in check the powers of the other two branches. In such a manner no one branch or combination of branches could exercise a tyranny over the nation.

The most important question to be resolved therefore was how much power would be granted to the executive branch. History had instructed that tyranny was most often born of an excess of power vested in the hands of a single ruler or in the hands of a few.

On this issue even those who favored a strong national government were largely united. Fear of despotism was high on the list of concerns of the framers in any new government that would include an executive. Thus they sought to create an executive whose powers were to be adequate to the task of carrying into execution mandates of the people's representatives brought together in a national Congress, but not so great as to permit a usurpation of the reins of state.

Thus as delegates embarked on discussions on the creation of a national executive magistrate, the focus would be not on how expansive the powers of that office should be, but rather on how any powers granted should be constrained. This was evidenced at every step as delegates focused on the nature and duties of the executive, whether on deliberations on the manner of selecting America's chief executive, or on the question of whether the nation's chief magistrate should be embodied in a single individual or in several, or on the very nature of the specific powers to be granted to the office. Perhaps among the delegates' greater concerns was the danger of too great a concentration of power in the hands of any potential American chief executive in the management of foreign relations and the power to go to war.

Delegates to the Philadelphia convention were well aware that foreign relations are the element most susceptible to abuse if in the sole hands of an executive, whether monarch or president. They also were aware that by virtue of their interaction with foreign nations, monarchs were in control of information related to the interplay of events among nations. By shaping and selectively releasing such information, whether for reasons of military glory, revenge, or ambition or the result of secret agreements with foreign powers, or to focus attention away from domestic concerns, monarchs often were able to engage in foreign wars that were not sanctified by justice and that frequently impoverished their peoples. Even Alexander Hamilton, perhaps the most vigorous proponent of a strong national government, warned of the dangers of committing intercourse with the rest of the world to the sole disposal of a president.

Thus in foreign affairs and on issues of war and peace, power was to be shared between Congress and the executive. Power was to check power. Ambition was to check ambition. The president could receive ambassadors and ministers of other nations but could appoint American ambassadors and other senior government officials and make treaties with other nations only with the advice and consent of the Senate. The president was to serve as commander in chief of the armed forces, but such forces were to be few in number, raised and supported only at the behest of Congress. And only Congress could call state militias to federal service and declare wars.

Such was the arrangement that served our nation well for the first one hundred years of its existence. Relations between Congress and the executive branch were characterized by comity, each branch respecting the prerogatives of the other and each carefully guarding those powers and prerogatives granted to it by the Constitution. There were, of course, exceptions to this general pattern of behavior and some were notable. But they were indeed exceptions, not the general rule, and often understood to be exceptions to be carefully circumscribed.

Over the past hundred-plus years this system of shared powers, of checks on the powers of America's chief executive, has eroded, particularly in foreign relations, at first slowly and later massively. Today presidents act as if the sole authority granted to the representatives of the people is to accede to their wishes, supporting and funding whatever foreign endeavors in which they choose to engage. Largely in control of information and intelligence and powerful within their own parties in a system of party politics, they use that control and power to manage the views of Congress and the public, defining events, identifying crises, and mobilizing the nation's resources according to their preferred views and outcomes. In the movement of U.S. military forces into harm's way and indeed in engaging those forces in combat, they largely ignore Congress, claiming an inherent right to deploy forces anywhere in the world and to initiate hostilities according to their preferred game plan.

It would be unfair to lay the blame entirely at the feet of America's presidents. Presidents have done just what the framers of the Constitution had expected. They have sought to maximize their power in order to accomplish what they more often than not honestly viewed to be in the interest of the nation. The Courts have on occasion assisted the aggrandizement of presidential power. However, the lion's share of the blame rests with Congress.

This book is about how over time Congress has grown comfortable in its acquiescence to presidential assertions of power and has come to abdicate its constitutional responsibilities in the arena of foreign affairs and war.

Introduction

I recognize my own personal biases in favor of republican forms of government: where diverse views are afforded a hearing at the highest levels, where the views of many are preferred to the views of one, and where the conjoined deliberative processes involving the people's representatives, while not yielding what in the eyes of one or a few is the perfect solution, by virtue of a full exploration of alternatives is likely to result in better decisions, not only for the legitimacy they bestow, but also for the power of the cognitive processes engaged.

I also recognize the hazards in any research of this kind that attempts to ascertain the mindset of those who embarked on efforts to improve on the Union that had been created by the Articles of Confederation. It is simply not possible at this time to fully comprehend the nature of the situation the nation was confronting as those who gathered to amend the articles understood it. Nor is it possible to fully understand the concerns, objectives, politics, or interpersonal and group dynamics that resulted in comments made or not made by those who crafted the Constitution, as well as by those in the various states who had been called upon to ratify the document that emerged after nearly three months of deliberations in Philadelphia that fateful summer of 1787. Written records too often are as notorious for what they reveal as for what they fail to reveal. Among the questions often raised are these: How accurately were words spoken captured by those who chronicled events? How frequently was the record of events tainted with their own biases? What did they fail to record and why? How did informal deliberations among the framers of the Constitution affect what was said at formal meetings? Did silence on the part of delegates signal agreement or disagreement with comments made by others?

Perhaps equally important, the document that issued from deliberations in Philadelphia in 1787 was a product of a different historical space and time. Times have changed. The usage and meaning of words have changed. The situation confronting the delegates is not analogous to that of today.

On the other hand, though difficult, it is not impossible to capture the general sentiment, the broad outlines of concerns and objectives of those who met in Philadelphia and at the various state ratifying conventions. So while I am aware of the dangers lurking in the waters I have chosen to tread, I also believe that on issues of war and peace, the intent of the framers and those involved in the ratifying process come through so clearly that few historians will find reason to disagree.

The larger question is how well the branches of government have functioned to preserve the system of checks and balances of power designed by the Founding Fathers to preclude the exercise of arbitrary power by any one branch.

The first chapter examines the intellectual origins of the Constitution. The story of the drafting of the American Constitution does not simply begin with the debates of those who gathered in the heat of Philadelphia from mid-May through mid-September 1787. Rather it has its roots in the history of human political and social organization. Many of those who gathered to amend the Articles of Confederation were well aware of the thoughts of ancient writers on politics such as Plato, Socrates, Polybius, and Cicero. They also were products of the Enlightenment, whose many writers often explored and expanded on ideas presented by those who had gone before them. Perhaps equally important, they were aware of the evolution of government in England from its early Anglo-Saxon roots, as well as the dangers that had confronted and undermined earlier attempts at republican forms of government.

Chapter 2 traces the concerns that grew from the failures of the Articles of Confederation and the transformation of those concerns into an entirely new document. The chapter outlines the factors that led to an extension of the powers of the federal government, as well as the factors that led to a system that incorporated both the concept of a separation of powers and that of checks and balances. This chapter is not intended to be a comprehensive examination of either all the commentary, points, and counterpoints that impacted the thinking of those who wrote the Constitution or the subsequent debates that took place during the ratification process. Rather, the chapter focuses on what by my examination are the central issues of concern of those who wrote and ratified the American Constitution on issues affecting foreign relations, treaty making, and war and peace. This effort by its very nature is necessarily as limited as the literature is vast. As Bernard Bailyn has noted, "No one has mastered all the useful writings on the Constitution; and no one ever will. There is too much; there is movement in too many directions at once; too many disparate issues are alive and flourishing independently of each other."

The last four chapters trace the evolution of the struggle between Congress and the executive branch over access to information, as well as the relationship between the two branches of government in the development of foreign policy, including issues of war and peace. They also examine the role the Courts have played in defining those relationships.

Chapter 3 examines the first one hundred years of the Republic, concluding that, with few exceptions, comity characterized relations between Congress and the executive branch, with each branch generally respecting the constitutional prerogatives of the other.

Chapter 4 notes that as the 19th century was drawing to a close, global imperial competition conspired with events in the Western hemisphere to propel the United Sates onto the world scene. As a result, in the late 19th and early 20th centuries global issues began to cast the presidency into the foreground. Presidents were increasingly willing to take a more strident approach in addressing events that threatened U.S. interests at home and abroad. The Courts began to take a more expansive view of presidential powers, and Congress increasingly acquiesced to presidential encroachments on its prerogatives.

Chapter 5 examines the sharp rise in presidential power with the advent of the nuclear age, the onset of the Cold War, and the potentially deadly competition between the United States and the Soviet Union that ensued. It also addresses the role the Courts have played in the growth of and limits on presidential power. The chapter also examines initial acquiescence by Congress to the usurpation of its powers by the president and then the resurgence of congressional power in the wake of discoveries of executive branch abuses resulting from an overextension of executive prerogatives.

The final chapter traces the reemergence of nearly unconstrained presidential powers in the field of foreign policy and war making in the post–Cold War period and the continued acquiescence of Congress.

The author would like to thank all of those who have gone before him and paved the way for this effort. At the risk of offending those not mentioned, the author still feels it necessary to mention those whom he relied on most heavily. So a note of appreciation is in order for contributions to my thinking made by David Gray Adler, Christopher Andrew, Bernard Bailyn, Raul Berger, Edward S. Corwin, Louise Fisher, Larry N. George, Gene Healy, Mark J. Rozell, Andrew Rudalevige, Arthur Schlesinger, Jr., Frank J. Smist, Jr., Britt Snider, Abraham D. Sofaer, and Gordon S. Wood, as well as for the enormous work that went into compiling the *Records of the Federal Constitution* by Max Farrand.

A few additional comments are in order. The book does not deal with the broader aspects of the power relationships among the three branches of government. Nor does it systematically address all aspects of presidential power. Its focus is principally on the relations as they have developed between the legislative and executive branches in the field of foreign relations and war making and information sharing attendant to decisions on such issues.

CHAPTER 1

Intellectual Origins of the American Constitution

As delegates were convening in the State House in Philadelphia in mid-to late May 1787, they were painfully aware that the future of the United States and indeed the grand American experiment with a republican government were at stake. The 13 colonies had risen in revolution against England and defeated a superpower. However, even before the end of the war, the former British colonies in America had begun to show strains. Under the Articles of Confederation and Perpetual Union, they had forged a nation managed by a central government whose principal legislative and executive arm was a congress formed of representatives from the 13 states. Though the articles had granted to this national congress extensive powers, the powers granted were primarily limited by an inability of Congress to enforce its decisions. By the end of the war in 1783, the danger signs of disintegration had begun to emerge.

Gathered in Philadelphia with their thoughts focused on the task of forging a more perfect union, delegates to the convention were influenced by a variety of factors. But above all, these were practical men. They were keenly aware of the failings of the Articles of Confederation and understood the strengths and limitations of the governments in the various states from which they came. Thirty-nine had served in the federal Congress at one time or another. Eight had worked in state constitutional conventions, while seven had served as governors.[1]

These also were learned men. A third of them had attended Harvard, Yale, or the College of New Jersey (Princeton). Others had attended colleges in England, Scotland, and the Netherlands or noteworthy institutions in the colonies. Even the youngest delegate, 26-year-old Jonathan Dayton of New Jersey, was a Princeton graduate at the age of 16. They were all products of the Enlightenment. They were men of reason. Furthermore, many of them were well acquainted with the ideas of governance that developed among the Greeks and Romans,[2] reflected in the writings of men like Polybius and Cicero and refined and often redefined during the Enlightenment by the likes of Thomas Hobbes, John Locke, Jean-Jacques Rousseau, and particularly Charles-Louis de Secondat, baron de La Brède et de Montesquieu. Perhaps more importantly, they were aware of the strengths and weaknesses of political organization as it had developed in England since the Angles arrived in the fifth century.

FAILINGS OF THE ARTICLES OF CONFEDERATION

Delegates to the Philadelphia convention were particularly concerned about the failings of the Articles of Confederation. The articles, completed in the summer of 1777 and adopted by the Second Continental Congress in November of that same year, had served as the nation's de facto constitution prior to their ratification in 1781. However, as time progressed, it became increasingly evident that the articles were inadequate to the task of governance of the new union of states. Unable to garner sufficient funds from the states to pay its debts, Congress was so poor that it was unable to afford the cost of printing its own proceedings.[3] Bereft of the power to tax the states directly, lacking the national wherewithal to manage its trade or provide for the collective defense of the nation, powerless to enforce its decisions on the states, and reeling from the pall of Shays's rebellion (see "Shays's Rebellion"), the newly formed United States was teetering on the

SHAYS'S REBELLION

In August 1786 farmers in central and western Massachusetts discarded their plowshares and took to their muskets in armed insurrection. The group included veterans of the Continental Army who had fought for their country, risked their lives, and lost their limbs, often for little or no pay, only to return home to see their livestock and property confiscated and many of their fellow farmers imprisoned. Unable to pay their debts, with no prospect of receiving back pay owed to them by the national government, they united under Daniel Shays, a former captain in the American revolutionary army. They demanded protective legislation and a reduction in taxes. They also forcibly acted to prevent courts from sitting and acting on judgments to enforce debt collection sought by wealthy businessmen to whom their debts were owed. Though the rebellion was put down in February 1787, it struck fear into the heart of many, underscored weaknesses of the Confederation, and tipped the scales in favor of those who sought a stronger central government.

brink of failure. One Briton was reported to have remarked: "What can the Americans do? They have neither government nor power."[4] As concerns grew, so grew an awareness that something indeed had to be done.[5]

George Washington, retired since resigning his commission following the end of the revolution, was well aware of the defects in the federal system created under the articles. Responding in August 1786 to a letter from John Jay, Washington, reflecting his concerns over the future of the Union, wrote:

We have errors to correct. ...I do not conceive we can long exist as a nation, without having lodged somewhere power which will pervade the whole Union in an energetic manner.

Washington also expressed his concern over the national government's inability to garner funds from the states to pay national debts or meet treaty obligations:

...requisitions are a perfect nihility, where thirteen sovereign, independent disunited States are in the habit of discussing & refusing compliance with them at their option. ...If you tell the Legislatures they have violated the treaty of peace and invaded prerogatives of the confederacy they will laugh in your face.

Concerned that the failures of the articles might lead to "disasterous [sic] contingencies," including a return to a monarchial form of government, he wrote to Jay: "What a triumph for advocates of despotism to find that we are incapable of governing ourselves. ..."[6]

In September 1786, at the Annapolis Convention called to address defects in the federal government that resulted in limitations to trade and commerce, Alexander Hamilton of New York introduced a resolution calling for the convening of a special convention to meet in Philadelphia in May 1787 to amend the Articles of Confederation in order to correct a number of serious defects. Keenly aware of the seriousness of the situation, delegates unanimously approved the resolution. Though only 12 delegates from five states attended the Annapolis convention, Hamilton's resolution captured a surging interest in amending the articles to meet the exigencies confronting the young nation.[7]

In April 1787 James Madison outlined 12 "Vices of the Political System of the United States," which pointedly suggested a nation in disarray. Among other things, Madison noted that states had regularly failed to comply with the requisitions [of men and money] of the Union; encroached on federal authority (e.g., wars and treaties of Georgia with the Indians and congressionally unapproved compacts between states); trespassed on each others' rights; failed to act in concert where required in matters of common interest; often ignored acts of Congress; and violated the laws of nations and treaties, including violations of the peace treaty with England

and the treaties with France and Holland.[8] The following month, Secretary of War Henry Knox wrote to New Hampshire president (governor) General John Sullivan, urging him to send delegates to the Philadelphia convention, stressing the urgency of the situation by emphasizing that he was "impressed most fully that we are verging fast to anarchy...."[9]

As delegates began assembling in Philadelphia in May 1787 the air was filled with anticipation. Though the convention opened on May 14, 1787, substantive issues were not considered until May 29, when Governor Edmund Randolph of Virginia addressed the convention, soundly condemning the Articles of Confederation. Sounding the alarm, Randolph said: "The confederation fulfilled *none* [italics in original] of the objects for which it was framed."[10] Randolph further observed that the U.S. federal system ought to secure the nation against foreign invasion and against dissentions between member states, or seditions in particular states. Among the criticisms leveled by Randolph, the federal government was able to provide for neither security against foreign invasion nor the ability to check quarrels between the states or rebellions within a state. It could not raise an army since it was without money. It was not superior to state constitutions and thus unable to defend itself against encroachments from the states and equally incapable of punishing states for transgressing laws of nations or for violating treaties.[11] Hamilton also signaled serious concerns about the future of the United States. Madison wrote in his notes on the convention that Hamilton "sees the Union dissolving or already dissolved—he sees evils operating in the States which must soon cure the people of their fondness for democracies."[12]

To remedy the situation, Randolph proposed a series of resolutions that became known as the Virginia Plan.[13] Among the principal features of the plan, there was to be a national legislature composed of two houses, and a national executive and national judiciary both chosen by the national legislature. As delegates deliberated over the next several months on the nature of those institutions and the powers they were to possess, their discussions were further influenced by English constitutional traditions of government and their experiences in the colonies, as well as by a new wave of thinking that had been developing in Europe since around the middle of the previous century, with roots in classical antiquity. As one historian put it: "It seemed indeed to be a peculiar moment in history when all knowledge coincided, when classical antiquity, Christian theology, English empiricism, and European rationalism could all be linked."[14]

ENGLISH CONSTITUTIONAL TRADITIONS

Among the more notable of the English constitutional traditions that informed the Founding Fathers of the American Republic and the framers of the American Constitution were the Magna Carta, the Petition of Right, the Habeas Corpus Act, the English Bill of Rights, and the Act of

Settlement. The U.S. national as well as state constitutions reflect many of the ideas set forth in these documents, and some even have phrases that are directly traceable to one or more of them.

Magna Carta

The Magna Carta, or "Great Paper," sometimes referred to as the Magna Carta Libertatum (Great Charter of Freedoms) or the Great Charter of the Liberties of England, was forced, under threat of civil warfare, on King John in 1215 by his barons. Though earlier English kings had granted concessions to barons, the Magna Carta was the first time the king was forced to sign a document that limited his powers and, at least in theory, bound the king and his heirs in perpetuity to protect the rights of Englishmen as specified in the charter. The Magna Carta was renounced by the king upon the departure of the barons from London and condemned by Pope Innocent III as "not only shameful and demeaning but also illegal and unjust, thereby lessening unduly and impairing his [the king's] royal rights and dignity."[15] Nevertheless, after Henry III, John's nine-year-old son was crowned king following John's death in October of the following year, leading nobles and clergymen ruling on Henry's behalf reissued an amended charter in the king's name later that year and again in 1217. Henry III upon reaching majority reissued a shortened version in 1225. Edward I, Henry's successor, reconfirmed the charter in its amended form in the Confirmatio Cartarum of 1297. Though modified somewhat to the king's favor, the charter established a benchmark for the limitations on the power of the king and became the symbol of resistance to tyrannical rule.

Petition of Right

The 1628 Petition of Right was an early 17th-century manifestation of a continuing struggle between the Parliament and the king over the powers of Parliament and the rights of Englishmen. From the time of Edward I, who ruled England from 1272 to 1307 through the 16th century, the powers of Parliament grew. Kings who wished to increase taxes or undertake major reforms often had to convene Parliament to obtain its concurrence.

But in 1625, following the death of his father, James I, Charles I inherited the throne. Seeking funds for war with Spain, he convened Parliament. Parliament, suspicious of the king's religious and foreign policy and reluctant to provide the monarch with authority to collect more taxes unless it was given a hand in supervising expenditures, only partially funded the conflict and placed a limit on his ability to collect taxes on wine and imports.[16] Charles promptly dissolved Parliament on August 12. He disregarded limits placed on his authority to collect taxes on wine, sought to raise money on the crown jewels, and attempted to diminish opposition in Parliament by appointing them sheriffs—since as officers of the crown they would be ineligible for membership in Parliament. Moreover, hoping that his success in the war with Spain would persuade Parliament to be more generous, he sent a military expedition against Cadiz. The expedition was an utter failure.

Determined to continue the war with Spain and also engage in war with Catholic France, which was suppressing the Huguenots (see "The Huguenots"), and in urgent need of funds to reequip the British Fleet and rearm his ground forces, Charles reluctantly reconvened Parliament in February 1626. Parliament balked once again and Charles once again dissolved Parliament. Still in need of money, Charles continued to collect taxes without parliamentary authority by cajoling or forcing subjects to provide him money, imprisoned people without charging them with a crime, and resorted to the quartering of troops in civilian homes in areas of the country where his opponents were predominant.

By the summer of 1627, Charles had engaged the French in a conflict. After a disastrous defeat, Charles, seeking additional funds to continue the war effort, again summoned Parliament in the spring of 1628. Members of Parliament, angered by the king's usurpation of power, soon dropped consideration of the king's request and set forth its grievances in a Petition of Right.

In the petition, the Parliament set out specific liberties of Englishmen upon which neither the king nor his commissioners should infringe. The petition mentioned such rights as the right not to be coerced to give money to the king or be imprisoned, confined, or otherwise molested for failing

THE HUGUENOTS

The Huguenots were French Calvinists, who had often been persecuted by Catholics in France. Most famous of these persecutions became known as the Saint Bartholomew's Day Massacre, which took place the night of August 23, 1572, as Catholics killed thousands of Huguenots in Paris. Many others were killed in other French towns in the days that followed. Conflict between Catholics and Huguenots abated following the 1598 Edict of Nantes signed by King Henry IV, which established Catholicism as the state religion but granted the Protestants a degree of political and religious freedom to practice their religion in 20 French cities. However, the Edict of Nantes was increasingly ignored under the reign of Louis XIII (1610–1643) and his chief minister, Cardinal Richelieu. One by one the free cities fell to the forces of the Cardinal, with the last and most important stronghold, La Rochelle, taken in 1629.

See "Who Were the Huguenots?", http://webspace.webring.com/people/ph/huguenot/hist-hug.htm

to do so; the right of an Englishman to be protected from imprisonment or seizures of property "but by lawful judgment of his peers, or by the law of the land"; freedom from imprisonment without showing cause; no quartering of soldiers against the will of the people whose homes are involved; and no one put to death, except under the statutes and laws established in this realm, either by the customs of the realm or by acts of Parliament.

Habeas Corpus Act

The Habeas Corpus Act passed by the English Parliament later in the same century codified and strengthened the right of a person being held as a prisoner to be brought before a court to determine whether he had been imprisoned lawfully and, if not, the right to be released from custody. The 1679 act capped a four-centuries-old tradition established during the reign of King Henry II in the 12th century. The right was executed by a *writ* issued with the force of a court demanding a prisoner be brought before the court. In the years following the 1200s, the king's commissioners frequently had violated this right. The commissioners of King Charles II (who ruled England from 1661 until his death in 1685) were no more respectful of those rights than others in the past. They often greatly delayed responding or found ways to avoid responding to writs of habeas corpus altogether. Now it would be law, not simply one of the many articles that represented the constitutional tradition. Hence the king's commissions could no longer easily ignore it. British jurist Albert Venn Dicey (1835–1922) wrote that the Habeas Corpus Acts "are for practical purposes worth a hundred constitutional articles guaranteeing individual liberty."[17]

Bill of Rights

The English Bill of Rights, or An Act Declaring the Rights and Liberties of the Subject and Settling the Succession of the Crown, often has been seen as the predecessor not only to the American Bill of Rights, but also to such documents as the United Nations Universal Declaration of Human Rights and the European Convention on Human Rights. The Parliament of England passed the Bill of Rights in 1689. The act, following the revolution in which King James II was dethroned (1688), culminated a century-long struggle between the Stuart kings and the Parliament of England. It delineated acts of King James II that were "utterly and directly contrary to the known laws and statutes, and freedom." The act, which William III and Mary II (daughter of James II) accepted upon taking the throne, confirmed the traditional rights and liberties of Englishmen, asserting that those rights were "true, ancient, and indubitable." Included among those rights and liberties were freedom of speech in Parliament, freedom to elect members of Parliament without royal interference, and freedom for Protestants to bear arms for their defense, as well as freedoms from royal interference with the law, from taxation except by agreement with the Parliament, and from a standing army during peacetime. The Bill of Rights became one of the fundamental features of British constitutionalism and had a great influence on the Founding Fathers of the American Constitution.

Act of Settlement

The Act of Settlement of 1701 was an act of the Parliament of England to settle the questions of succession to the English throne. However, the law also included several provisions, which further enhanced the role of the English Parliament. In this regard, the act underscored the supremacy of the laws of England and the requirement of all succeeding "Kings and Queens" and "all their officers and ministers...to administer the government...according to said laws." It effected the separation of the judiciary from the direct control of the monarch by making the removal of judges conditioned on "the address of both Houses of Parliament." The act also established, under certain circumstances, that a decision to go to war would require Parliament's consent.

That in case the Crown and imperial dignity of this Realm shall hereafter come to any person, not being a native of this Kingdom of England, this nation be not obliged to engage in any war for the defence [sic] of any dominions or territories which do not belong to the Crown of England, without the consent of Parliament.

Thus by the early 18th century, most Englishmen in Britain and in the colonies were well acquainted with concepts derived from the English constitutional tradition. Those concepts included the notion that there are limits to a monarch's powers. Neither kings and queens nor their officers and ministers could act in a tyrannical manner. The people had certain immutable civil and political rights that were "ancient and indubitable." The Parliament was the supreme law-making body, and monarchs and their commissioners had a responsibility to administer government according to the laws. And, under some circumstances, the decision to go to war required the consent of Parliament.

THE COLONIAL EXPERIENCE

In spite of their knowledge of the evolution of English governance and the struggles and the traditions that emerged, circumstances differed in America. Hence ideas of governance in colonial America sprouted in directions often different from those in England, reflecting political, economic, and social conditions that frequently diverged from, were somewhat more chaotic than, and sometimes stood in sharp contrast to those of the mother country. Among the more significant were differences in approach to ideas about the rights of individuals and the very nature of sovereignty of the state and of parliamentary representation.[18]

Rights of Individuals

The belief that there exists a "natural law" derived "from some objective and external reality, not subject to the arbitrary will of the ruler or the people" and that is universally applicable in human affairs and superior to human-made or customary law has had a long history dating back to classical antiquity. Indeed, Cicero's success in arguing before a Roman court that one of Rome's laws was unlawful since it was contrary to natural law, "created a legal precedent that endured throughout the western world for two millennia."[19] Thus, "natural law," and the natural rights of individuals so derived from that law, came to be seen as the best defense against tyranny. Indeed, as discussed previously, this concept was well understood and accepted in England.

However, by the mid-18th century it was the Parliament in which unfettered power was increasingly seen to reside. Sir William Blackstone, jurist, legal scholar, and one of the most knowledgeable men on English common law, writing in the mid- to late 1760s, captured the sentiment of the time, contending that supreme and absolute power in England was vested by the constitution in the legislature. The underlying concept was simple and straightforward. Somewhere in the state there must be a supreme or absolute power, some authority beyond which there was no appeal. For Blackstone that authority was the English Parliament. Blackstone went on to define the constituent parts of Parliament as

the king's majesty, sitting in his royal political capacity, and the three estates of the realm; the lords spiritual, the lords temporal (who sit, together with the king, in one house) and the commons, who sit by themselves in another.[20]

For the colonial Americans, the problem with such an approach to governance was that if the government were supreme, what then would serve as a roadblock to tyranny? Of course, the colonials as well as the British in England knew that Parliament was restrained in its actions by a constitutional framework made up of a sum total of institutions, statutes, laws, court judgments, customs, and treaties knit together over time, which formed the underlying basis for the general system of English governance. This was the so-called constitution that guided Parliament and thus served as guardian of man's natural rights. However, there was no written constitution. Thus, if Parliament were supreme, as Blackstone and others had contended, then Parliament could change the constitution simply by passing new acts.

As political thinking further developed in the colonies on this subject, Americans not only began to view the constitution, not the Parliament, as the supreme and absolute authority, but also came to believe that there was a need for a written document that identified those natural rights that man enjoyed by virtue of being man. Typical of the transformation of thought that was occurring among American colonists, Reverend John Joachim Zubly, a revolutionary pamphleteer; Calvinist minister from Savannah, Georgia; and staunch supporter of the rights of American colonists,[21] declared in 1769 that the existing Parliament "derives its authority and power from the constitution, and not the constitution from Parliament."[22] By 1775, the constitution, it was argued,

...was "certain great first principles" on whose "certainty and permanency...the rights of both the ruler and the subject depend; *nor may they be altered or changed by the ruler or people, but [only] by the whole collective body...nor can they be touched by the legislator.*"[23] [emphasis added]

Thus the primary function of the constitution came to be seen as the instrument that delineated the boundaries of governmental power. However, since England had no written constitution, there was no firm guide, no undeniable permanently established set of great first principles upon which to judge actions of the government. From this the colonists concluded that if tyranny were to be prevented, if the rights of man were not to be trampled, there ought to be "some written charter" that "*guaranteed* not *granted*" all the great "inalienable, indefeasible rights inherent in all people by virtue of their humanity,"[24] in other words, their natural rights.

Concept of Sovereignty

As questions about protecting the inalienable rights of man arose, so did questions about wherein resides the sovereignty of the state. The concept of sovereignty as it evolved in England in the 17th and 18th centuries began to diverge from previously held concepts. In part derived from classical political theory, earlier concepts of sovereignty included the notion that in every political unit there must reside a single, "undivided, final power, higher in legal authority than any other power, subject to no law, a law unto itself." It also included the notion that such a supreme authority was still constrained by "important limitations derived from its legal, religious, and pre-national origins." Sovereignty did not signal arbitrary, unrestrained power. Action by the state still was to be guided by and "embody the law of nature and of God."[25] However, during and following the period of the English Civil War (1642–1651), fought between supporters of the Parliament and supporters of the king, Professor Bernard Bailyn notes:

In the desperate necessity to isolate a reliable source of order, the permeation of might with right ended; a generation of cold-eyed analysts stripped the idea of sovereignty of its moral and legalistic qualities and laid bare the doctrine of naked force.[26]

Immediately prior to the English Civil War, Charles I ruled England from 1625 until his execution in 1649. Often at odds with Parliament over a variety of issues and frequently frustrated in his efforts to get approval from a reluctant Parliament to collect taxes to support his war efforts, Charles dissolved Parliament for a fourth time in 1629, never to summon it again, and ruled by royal prerogative. Thus ensued what many English Whigs called the "Eleven Years Tyranny." However, as Professor Bailyn suggested, in these troubled times opinion was shifting. Rule by royal prerogative or personal rule of the king was increasingly accepted as a legitimate exercise of the absolute power of the king, particularly by those in favor of monarchial rule. Indeed, Church of England ministers Roger Maynwaring and Robert Sibthorpe were both asserting at the time a doctrine of divine right: "The King was God's representative, and that all his commands (except those directly contrary to the word of God) should be obeyed."[27] Philosophers like Thomas Hobbes, Robert Filmer, and others reinforced such ideas through their strong support of the doctrine of absolute power and their contention that limited monarchy meant anarchy.

Such ideas, however, did not go without challenge. While it might be conceded that for peace and tranquility absolute power resides somewhere in every political unit, the question remained open as to which individual or what body held such absolute power. Some feared the potential for despotism should such power reside in the king. Writing in 1642, the year the English Civil War began, Henry Parker, English barrister and political writer, suggested an alternative. He reasoned that from the argument that there must reside an absolute, arbitrary, unfettered power somewhere in every state, if such power fell to "one man or to a few there may be the danger in it, but the Parliament is neither one nor few" and is "equally and geometrically proportioned" in composition with all the estates contributing to its efforts. Hence, "no inconvenience" would result from placing such power in the hands of Parliament.[28] With these words Parker advanced "for the first time in English history a theory of Parliamentary sovereignty."[29]

This division between those who believed the Crown was the repository of absolute power and those who saw Parliament as that repository was one of the issues at the heart of the English Civil War, or, more correctly, English civil wars.[30]

By the time of the Restoration of the English monarchy, Henry Parker's view that absolute, arbitrary, unfettered power must exist somewhere in every state and that the safest place for that power was Parliament had flourished. Moreover, it continued to persist as the predominant view following the Glorious Revolution, or the Revolution of 1688, as it is sometimes called, that saw the removal of James II, the last Catholic monarch of England. Parliament was seen as sovereign, "a body absolute and arbitrary in its sovereignty; the creator and interpreter, not subject, of law; the superior and master of all other rights and powers within the state."[31]

This approach to sovereignty became the foundation of the English Parliament's claim of authority over the American colonies and was embodied in the Declaratory Act of 1766, which stated that "Parliament assembled, had, hath, and of right ought to have, full power and authority to make laws and statutes of sufficient force and validity to bind the colonies and people of *America,* subjects of the crown of *Great Britain,* in all cases whatsoever."[32]

However, the American colonial experience ran counter to the conception that absolute power resided in a single body. Though "presumably ruled by a single, absolute, undivided sovereign," the American colonies had come to enjoy an "extreme decentralization of authority within the empire." They maintained law and order. They set the rules of daily life, including rules concerning the production and distribution of wealth, personal conduct, and the worship of God. Local common law courts administered justice. Indeed, even the power to tax had been in the hands of colonial representative assemblies. Parliament, in fact, had never exercised total control. Sure the home country had collected fees, dues, and rents, usually "incidental to the regulation of overseas trade." Sure Parliament "made appointments to high office," "laid down rules and policies for colonial officials to follow," and exercised its authority over a wide variety of other aspects of colonial life. But generally Parliament acted in areas "beyond the competence" of local colonial authorities. This was far from the exercise of absolute power.[33]

So, while those who favored the unfettered power of Parliament continued to ridicule the concept of an *imperium in imperio* or two sovereign entities within the same state, Americans searched for a pragmatic and acceptable division of powers and responsibilities between the Parliament and local colonial agencies. First, colonists focused on the distinction between things internal and things external. Parliament would have exclusive jurisdiction over matters of a general nature that confronted the empire—such as commerce and foreign affairs. Colonial assemblies would exercise exclusive jurisdiction on issues specific to the colonies. Bernard Bailyn has noted:

Not only did it appear to separate out conveniently the powers that had been exercised for so long by the colonists' own Assemblies and those that had been exercised by Parliament, but it did so echoing the words of some of the most respected authorities on the question of government.[34]

Unfortunately, it became increasingly evident that no clear distinction could be made between internal and external. If Parliament couldn't levy internal taxes, could it then levy duties on products entering or leaving the colonies? Would this not have the same effect as an internal tax?[35]

John Dickinson in his 1768 *Letters from a Farmer in Pennsylvania* suggested another solution. He contended that the legislature of an empire was different from the legislature of a nation. Parliament's power over the American colonies extended only to that power necessary to maintain essential connections to the empire.[36] It was becoming an increasingly common belief, among those concerned about the power of the British Crown, that the British Parliament could not be supreme in every respect. Councilors of the two Houses of the Massachusetts Assembly replied to lieutenant governor and loyalist Thomas Hutchinson of Massachusetts assertions supporting the supreme authority of the British Parliament. They argued that there is no such thing as total absolute authority: "supreme or unlimited authority can with fitness belong only to the sovereign of the universe." Fearing the consequences of an uncontrolled supreme power, whether of a nation or a monarch, they suggested the need to separate the permissible from the forbidden powers of that body.[37]

Others, like Calvinist minister Moses Mather of Connecticut, suggested a concept of two separate realms of legislative power. Mather argued that this would mean total exclusion of British parliamentary power from the colonies, but not necessarily the total elimination of all ties with England, since both Parliament and the colonial assemblies would remain united under the same king.[38] By the mid-1770s, an earlier view, promoted by several, including James Wilson, American lawyer and scholar, a future member of the Continental Congress and a major force in the crafting of the American Constitution, was gaining support. That view held that the absolute sovereignty of the British Parliament did not extend to the colonies, but rather that it was constrained constitutionally by the powers reserved to the colonial assemblies in a kind of imperial federalism.[39]

However, it was Benjamin Franklin who had hit the nail on the head. While in England following the British Parliament's imposition of the Stamp Act of 1765, Franklin explained to his British colleagues that the colonists were not denying the right of Parliament to lay duties to regulate commerce. Rather, Franklin contended what they objected to as "unconstitutional and unjust" was Parliament's effort to "to lay internal taxes," for such a right "was never supposed to be in Parliament, as *we are not represented there*" [emphasis added].[40] It was this concept that sovereignty resided not in Parliament per se but ultimately in the people that coursed through American thought at the time.

But if the people were sovereign, by what mechanisms were they to express their sovereignty? How were their views to be heard in government?

Concepts of Representation

In medieval England, Parliament was a place where communities could seek redress from the royal court. Those elected to Parliament were local men with local ties to their communities, whose task it was to advance the interests of their communities. They were held strictly accountable to and closely controlled by their constituents, who often issued very specific instructions as to the powers their elected officials had and the limits of permissible concessions they could make. Thus representatives of the commons in the medieval Parliaments represented and spoke only for those who had elected them, not for the broader community.

But by the time institutions in the American colonies were developing, this practice was no longer the norm in England. As a result of changed circumstances, the electorate no longer strictly controlled those elected to Parliament. Members of Parliament no longer were there to merely represent the parochial interests of their constituents. Rather they now joined Parliament to advance the interests of all as well as their particular electorate. In the words of Edmund Burke:

[Parliament is not] a *congress* of ambassadors from different and hostile interests, which each must maintain, as an agent and advocate against other agents and advocates; but Parliament is a *deliberative* assembly of one nation, with one interest, that of the whole, where, not local purposes, not local prejudices ought guide, but the general good, resulting from the general reason of the whole.[41]

Circumstances, however, were different in the American colonies. Towns and counties were more like those of medieval England. They were largely autonomous, had "little reason to identify their interests with those of the central government" of the colony, and felt they had more to lose than to gain "from a loose acquiescence in the action of central government." Thus they "sought to keep the voices of local interests clear and distinct," and when believing it necessary, sought "to bind representatives to local interests."[42]

Such differences, of course, played out in the struggle between England and the colonies, especially in the arena of taxation. "No taxation without representation" was an old principle in English history. It meant that Parliament had to pass all taxes. Though the American colonies selected agents to speak for them in England, many of those selected felt equally or perhaps more a part of a constituency in England than they did a part of the colony from whence they were dispatched or represented. Thus the colonies came to believe, or at least argue, that they were not represented in the English Parliament and therefore laws taxing the colonists as well as other laws pertaining only to the American colonies were unconstitutional. To be so bound would be nothing less than oppression.

The English Parliament, for its part, believed that it represented the views of all Englishmen. Though in England only 3 percent of the men could vote, thus limiting representation in Parliament, it was argued that most people in England were "virtually" represented in Parliament. This concept of virtual representation was based on the belief that men without the vote were virtually represented in Parliament by those who had been elected by similar voters. Since there were some farmers, some merchants, and so forth who voted for members of Parliament, the theory went that therefore all farmers, all merchants, and so forth were virtually represented. Hence advocates of virtual representation in England argued that in the American colonies, men who owned property in North America voted for members of Parliament—some, indeed, sat in Parliament. Thus, these advocates held that as with Englishmen in England, the interests of the colonists were virtually represented in Parliament. Accordingly, laws made in England bound all Englishmen, whether in England or elsewhere. Hence, decisions involving issues internal to the colonies, including taxation, were a proper purview of the Parliament acting in the general interest of all.

This theory, attacked even by some in England, was totally rejected in the colonies as irreconcilable with their republican belief that government derives its just powers from the consent of the governed. For the colonies, the view emerged that the binding power of law flowed from the continuous assent to the law by the subjects through their representatives and that the only reason a free and independent man was bound by human laws was because he bound himself. Indeed, government had no separate existence apart from the people. It gained its authority and, ipso facto, its legitimacy from their continuous consent.[43] Reflecting this view, John Adams, though not yet believing in full independence from Britain, wrote in a letter to the *Massachusetts Gazette* in February 1775 under the nom de plume "Novanglus: "Metaphysicians and politicians may dispute forever, but they will never find any other moral principle or foundation of rule or obedience than the consent of governors and governed."[44]

Such ideas grounded in the colonial experience found ally with the concepts of inalienable rights and sovereignty that were emerging in colonial America and were further reinforced by the thinking of the writers during the Age of Enlightenment.

AGE OF ENLIGHTENMENT

The 17th and 18th centuries saw a blossoming of ideas based on observation and reason that added impetus to trends already under way in England. From the time of Justinian I, who, in the early sixth century a.d., alarmed by ideas he considered at odds with Christian beliefs, had closed all philosophy schools, religious faith had become the accepted means of obtaining knowledge. Investigation largely consisted of interpreting the Bible or at best postulating high principles. With the Enlightenment came the application of scientific study, careful examination, and the use of reason in efforts to understand the universe and those who inhabit it.

The intellectual roots of the Enlightenment extend back in time to antiquity and to such classical thinkers as Thucydides, Plato, Aristotle, Polybius, and Cicero. All emphasized the importance of reason and in governance also stressed the supremacy of a mixed constitution and the need for a separation of the powers of government. Plato also held that "all men are by nature equal, made all of the same earth by one Workman" and was against placing too much power in the hands of a single body of government. Aristotle believed, "The only stable government is the one in which all men are equal before the law."

Polybius and Cicero, like Aristotle, preferred a mixed government. Both were well schooled in the weaknesses and strengths of the Roman senate and various Roman citizen assemblies (Curiata, Centuriata, and Tributa) as checks on the power of the executive branch of elected magistrates.[45] Both studied and wrote during the Roman republic (c. 510 b.c.– c. 27 b.c.), a time during which only the Roman centuriate assembly could elect the executive (consuls, praetors, and censors)[46] and only the centuriate assembly could declare an offensive war.[47] Polybius, reflecting as Aristotle had done on ideas of governance advanced by Plato, outlined three simple forms of government—monarchy, aristocracy, and democracy, each degenerating over time into corrupted forms—tyranny, oligarchy, and mob rule, respectively. For Polybius the answer to the question of how to avoid such a degeneration could be found in the mixed-constitution Roman republic, "a single state with elements of all three forms of government at once: monarchy (in the form of its elected executives), aristocracy (as represented by the senate), and democracy (in the form of popular assemblies, such as the *Comitia Centuriata*)."[48] With each branch of government checking the strengths and weaknesses of the other two, no single branch possesses absolute power, and the danger of unchecked power is greatly reduced. Cicero introduced many of the ideas of the earlier great philosophers to Rome. An avid believer in the use of reason, he opposed the dictatorship of Julius Caesar, arguing the case for man's natural rights and advocating a return to the mixed government of checks and balances characteristic of the Roman republic. For Cicero such a government was "the most splendid conceivable."[49]

By the 17th and 18th centuries, men of learning began to reexamine such classical ideas and began to expand on and apply those as well as new ideas in the field of science and human endeavor.[50] Following on the efforts of men like Galileo (1564–1642) and Sir Isaac Newton (1643–1727), who believed that there was a natural order to the physical universe and that that natural order could be discovered through reason and scientific investigation, others began to reason that if the physical order of the universe could be uncovered through such methods, then perhaps the same pertained to uncovering the natural laws that regulated human existence. Those who espoused such ideas in France often called themselves Philosophes, or philosophers. Frequently meeting in Paris salons (reception rooms in private homes where they would gather for long afternoons or evenings of conversations, usually hosted by a wealthy woman from the nobility or upper bourgeoisie), these challengers to contemporary wisdoms were offered a chance to engage others with their ideas. Among the many French Philosophes were such well-known figures as Denis Diderot, Marquis de Condorcet, Baron de Montesquieu, Jean-Jacques Rousseau, and Voltaire. To be sure, not all of those involved in the movement were French. There were Dutchmen like Balthasar Bekker; Germans like Johann Wolfgang von Goethe, Johann Gottfried von Herder, and Immanuel Kant; Italians like Cesare Beccaria; and Russians like Nikolay Novikov. There were Englishmen like Thomas Hobbes and John Locke, Scots like David Hume and Adam Smith, Irishmen like Edmund Burke, and others from all over Europe. For the most part these men of the Age of Enlightenment emphasized empiricism and the use of logic and reason, reintroducing to Western culture a philosophy of knowledge first systematized by Aristotle and contending, as Newton had done, that all human certainty is based on evidence gathered through empirical observation. They had an abiding mistrust of religion and traditional authority and institutions. They were primarily concerned with the betterment of society and improvements in human existence. Among their beliefs was the need to reform "outdated human institutions and belief systems." Thus their focus was"overwhelmingly practical."[51]

Across the Atlantic many of the intellectual leaders of the American colonies were drawn to the Enlightenment. Men like Franklin, Washington, Hamilton, Madison, and Jefferson were powerfully attracted to and influenced by the ideas of the Enlightenment, often filtered through the radical social and political thought that emerged consequent to the English Civil War, the Commonwealth era, and the writings of such radical Whigs[52] as John Trenchard and Thomas Gordon and tempered by their own colonial experiences. Arguably, in terms of influence on the thinking in the American colonies in the arena of politics, Hobbes, Locke, Smith, and Montesquieu certainly are among those who had a significant impact on leading Americans. Hobbes, with his pessimistic view of human nature, contended that man, in the absence of government—that is, in a state of nature—was constantly at war. Hobbes wrote that the life of man in a state of nature (that is, in the absence of some ruling force) was "solitary, poor, nasty, brutish, and short."[53] Therefore, for human progress, man joined with others in an unwritten social contract in which he relinquished his rights to a higher authority for peace, security, and the common good.

Like Hobbes, Locke endeavored to discover the "natural order" of humankind and the natural rights of individuals. However, Locke had a more optimistic view of human nature than did Hobbes. As with Hobbes, Locke saw man entering into an unwritten social contract, but the nature of that contract was much less restrictive. Man, the individual, retained much greater freedom, including the freedom to dissolve the "social contract" should the rulers wield arbitrary power. This was clearly reflected in the views of those who chose to break away from England. In this regard, the Founding Fathers rejected Hobbes's argument that the government had absolute power over its subject. Instead, they embraced Locke's belief in unalienable rights and limited government.

The ringing language of the American Declaration of Independence is testimony to many of the ideas that flowed from the long line of thinking that led to the Americas primarily through England and France.

We hold these truths to be self-evident, that all men are created equal, that they are endowed by their creator with certain unalienable rights, that among these are life, liberty, and the pursuit of happiness. That to secure these rights governments are instituted among men, deriving their just powers from the consent of the governed. That to secure these rights, Governments are instituted among Men, deriving their just powers from the consent of the governed,—That whenever any Form of Government becomes destructive of these ends, it is the Right of the People to alter or to abolish it, and to institute new Government....

However, if Locke set the general political tone for American governance, Hobbes, as well as Adam Smith, introduced cautions not to be lightly disregarded. Smith, though not as pessimistic as Hobbes, saw man as principally motivated by self-interest, though the outcome could be positive. He wrote:

he intends only his own security; and he is in this, as in many other cases, led by an invisible hand to promote an end which was no part of his intention...by pursuing his own interest he frequently promotes that of the society more effectually than when he really intends to promote it.[54]

Smith also believed businessmen would exploit the state to their advantage. In *The Wealth of Nations*, his *opus magnum* first published in the year of the signing of America's Declaration of Independence, Smith wrote:

The proposal of any new law or regulation of commerce which comes from this order ought always to be listened to with great precaution, and ought never to be adopted till after having been long and carefully examined, not only with the most scrupulous, but with the most suspicious attention. It comes from an order of men whose interest is never exactly the same with that of the public, who have generally an interest to deceive and even to oppress the public, and who accordingly have, upon many occasions, both deceived and opposed it.[55]

Men like Benjamin Franklin, Alexander Hamilton, James Madison, and others shared some of the pessimism exhibited by Hobbes and Smith. For example, speaking during the federal convention of 1787 Franklin noted:

Sir, there are two passions which have a powerful influence on the affairs of men. These are ambition and avarice, the love of power and the love of money. Separately each of these has a great force in prompting men to action; but when united in view of the same object, they have in many minds the most violent effects.[56]

Likewise, Madison wrote in *Federalist Paper No. 51*: "If men were angels, no government would be necessary. If angels were to govern men, neither external nor internal controls on government would be necessary." But as Madison and others so well recognized, men are not angels. Hence, there was a need to construct a government that preserved individual liberty, while providing for needed order and guarding against tyranny of the rulers over the ruled.

Reflecting similar concerns, staunch anti-federalist Robert Yates, under the non de plume Brutus, wrote: "It is a truth confirmed by the unerring experience of the ages, that every man, and every body of men, invested with power, are disposed to increase it, and to acquire a superiority over every thing that stands in their way."[57]

Thus as the delegates gathered in mid- to late May in Philadelphia to amend the Articles of Confederation amid growing concerns over its failures, they came armed with ideas of governance that dated to ancient Greece and Rome, a sound understanding of English constitutional traditions, and their own experiences in the colonies. The delegates also brought with them the ideas of the Enlightenment to which many Americans had already contributed.[58] Indeed, the language of natural law, of inherent freedoms, and the need to protect from tyranny that might threaten the private rights of individuals was in their mind's eye as they met in Philadelphia 11 years after declaring independence from Britain. Their task was now to decide how a government managed by imperfect human beings should be designed to accomplish such objectives. Here Montesquieu's further development of the ideas of mixed governments, with its checks on and balances of power that were first introduced in classical antiquity, proved valuable. Nevertheless, though those who gathered in Philadelphia in May 1787 drew ideas of governance from antiquity, the English constitutional traditions, and the Enlightenment writers, they did not accept blindly what had gone before them. Classical as well as recent formulations were to be examined in every detail. Old maxims were there to accept, reject, or modify as the American predicament demanded. It was an exercise of the most extraordinary and exhilarating kind.

CHAPTER 2

The Constitutional Convention: Forging a Nation

As the delegates began their work in May 1787, of course they did not start with a blank slate. The United States already had a constitution. Their task, as it was initially proposed, was to amend that document. Though many at the time thought that the Articles of Confederation had serious flaws, it did embody principles that would not warrant rejection. Indeed, its construction had reflected many of the great concerns that troubled those who wrote the document that was adopted by the Second Continental Congress on November 15, 1777,[1] and ratified in 1871. It was a document designed to limit the power of the national government and thus preserve the rights of the states and the people. It was a document that tightly circumscribed the executive powers of the central government. Furthermore, it was crafted so that the executive powers, as limited as they were, resided with the representatives of the states sitting as the U.S. Congress and the task of carrying through with the actions of Congress was largely left to the individual states. Though every state was obliged to abide by the determinations of Congress, there was no central mechanism for Congress to enforce its decisions on the states. There was no national court system. There was no executive branch of government. There was a president, but he was simply the presiding officer of the Congress. Nevertheless, Congress did have some significant, though not always enforceable, powers.

POWERS OF CONGRESS UNDER THE ARTICLES

Under the articles Congress was given a number of sole and exclusive powers, among which were to print money (regulate the alloy and value of coin), to fix standards of weights and measures throughout the United States, to regulate trade and manage all affairs with the Indians, to establish and regulate a postal system throughout the United States, to serve as a last resort on appeal in disputes between "States concerning boundary, jurisdiction, or any other causes whatever," and acting through a "Committee of the States,"[2] to build and equip a navy, and to make requisitions from each state for an army.

On issues of war and peace, the articles gave Congress "the sole and exclusive right and power of determining peace and war." The only exceptions appeared in the sixth article.

No state shall engage in any war without the consent of the United States Congress assembled, unless such a state be actually invaded by enemies,...and the danger is so imminent as not to admit of a delay, till the United States in Congress assembled can be consulted.

Under the articles, Congress also had the sole and exclusive right of "sending and receiving ambassadors—entering into treaties of alliance;...[and] of granting letters of marque[3] and reprisal in times of peace."

While the articles had served the nation adequately during the war, they were failing the nation during peace. Soon after the convention began in 1787 it became evident that more would need to be done than crafting a simple amendment.

Edmund Randolph's initial assault on the articles as he introduced the Virginia Plan on May 29, just 15 days after the formal opening of the convention (see chapter 1), was just the tip of an iceberg of criticism of the failings of the articles. Joining the convention the next day, Roger Sherman of Connecticut argued that the articles had not given sufficient power to Congress, and additional powers were necessary.[4]

Within two weeks, William Patterson of New Jersey introduced what became known as the New Jersey Plan. The plan would significantly amend the articles, though not create a truly national government. Like the Virginia Plan, the New Jersey Plan would add to the powers of Congress and create a federal executive as well as federal judiciary. Unlike the Virginia Plan, which had two chambers, in each of which the number of state representatives was based on each state's population, thus favoring the more populous states, the New Jersey Plan, favored by the less populous states, recommended a single house, with members selected by the states and with each state having one vote, thus retaining the essential structure of Congress as established in the articles. The plan, however, did recognize the deficiencies in the powers of Congress, granting it such additional powers as those of raising a revenue, levying duties on all goods or merchandises of foreign growth or manufacture, and regulating trade with foreign nations.[5]

Responding to Patterson's proposal, Randolph, once again, assailed the articles. According to the notes of James Madison, Randolph "painted in strong colours [sic], the imbecility of the existing confederation, & the danger of delaying a substantial reform."[6] Later that same day, Randolph said that he would consent to any mode of government that will preserve the nation. Adding substance to his concerns, he went on to note:

France, to whom we are indebted in every motive of gratitude and honor, is left unpaid the large sums she has supplied us with in the day of our necessity—Our officers and soldiers, who have successfully fought our battles—and the loaners of money to the public, look...for relief.

The bravery of our troops is degraded by the weakness of our government....we have found that the powers granted to congress are insufficient. The body of congress is ineffectual to carry the great objects of safety and protection into execution.[7]

Randolph, in further frustration, noted that state assemblies were constantly encroaching on the powers of Congress. Congress had too many members to serve as an effective executive, and additional powers granted to Congress would never be sufficient to protect the United States against foreign invasion.[8] Alexander Hamilton of New York, also concerned about this lack of power at the national level, argued that states "constantly pursue internal interests adverse to those of the whole [nation]" and when a state's particular plans are in conflict with those of Congress, state plans "invariably prevail."[9]

James Madison contended that the violations of the federal articles by the states had been numerous and notorious. Among the most notorious, Madison pointed to an action by New Jersey, the very state proposing the retention of a national legislature similar in composition to the one that was failing the confederation. New Jersey, he noted,

expressly refused [italics in original] to comply with a constitutional requisition of Congs.—and yielded no farther to the expostulations of their deputies, than barely to rescind her vote of refusal without passing any positive act of compliance.[10]

In further evaluating the New Jersey Plan, Madison alluded to other weaknesses of the national legislature under the articles, contending that states, with impunity and in direct conflict with the articles, violated the laws of nations and treaties, encroached on federal authority, and trespassed on the rights of other states. He further noted, the articles could not secure the internal tranquility of the states, as demonstrated by insurrections in Massachusetts [i.e., Shays's Rebellion], nor could it secure the Union against the influence of foreign powers over its members.[11]

Sherman probably summed up the general feeling that existed among delegates as they began the arduous task of forging a stronger, more effective, and more united union. Addressing the delegates on June 20, he said:

Congs. carried us thro' [sic] the war, and perhaps as well as any Govt. could have done. The complaints at present are not that the views of Congs. are unwise or unfaithful, but that their powers are insufficient for the execution of their views. The national debt & the want of power somewhere to draw forth the National resources, are the great matters that press. All the States were sensible to the defect of power in Congs.[12]

Reflecting a similar view earlier that same day, Luther Martin of Maryland confessed that "when the confederation was made, congress ought to have been invested with more extensive powers."[13]

Of course some delegates were apprehensive over prospects that too much power might be granted a national legislature. Many delegates were aware of the abuses of legislative power at the state and local levels following the revolution, as well as legislative incompetence at the national level. Prior to the convention, Madison wrote to Thomas Jefferson that Congress had mismanaged its power under the confederation.

As the convention was getting under way, Jacob Brown of Delaware, perhaps offering at least a glimpse of concern over the powers that the national government might be granted under an amended articles or a newly formed constitution, wrote in a letter to Thomas Collins dated May 23, 1787: "Two Legislative Branches and one Executive seems to be a prevailing sentiment; but how extensive their powers will be a weighty subject of consideration."[14]

Nevertheless, as the convention proceeded there seemed to be a general willingness to grant the national legislature much more extensive powers than had been granted to it under the articles. The principal question then to be addressed was what powers should be vested in the Congress and how should they be defined.

EXTENDING THE POWERS OF CONGRESS

After intense deliberations on the Virginia and New Jersey plans and the interjection of an alternate plan by Alexander Hamilton, by June 25 delegates had settled the issue of the number of branches of the national legislature and its method of election of the legislators in each with what later became known as the "Connecticut Compromise" or "Great Compromise." There would be two house of Congress, one elected by the people of the several states, the other elected by the state legislatures. By August 6 John Rutledge of South Carolina delivered the report of the Committee of Detail. Among other things the report outlined the powers the committee recommended be given to the national legislature (see Committee of Detail Report).[15]

By August 17 delegates changed the wording suggested by the committee, replacing the power to "make" war with the power to "declare" war.[16] The following day the powers of Congress were further amended. Congress would be given not only the power to "raise" armies but also to "support" them. The power of Congress to "build and equip fleets," both of which were considered physical efforts, was changed to "provide and maintain" fleets. The national legislature was also given the power

COMMITTEE OF DETAIL REPORT

Recommendations on the Powers of Congress (Abridged)

- To lay and collect taxes, duties, imposts, and excises;

- To regulate commerce with foreign nations, and among the several states;

- To coin money;

- To establish post offices;

- To borrow money and emit bills on the credit of the United States;

- To constitute tribunals inferior to the Supreme Court;

- To make rules concerning captures on land and water;

- To subdue a rebellion in any State, on the application of its legislature;

- To make war;

- To raise armies;

- To build and equip fleets; and

- To call forth the aid of the militia, in order to execute the laws of the Union, enforce treaties, suppress insurrections, and repel invasions.

"to make rules for the government and regulation of the land and naval forces."[17] Thus, by mid-August, the powers granted to the national legislature were a substantial improvement over those that had been granted to the Congress under the Articles of Confederation. As the convention was drawing to a close, delegates made a few additional changes. To the power "to declare war" was added "and grant letters of marque and reprisal." To the power "to lay and collect taxes, duties, imposts, and excises" was added the phrase "for the common defence and general welfare." Also, Congress was given the power not only to regulate commerce "with foreign nations, and among the several states" but also "with the Indian tribes."

Extending the powers of the national legislature was not done without trepidation. Anti-federalists feared a national government with too much power. This was certainly evident in deliberations over the size of any standing army and over the control and regulation of militias. It also was evident during the state ratification debates.[18]

Nevertheless, the delegates completed a document that significantly expanded the powers of the national legislature. However, when delegates undertook discussions on the nature and powers of the executive, there was no general willingness to grant the executive extensive powers.

FEAR OF DESPOTISM

Fear of the tyranny that arises from excessive power in the hands of a nation's executive was foremost in the minds of many delegates as they met in Philadelphia. They were aware that English kings often took back with one hand powers they had conceded to Parliament with the other. Kings all too frequently were able to do so by exercising their prerogative powers, which in earlier years included the king's ability to convene and dissolve Parliament at his convenience (see "Prerogative Powers"). Delegates, also aware of their own colonial experiences, had reasons to be concerned about an executive without effective limits on executive power. For example, Thomas Hutchinson[19] had established an elaborate patronage machine that was viewed by men like John Adams as a serious threat to liberty. Many in the colonies held the view that Hutchinson and his ambitious allies had managed, by accumulating a massive plurality of offices through patronage, to engross the power of all branches of the

PREROGATIVE POWERS

In 1690 John Locke in his second essay concerning civil government set the case for the prerogative powers of the executive. "Where the legislature and executive power are in distinct hands, as they are in all moderated monarchies and in well-framed governments, there the good of the society requires that several things should be left to the discretion of him that has the executive power. For the legislators not being able to foresee and provide by laws for all that may be useful to the community, the executor of the laws, having the power in his hands, has by the common law of Nature a right to make use of it for the good of the society...."*

Three quarters of a century later Sir William Blackstone outlined the king's prerogative powers. Among those powers, the king "has the sole power of sending ambassadors to foreign states, and receiving ambassadors at home," has the power "to make treaties, leagues, and alliances with foreign states and princes," and "has the sole power of raising and regulating fleets and armies." He also has the prerogative powers of "directing ministers of the crown to issue letters of marque and reprisal," serving "as the generalissimo, or first in military command, within the kingdom," and "the sole prerogative of making war and peace." Additionally, the king "has the prerogative of rejecting such provisions in parliament as he judges improper to be passed," is "not bound by any act of parliament," is entrusted "with the whole executive power," is "the arbiter of commerce," and "has alone the right of erecting courts of judicature."**

*John Locke, *Second Treatise of Civil Government*, 1690, sec. 159.
**Sir William Blackstone, *Commentaries on the Laws of England*, bk. 1, chap. 7, 245–63.

Massachusetts government, thereby building a "foundation sufficient on which to erect a tyranny."[20] This was perhaps especially true as Hutchinson served as lieutenant governor under Governor Francis Bernard, who took his post in 1760 and not only had executive authorities but also held veto power over the legislature, and most assuredly when Hutchinson himself ascended to governor in 1771.

Thus, even before delegates undertook substantive discussions on the nature and duties of an executive, some were expressing their concerns over the dangers of forming an office that might be too powerful. For example, before his arrival at the convention, William Pierce of Georgia, in a letter to George Turner, an English-born soldier, land speculator, jurist from South Carolina, and member of the Society of Cincinnati,[21] wrote on May 19, 1787:

Upon whatever principles a Government is founded, whether rights are equally distributed among the People at large or among a few, some respect ought to be paid to the temper of the People, as produced by one or the other of these rights. To depart from the general freedom of our Governments [indecipherable phrase] and to step into a Monarchy, which will at times be despotic, would plunge the States into a tumult infinitely worse than anarchy itself: torrents of blood would follow the confusion.[22]

This is not to suggest that delegates did not harbor fears of the possible tyranny of legislatures. As Gordon S. Wood has noted:

By the mid-1780s many Americans were convinced that the state legislatures and majority factions within those were the greatest source of tyranny in America.[23]

During the convention and often in the debates that preceded ratification by the states, however, concerns over the dangers of vesting too much power in an executive were manifest in nearly every aspect of discussions surrounding the creation of a national executive, from the very nature of the executive to the powers to be extended to that office.

ON THE NATURE OF THE EXECUTIVE AND HIS SELECTION

On Having One Person or More than One Serve as Chief Executive

Though early in their deliberations delegates settled on a single executive, there was evident concern over the potential power of such an executive. James Wilson of Pennsylvania, a leader among those favoring a single executive, argued that a single executive magistrate at the national level would give the "most energy, dispatch and responsibility to the office."[24]

On the other hand, several delegates, conspicuous among them Edmund Randolph, offered countering arguments over the efficiency of a single executive. He said that there was "no motive to be governed by the British governmt. [sic] as our prototype." He further contended that he "could not see why the requisites for the Executive department, vigor, dispatch & responsibility could not be found in three men, as well as in one man." To which Wilson responded: "Unity in the Executive instead of being the fetus of Monarchy would be the best safeguard against tyranny,"[25] presumably in the belief that with a single executive there would be a clear line of accountability. Three days later, on June 4, 1787, on the day state delegations approved a single executive by a vote of 7 to 3, Wilson reminded the delegates that having a single magistrate is not the same as having a king. Indeed, all 13 states have a single magistrate at the head of their respective governments. Though Sherman acknowledged that each state had a single magistrate and wished the same policy to prevail at the national level, he also expressed some reservations. As a further limitation on the power of the executive, Sherman noted: "In all of the States there was a Council of advice, without which the first magistrate could not act."[26]

George Mason of Virginia also apparently shared the concerns of those opposed to a single executive. In a draft document prepared during these discussions, Mason wrote: "I believe there is a general tendency to a strong Executive, and I am inclined to think a strong Executive necessary. If strong and extensive powers are vested in the Executive, and that executive consists only of one person, the government will of course degenerate...into a monarchy—a government so contrary to the genius of the people that they will reject even the appearance of it."[27]

Ultimately, delegates settled on a single executive. As had been recommended by the Committee of Detail on August 6, 1787, the title of the nation's chief executive would be the "President of the United States of America." But the title itself spoke of the concerns of the delegates. In the usage of the time, the term "president" commonly signified presiding officer, "almost to the exclusion of any executive powers."[28]

On the Method of Selecting the Executive

When delegates turned their attention to the method by which the executive should be chosen, a number of delegates felt that the nation's chief magistrate should be chosen by the legislature, have a relatively long term in office, but must not be eligible for reelection. Roger Sherman "considered the Executive magistracy as nothing more than an institution for carrying the will of the Legislature into effect, that the person or persons ought to be appointed by and accountable to the Legislature only."[29] According to Sherman, this would make the Executive "absolutely dependent" on the legislature whose will it was that was to be executed. For Sherman, an executive independent of the legislature was the very essence of tyranny.[30]

Charles Pinckney of South Carolina held a similar view, contending that by such a process "respect will be paid to the character best qualified to fill the Executive department of Government."[31] John Rutledge, also from the South Carolina delegation, suggested that only the second branch of the national legislature should elect the executive.[32]

Responding to those who suggested that perhaps the executive should be chosen by electors, Hugh Williamson of North Carolina "observed that if the Electors were to chuse [sic] the Executive it would attend with considerable expense and trouble; whereas the appointment made by the Legislature would be easy, and in his opinion, the least liable to objection."[33]

Of course there were those who opposed election by the national legislature. Among those, Wilson was initially in favor of appointment of the executive by the people. He sought "to derive both branches of government from the people without the intervention of the State Legislatures...in order to make them as independent as possible of each other, as well as of the States."[34] Mason favored Wilson's idea of election by the people but thought it impractical.[35] The next day Wilson altered his position, proposing a system of electors chosen at the state district level, in lieu of a direct popular election. Elbridge Gerry of Massachusetts argued that if the national legislature were to choose the executive there "would be a constant intrigue kept up for the appointment" with both legislature and candidates bargaining for position and "votes would be given by the former under promises or expectations of the latter, of recompensing them by services to members of the Legislature or to their friends."[36]

On June 2 state delegations initially accepted the proposal for the election of the executive by the national legislature for a term of seven years, voting 8 to 2.[37] Nevertheless, the debate continued. Gouverneur Morris of Pennsylvania, firmly against an executive chosen by the national legislature, declared that if that body could appoint and impeach the executive, the executive "will be the mere creature of the Legisl [sic]." Thus he believed that the executive "ought be elected by the people at large, by the freeholders of the Country."[38] He further concluded, "If the Executive be chosen by the Natl. Legislature, he will not be independent on it; and if not independent, usurpation & tyranny on the part of the Legislature will be the consequence."

Madison, also concerned about an executive dependent on the legislature, supported the arguments made by Morris maintaining that a separation between the various branches of government, including the judiciary, was essential to the preservation of liberty. He held:

The Executive could not be independent of the Legislature, if dependent on the pleasure of that branch for re-appointment....In like manner a dependence of the Executive on the Legislature would render it the Executor as well as the maker of laws; & then according to the observation of Montesquieu, tyrannical laws may be made that may be executed in a tyrannical manner.[39]

Madison further added:

Experience has proved a tendency in our governments to throw all power into the Legislative vortex. The Executives of our States are in general little more than Cyphers; the legislatures omnipotent. If no effectual check be devised for restraining the instability & encroachments of the latter, a revolution of some kind or other would be inevitable.[40]

Nevertheless, on July 17 state delegations, once again, voted in favor of an Executive "to be chosen by the national Legislature." This time the vote was unanimous. However, the tide was beginning to turn against the election of the Executive by the Legislature. Within two days, delegations voted to reconsider their previous decision. Wilson reflected: "It seems to be the unanimous sense that the Executive should not be appointed by the Legislature, unless he be rendered in-eligible a 2d time:... the idea gaining ground, of an election mediately or immediately by the people."[41] That same day delegations voted 6–3, with one state delegation divided, in favor of an Executive "to be chosen by electors appointed for that purpose." They also voted 8–2 that the electors were to be chosen by the legislatures of the states,[42] only to reverse themselves, voting 7–4 on July 24 against having the supreme executive selected "by electors appointed for that purpose by the Legislatures of the State" and in favor of election by the national legislature.[43]

The issue arose again following the report of the committee of detail on August 6, which once again reaffirmed election of the executive by the legislature.[44] A move to substitute election by the people instead of the legislature was defeated 2–9 on August 24. At the same time delegates voted to make the selection by a majority in a joint ballot, while turning down an effort to have the executive chosen by electors chosen by the people instead of the legislature.[45]

On selection of the executive by the people, George Mason perhaps had captured the sentiment of many of the delegates on this issue when he said:

It would be as unnatural to refer the choice of a proper character for the chief Magistrate to the people, as it would, to refer a trial of colours to a blind man. The extent of the Country renders it impossible that the people can have the requisite capacity to judge of the respective pretensions of the Candidates.[46]

The delegates also were concerned that the people would always choose someone from their own state.[47]

However, concern among the delegates that, if the executive were chosen by the national legislature, the independence of the executive would be circumscribed kept the issue alive. Once again Morris arose to oppose the election of the president by the legislature, arguing that it would lead to legislative tyranny. He then moved that the president "shall be chosen by Electors to be chosen by the people of the several States." David Carrol of Maryland seconded his motion. Though the motion was defeated, the vote was a close five in favor and six against.[48]

When the issue was again addressed on September 4 opposition to legislative selection of the executive continued to grow. The Committee of Eleven reported in favor of the election of the president and vice president by electors appointed by each state, with each state having a number of electors equal to the total number of Senators and members of the House of Representatives to which each state was entitled. The electors would meet in their respective states and vote for two persons, one of whom was not from their state. The candidate gaining a majority of the electors' votes would be president. If there were a tie, the Senate would choose one of them to be president. If no candidate had a majority, the Senate would chose from among the top five candidates. The person with the next greatest number would be vice president. Thus the idea of an electoral college was born.

Gouverneur Morris, commenting on the changing mood of the delegates, said: "No body had appeared to be satisfied with an appointment by the Legislature." He further noted: "Many were anxious even for an immediate choice by the people." Yet there existed an "indispensable necessity of making the Executive independent of the Legislature."[49]

Butler responded that the mode proposed by the Committee of Eleven, while "not free from objections, [was] much more so than election by the Legislature."[50]

Yet again views remained somewhat divided: Pinckney opposed having electors, who he felt, among other things, would not have sufficient knowledge of the fittest men. Rutledge opposed the plan, contending that since it was likely that no one person would have a majority, it would throw to the Senate the "whole power" of electing the president.[51] Wilson and Dickenson, in the event of a tie among electors or absence of a majority candidate, preferred that final selection be made by the entire national legislature instead of by only the Senate. Randolph was concerned that giving such influence over the election of the president to the Senate might result in a "dangerous Aristocracy."[52]

It wasn't until the last days of the federal convention that the issue was finally settled in favor of an electoral college.

ON THE POWERS OF THE EXECUTIVE

Power to Execute the Laws

On July 17 delegations to the federal convention approved unanimously granting the executive "the power to carry into effect the national laws."[53] However, from the outset of discussions leading up to this decision to grant such a basic function to the executive, delegates betrayed a concern over a potential usurpation of power by the executive. The issue of executive powers was first introduced as part of the Virginia Plan. That plan granted to a national executive "a general authority to execute the National laws," as well as the "Executive rights vested in Congress by the [Articles of] Confederation."[54] On June 1, delegates undertook discussions on the nature and powers of the executive. When the issue of executive power was first introduced to the delegates, Madison proposed an amendment to the wording of the Virginia Plan that would "fix the extent" of the powers of the executive. The proposed amendment, seconded by Wilson, would grant to the executive the power "to carry into effect the national laws, to appoint officers in cases not otherwise provided for, and to execute such powers (not Legislative nor Judiciary in their nature) as they may from time to time be delegated by the national Legislature."[55] Concerned that the executive might acquire powers not intended by the delegates, Charles Cotesworth Pinckney proposed adding the words enclosed by parentheses to the amendment in order to preclude the legislature from delegating improper powers to the executive. Randolph, apparently harboring similar concerns, seconded Pinckney's motion.

Though the delegates decided against the explicit limitation of executive power as suggested by Madison and amended by Pinckney beginning with the clause "to execute such powers not Legislative nor Judiciary," they did so primarily because they thought it unnecessary since the power of the executive was already limited implicitly to the "power to carry into effect the national laws." Madison remained unconvinced. He saw no inconvenience in retaining the explicit limitations since "cases might happen in which they might serve to prevent doubts and misconstructions."[56] It clearly was evident that delegates intended to constrain the powers of the executive.

On Issues of Foreign Policy, the Military, and War and Peace

Under the Articles of Confederation, the United States Congress had "the sole and exclusive right and power of *determining* [emphasis added] on peace and war ...; of sending and receiving ambassadors; entering into treaties and alliances;...granting letters of marque and reprisal...." States were not permitted to "engage in any war without the consent of the United States in Congress assembled," unless a state were "actually invaded by enemies," or had received certain advice of a resolution being formed by some nation of Indians to invade such state, *and the danger is so imminent as not to admit of a delay* [emphasis added], till the United States in Congress assembled can be consulted...." The task of the delegates to the federal convention was to determine which of these functions should be retained by Congress and which should fall to the executive.

The Virginia Plan merely provided for an executive who was "to enjoy the Executive rights vested in Congress by the Confederation," without stipulating just what those executive rights were. The New Jersey Plan was somewhat more specific. Besides granting the federal executive or executives (leaving aside whether the executive was to be a single individual or several individuals sharing power) the "general authority to execute the federal acts," it granted the executive(s) the authority "to appoint all federal officers not otherwise provided for, & to *direct* [emphasis added] all military operations; provided that none of the persons composing the federal Executive shall on any occasion take command of any troops, so as personally to conduct any enterprise as General, or in other capacity."[57] The New Jersey Plan clearly betrayed an evident concern over the powers of the executive[58] that was played out during the deliberations that followed.

On the Appointment of Federal Officers and Ambassadors

On the question of who should appoint federal officers, delegates generally preferred the very limited position laid out in the New Jersey Plan. Wilson set forth his own views on this very early in the proceedings, maintaining: "The only powers he conceived strictly Executive were those of executing the laws, and appointing officers, not (appertaining to and) appointed by the Legislature."[59] Similarly, Hamilton asserted that the executive should have the sole authority to appoint heads or chief officers of the departments of finance, war, and foreign affairs, and the power to execute all laws passed. Hamilton did, however, recommend that the Senate have the power to approve or reject the appointments "of all other officers (Ambassadors to foreign Nations included)"[60] In mid-July delegations voted unanimously to vest the power "to appoint offices [sic] in cases not otherwise provided for" in the executive.[61]

However, in early August the Committee of Detail, composed of five members from five different states, whose task it was to create a constitution containing all issues agreed to by the convention, rendered its report. In that report the committee, while granting the executive the power to commission all officers of the United States and appoint officers in all cases not otherwise provided for by the Constitution, granted the Senate the power to appoint ambassadors.[62]

As the convention was drawing to a close, Sherman, expressing a concern over the dangers of excessive power in the hands of the executive, admitted that it was proper for many officers in the executive department to be appointed by the executive. But he contended that there were also many who should not be appointed by the president, such as general officers of the army in time of peace. Sherman argued: "If the Executive can model the army, he may set up an absolute Government; taking advantage of the close of a war and an army commanded by his creatures."[63]

In the end, delegates agreed to carefully circumscribe the power of the executive. The executive would have the power to nominate ambassadors, other public ministers and consuls, judges of the supreme court, and all other officers of the United States, whose appointments were not otherwise provided for and established by law. However, the appointment of such officials would require the advice and consent of the Senate. To the executive was also granted the responsibility to "*receive* [italics added] Ambassadors and other public Ministers" and to "Commission all the Officers of the United States."

On Treaties

Neither the Virginia Plan nor the New Jersey Plan mentioned whether the making of treaties with foreign powers was an executive or legislative function. On August 6, the Committee of Detail report specified that the Senate of the United States should have the power to make treaties.[64] If adopted, this would be a major departure from the traditions and practices of European and English monarchs, who held exclusive treaty-making powers. However, several delegates opposed this idea.

John Francis Mercer of Maryland maintained that the Senate ought not have the power of making treaties. This power, he argued, should belong to the executive department. However, treaties should not be final "til ratified by legislative authority."[65] Madison "observed that the Senate represented the States alone, and that the President should be the agent in Treaties."[66] Gouverneur Morris, though unsure whether the Senate should be given the power to make treaties, proposed an amendment to the effect that no treaty would be binding, which was not ratified by a law, thus making concurrence by both the House and the Senate a requirement. Dickenson agreed. Wilson seemed both opposed to fettering the government with the requirement that both houses would need to ratify a treaty and that the Senate alone should have the power to make treaties. With such differences among delegates further discussion was postponed and the issue referred to a committee.[67]

On September 4 the Committee of Eleven rendered its recommendations on a wide range of issues still under consideration. Section 4 of the report stated, among other things: "The President by and with the advice of the Senate, shall have the power to make treaties.... But no Treaty shall be made without the consent of two thirds of the Members present."[68]

When discussions resumed three days later on the issue of treaties, deliberations took an interesting turn. Madison moved and delegates unanimously agreed to insert after the word "Treaty" in the last sentence the words "except Treaties of Peace," arguing that treaties of peace should be made with less difficulty than other treaties. His amendment passed 8–3. He then proposed that treaties of peace require concurrence of two-thirds of the Senate, without concurrence of the president. On this he contended that the president "would necessarily derive so much power and importance from a state of war that he might be tempted, if authorized, to impede a treaty of peace." Butler, who seconded the motion, "was strenuously for the motion, as a necessary security against ambitious & corrupt Presidents."[69] Though the proposed amendments failed, they exhibited, once again, delegate concerns over a potential misuse of power by the executive.

Delegations finally agreed to accept the recommendation of the Committee of Eleven. Even Hamilton, perhaps the most vigorous of supporters of a strong executive, favored this sharing of treaty-making power.[70]

Nevertheless, issues remained to be resolved. How might a treaty be abrogated? Would a treaty, once made, require a two-thirds concurrence of the Senate as well as that of the president to revoke? What about agreements short of a treaty? Could the president alone make such agreements? The final document remained silent on these issues. The only reference to agreements other than treaties appeared in article I, section 10, which prohibited states not only from entering into treaties, alliances, or confederation and from granting letters of marque and reprisal, but also from entering into "any Agreement or Compact with another State, or with a foreign power" without the consent of Congress.

On the Militia

To understand the context in which deliberations took place over the nature and control of the militia, it is necessary to know that the framers of the Constitution eschewed a standing army. History, particularly English history of the seventeenth century, had demonstrated, and events leading up to the 1770 Boston Massacre (see "The Boston Massacre, 1770"), had confirmed that:

"Standing armies" were not national guards, protecting the people. They were janissary troops, palace guards, predatory mercenaries loyal to the power source—the Crown, the executive, the President, anyone of authority to whom they were loyal or who would pay them.[71]

Bernard Bailyn noted that for those who led the American Revolution, "The absolute danger to liberty lay in the absolute supremacy of 'a veteran army'... Their fear was not simply of armies but of *standing armies.*"[72]

Anti-federalists were concerned that if the national government had the power to "raise and support armies" either the president or the legislature might misuse standing armies to their own purposes, infringing on the liberties of citizens. During the state ratification debates some argued that Congress could nationalize state militias and use them for their purposes, that there was nothing to prevent the president from using state militias as if they were standing armies, deploying them to wherever his adventures

THE BOSTON MASSACRE, 1770

In 1768 British troops had been sent to Boston to enforce a series of laws passed by Parliament a year earlier. Collectively known as the Townsends Acts, the laws were designed to raise revenue, to create a more effective means of enforcing compliance with trade regulations, and to establish the precedent that the British Parliament had the right to tax the colonies. They also were passed to punish the province of New York for failing to comply with the 1765 Quartering Act, which permitted the housing of British soldiers in inns and other public and private buildings.

Upset about being taxed without adequate representation in the British Parliament and incensed that Britain was maintaining a standing army in the Americas after the defeat of the French in the French and Indian War, even though none was required before, the colonists resisted. To enforce the laws the British occupied Boston in 1768. The heavy British military presence in Boston resulted in a tense situation. In March 1770 a brawl broke out between the British soldiers and colonists. When a rioting crowd attacked, the British soldiers responded by firing their weapons into the crowd. Three colonists were killed instantly. Two died later.

The massacre was one of the most important events that turned colonial sentiment against King George III and British rule.

might lead him, and that only the goodness of men, not the goodness of the Constitution, stood in the way of such actions that might threaten the liberties of freemen. And for many anti-federalists, relying on the goodness of men was a hopelessly frail reed. Their principal concern was that "a standing army, once established will not be controllable."[73]

Thus as discussions got under way at the convention on the nature of America's military and its control, the focus was not so much on the question of whether the executive or the legislature should exercise authority, but whether there was a need for a standing military force and to what degree the states would assent to national control of state militias.

On the former, Mason said that he hoped there would be no standing army in peacetime, except perhaps a few garrisons.[74] Gerry was concerned that there was no check against standing armies in time of peace. While he noted that Congress under the Articles of Confederation was so constructed as to not be able to maintain an army, this would not be so under the new Constitution. Thus he proposed to limit any standing army to two or three thousand.[75] On the other hand, Pinckney had "scanty faith in Militia. There must be (also) a real [standing] military force."[76]

On the question of how much control over the militias states would be willing to relinquish, there was general agreement that militias should be uniformly and well trained and that this would require some centrality of control. However, Oliver Ellsworth of Connecticut contended, "The whole authority over the Militia ought by no means to be taken away from the States whose consequence would pine away to nothing after such a sacrifice of power." Sherman noted: "States might want their Militia for defence [sic] agst. [against] invasions and insurrections, and for enforcing obedience to their laws," contending that they will not give up this point. Dickenson was of the opinion that "the States would never nor ought give up all authority over the Militia," suggesting that only one-fourth of the militia come under the central government at any one time, but by the rotation of militia, all would be similarly disciplined (trained).[77]

On the other hand, Pierce Butler preferred that the entire militia come under the authority of the national government, which was charged with the general defense of the nation.[78] Mason, initially holding a similar view, thought the militia ought to be prepared for the public defense. However, he maintained that, since the 13 states would never concur on any uniform system for training of the militia, delegates ought to consider remanding to the national legislature "a power to regulate the militia."[79] Mason later altered his view, asserting that the national government should be charged only with making laws for regulating and training the militia, with only one-tenth of the militias coming under federal control in any one year. Mason also maintained that it should be left to the states to appoint all militia officers.[80]

On August 21 William Livingston of New Jersey reported for the Committee of Eleven, recommending that the legislature of the United States have the power "to make laws for organizing, arming, and disciplining the militia, and for governing such part of them as may be employed in the service of the United States, reserving to the States respectively, the appointment of the Officers, and the authority of training the militia according to the discipline prescribed by the United States."[81] It was this formulation with minor changes in wording—a formulation that favored Congress over the executive—that found its way into the new Constitution. There would be no sizable standing army. America's regular military would be limited. The militias were to be America's army, and Congress would provide for their organization, arming, and training when they were called to federal service. However, power was shared. It was the president who would serve as their commander in chief when militias were called into the service of the nation.

On War and Peace

Perhaps the most intensive discussions over the powers of the executive focused on the president's power on issues of war and peace. Madison contended that the first task of the legislature is "to protect the people agst. [against] their rulers."[82] Among Madison's major concerns was the misuse of powers granted to a national executive during times of conflict, especially if coupled with a standing army.

> In time of actual war, great discretionary powers are constantly given to the Executive Magistrate. Constant apprehension of War, has the same tendency to render the head too large for the body. A standing military force, with an overgrown Executive will not long be safe companions to liberty. The means of defence [sic] agst. [against] foreign danger, have been always the instruments of tyranny at home. Among the Romans it was a standing maxim to excite war, whenever a revolt was apprehended. Throughout all Europe, the armies kept up under the pretext of defending, have enslaved the people. It is perhaps questionable, whether the best concerted system of absolute power in Europe cd. [could] maintain itself, in a situation, where no alarms of external danger cd. [could] tame the people to the domestic yoke.[83]

Aware of the dangers of the tyranny of despots, in nearly every instance the framers of the Constitution favored placing powers of war and peace in the hands of the legislative branch rather than in the executive branch, often placing significant restrictions on the powers of the executive. When delegates agreed on the final document to be forwarded to the states for ratification as the new Constitution of the United States, they had made the president the "Commander in Chief of the Army and Navy of the United States, and of the Militia of the several States, when called into actual Service of the United States."[84] To Congress, however, they granted such powers as the power to declare war, grant letters of marque and reprisal, raise and support armies, provide and maintain a navy, make rules for the government and regulation of the land and naval forces, provide for the calling forth of the militia to execute the laws of the Union, suppress insurrections, and repel invasions, and to provide for the organizing, arming, and disciplining of the militia.

The message from the federal convention delegates could not have been clearer. The national legislature was to be the supreme decider on issues of war and peace.

In deliberations over which executive powers exercised by Congress under the articles would be transferred to a newly formed executive, Charles Pinckney, though in favor of a vigorous executive, expressed concern that if the power of war and peace granted to Congress under the articles were transferred to America's chief executive, it "would render the Executive a Monarch of the worst kind, towit an elected one." Similarly, Rutledge "was for vesting the Executive power in a single person, tho' [sic] he was not for giving him the power of peace and war."[85]

Further reinforcing a preference for limiting the authority of the president on issues of war and peace, Wilson said that he "did not consider the Prerogatives of the British Monarch as a proper guide in defining Executive powers." He believed that some of these prerogatives were of a legislative nature, among which were the powers of war and peace. As noted previously, Wilson maintained: "The only powers he conceived strictly Executive were those of executing the laws, and appointing officers, not...appointed by the Legislature."[86] According to Wilson, the "making peace and war are generally determined by Writers on the Laws of Nations to be legislative powers."[87] Madison agreed with Wilson's defining of executive powers, arguing that executive powers "do not include the Rights of war & peace." Madison contended that "the powers shd. [should] be confined and defined—if large we shall have the Evils of elective Monarchies."[88]

Even Alexander Hamilton, one of the strongest proponents of executive power, favored constraining the power of the executive when it came to war-making authority. Hamilton argued that the power of the executive should be limited to "the direction of the war when authorized or begun," while maintaining that the Senate should have "the sole power to declare war."[89]

When the Committee of Detail rendered its report on August 6, it had granted the power to make war to the "Legislature of the United States." The following week discussions among the delegates revealed concerns over the implications of granting war-making authority to a deliberative body. Charles Pinckney was opposed to granting the power to make war to the entire legislature for fear that its proceedings would be too slow. Concerned that the members of the House were too numerous for that body to act expeditiously, Pinckney preferred that the power to make war be vested in the Senate, which also would be "more acquainted with foreign affairs, and most capable of proper resolutions.[90]

Butler, on the other hand, "was for vesting the power [to make war] in the President, who will have all the requisite qualities, and will not make war but when the Nation will support it." At that point Madison and Gerry made a motion to insert the word "declare," striking out "make" war, thus leaving the executive the power to repel sudden attacks. Such an approach would be consistent with the concept of extant or *imminent danger* that had been established under the articles, by which states were permitted to engage in war if attacked or under the threat of imminent attack. Sherman agreed: "The Executive shd. [should] be able to repel and not commence war." For emphasis Gerry noted that he "never expected to hear in a republic a motion to empower the Executive alone to declare war."[91]

Mason also was against giving the power of making war to the executive, because it could not safely be entrusted. He also did not favor giving it to the Senate because "it is not so constructed as to be entitled to it," presumably referring to the fact that the Senate represented the states, not the people, whose interests the government is obliged to protect. In an attempt to clarify the issue, King remarked that "make" war might be understood as to "conduct" it, which he considered to be an executive function.[92]

On the same day that discussions were undertaken, the motion granting the national legislature the power to "declare" rather than "make" war passed 8–1 with one absention. On this issue there seems to have been very little debate. One possible reason is that with minor exceptions all were generally in agreement, though the grounds for New Hampshire's negative vote and the abstention by the Massachusetts delegation are not referenced in *The Records of the Federal Constitution.*

Thus by the end of the federal convention the intent of the delegates was evident. To preclude the exercise of arbitrary power on the part of the executive, Congress was to have the power to declare war. It is important to note here that at the time of the drafting of the American Constitution, formal declarations of war already had fallen into disuse. For example, there was no formal declaration of war when England and France went to war in 1778. However, according to James Kent, a prominent jurist at the time, what was essential was "some formal public act, proceeding directly from a competent source" announcing the changed nature of relations. Of course, that competent source, according to Kent, was Congress.[93]

The task of the executive was to carry out the wishes of Congress. If that meant war, then it fell to the executive to conduct the war, which had been lawfully declared by Congress. Though not mentioned specifically in the Constitution, presumably the president also had the power to repel sudden attacks. However, to Congress fell the power "to provide for calling forth the Militia to execute the Laws of the Union, suppress insurrections and repel invasions." The framers did, however, remain silent on such important foreign policy issues as the role of executive agreement, the recognition of foreign governments, and the control of information acquired by the executive branch that might prove essential to decisions of Congress.

Nonetheless, following the convention, as the Federalists went to work selling the Constitution to the American people, John Jay, in *Federalist Paper No. 4,* reconfirmed the rationale for limiting the power of the nation's executive, observing "that there are PRETENDED [emphasis in original] as well as just causes for war." Among the pretended causes, Jay noted:

absolute monarchs will often make war when their nations are to get nothing by it, but for the purposes and objects merely personal, such as thirst for military glory, revenge for personal affronts, ambition, or private compacts to aggrandize or support their particular families or partisans. These and a variety of other motives, which affect only the mind of the sovereign, often lead him to engage in wars not sanctified by justice or the voice and interests of his people.

Later, even in his heated 1793 defense of President Washington's Proclamation of Neutrality in the war between England and France, which some contended was a violation of our Treaty of Alliance with France, Hamilton, writing as "Pacificus" in the biweekly newspaper *Gazette of the*

United States, continued to recognize that it was "the right of the Legislature 'to declare war and grant letters of marque and reprisal,'"[94] the later tantamount to the authority to engage in hostilities short of a formal declaration.

Similarly, while engaging Hamilton on the issue of Washington's proclamation, Madison, responding as "Helvidius," agreed and went further, arguing that "the two powers to declare war and make treaties...can never fall within a proper definition of executive powers. The natural province of the executive magistrate is to execute laws, as that of the legislature is to make laws." Madison further reasoned: "All his acts therefore, properly executive, must presuppose the existence of the laws to be executed." However, neither a treaty nor a declaration war is "an execution of laws." Rather, they are to have "the force of a *law,* and to be carried into *execution,* like all other laws, by the executive magistrate" (italics in original). Moreover, Madison contended:

Those who are to *conduct a war* cannot in the nature of things, be proper or safe judges, whether *a war ought* to be *commenced, continued,* or *concluded.* They are barred from the latter functions by a great principle in free government, analogous to that which separates the sword from the purse, or the power of executing from the power of enacting laws. (italics in original)[95]

CONCLUSIONS

A careful examination of the records of the convention suggests that for much of the federal convention, the deliberations over the nature and powers of the executive are a story of concern over dangers of an overly powerful executive branch coupled with a determination to tightly circumscribe any wording in the new constitution that might permit an expansion of executive power beyond what the framers deemed appropriate. They had rejected Locke's formulation of a government of three branches—legislative, executive, and federated—in which the powers of the latter included "the power of war and peace, leagues and alliances, and all the transactions with all persons and communities without the commonwealth" and in its exercise of those powers was "always almost united" with the executive.[96] They had rejected Blackstone's conception of the sole prerogative powers of the executive, which included the power to make treaties, raise and regulate fleets and armies, make war and peace, and issue letters of marque and reprisal.

There was to be a sharing of power, or, as Hamilton put it, a "joint possession."[97] Hamilton, reflecting the views of many of those who supported the new Constitution, justified this sharing of power in *Federalist Papers Nos. 64, 70,* and *75.* In those papers he suggested that such characteristics necessary to the effective conduct of foreign policy as an accurate and comprehensive knowledge of foreign politics; a steady and systematic adherence to the same views; and a uniform sensibility to national character, unity, decision, secrecy, and dispatch are common to an executive rather than legislative bodies. On the other hand, he noted in *Federalist Paper No. 75:*

The history of human conduct does not warrant that exalted opinion of human virtue which would make it wise in a nation to commit interests of so delicate and momentous a kind, as those which concern its intercourse with the rest of the world, to the sole disposal of a magistrate created and circumstanced as would be a President of the United States.

Thus the historical record of the framing of the Constitution strongly supports the contention that for the framers, "The concept of presidential unilateralism in foreign affairs was intolerable."[98] As Pulitzer Prize–winning historian Arthur Schlesinger Jr. has written, "The Framers envisaged the conduct of foreign affairs as a partnership between Congress and the president, with Congress, when it came to warmaking, as the senior partner."[99] Indeed, to Congress had been given the lion's share of the powers of the national government. The president could recommend for Congress's consideration such measures as he might judge necessary and expedient and was charged with executing the laws, but to Congress fell the legislative power of the nation. The president could appoint ambassadors, other public ministers and consuls, judges of the Supreme Court, and most other officers of the United States and make treaties with foreign governments, but only with the advice and consent of the Senate, and to Congress fell the power to regulate commerce with foreign nations. The president served as commander in chief of the nation's armed forces, but to Congress fell the power to raise armies and provide for and maintain a navy, and only Congress could declare war. Perhaps above all, Congress was granted the power of the purse, as well as the power to impeach and try the president with the prospect of removal from office.

It was, as Bernard Bailyn has written, that the framers of the Constitution

continued to believe, as deeply as the militants of '76, that power corrupts; that, in the words of the conservative Edward Rutledge of South Carolina [signer of the Declaration of Independence], "the very idea of power included the possibility of doing harm"; that any release on the constraints on the executive—any executive—was an invitation to disaster.[100]

And so the framers of the Constitution had endeavored to create a practical document that built on the historical experiences of governance since ancient Greece and Rome, captured the failings as well as successes of the evolution of parliamentary government in England, and united the wisdoms of the Age of Enlightenment with efforts to eliminate tyranny in order to preserve the unalienable rights of man. They did not attempt to eliminate the tension that would exist between the branches of government, or for that matter, between the national and state governments. Rather, by virtue of the natural tensions of differing interests and approaches, the ability of any one branch of government to usurp power would be precluded.

CHAPTER 3

Laying the Foundation

If, as those who had crafted the Constitution had planned, there was to be a true sharing of power in the making of foreign policy, if Congress was to remain the senior partner in war making, and if the nation was to avoid allowing, as Hamilton had feared, having "its intercourse with the rest of the world" at the "sole disposal" of the president, then Congress would have to ensure that it was well-informed and determined to resist the inevitable efforts of chief executives to encroach upon the powers granted to it by the Constitution.

ON THE PROVISION OF INFORMATION

Generally speaking, in domestic affairs, members of Congress as representatives of the people are regularly informed by their constituents and other interested parties on issues of concern. Armed with such information, they often feel able to act competently. In foreign relations, it is the executive who sends ambassadors to and receives the ambassadors of foreign governments. It is the executive who is in contact with other nations during treaty negotiations. The executive branch, with its foreign missions, intelligence apparatus, and departments such as State, Defense, and Treasury tasked in whole or part to monitor events in foreign lands, has always possessed the lion's share of information. Hence, Congress is largely dependent on the president and other executive branch officials for information required for effective decision making.

The Constitution mandated that the president provide Congress with information. The president "shall from time to time give to Congress

Information of the State of the Union." This seemingly innocuous requirement left much unanswered. What did the framers mean by "from time
to time"? Was this a mandate that the president keep Congress continually updated on all issues foreign and domestic, or if not continually,
how often and in what manner? Did this phrase levy on the president
a requirement to provide Congress any and all information Congress
might request? What about sensitive or secret information? What about
information pertaining to operations within the executive branch? Under
what circumstances, if any, could the executive branch lawfully withhold
information?

Information has always been a key issue in legislative–executive branch
relations, particularly on issues related to foreign affairs. In a letter to
Thomas Jefferson in 1798, Madison warned:

The management of foreign relations appears to be the most susceptible of abuse,
of all the trusts committed to a Government, because they can be concealed or disclosed, or disclosed in such parts & at such times as will best suit particular views;
and because the body of the people are less capable of judging & are more under
the influence of prejudices, on that branch of their affairs, than of any other.[1]

Self-sufficient and seeking to avoid involvement in European wars, the
United States had less of a need for foreign intelligence and, more generally, for information about other nations than did the great powers of
Europe.[2] Indeed, the United States had no professional intelligence organization until 1863, when the Bureau of Military Intelligence was created
during the Civil War, only to be disestablished at war's end. Nevertheless,
questions concerning the communication of information between the executive and Congress surfaced early in the republic.

St. Clair and Gouverneur Morris

Perhaps the earliest episode in which Congress requested information
from the executive branch occurred in 1792 as a result of a failed military
campaign against Native Americans in the Ohio Valley. In November 1791,
during the Northwest Indian War (1785–1795), Major General Arthur St.
Clair and his forces had engaged the Western Confederacy of American
Indians and suffered the worst defeat ever inflicted on the U.S. Army. The
following March the House of Representatives initiated an investigation
of the events. Pursuant to its investigation, the House requested documents from the War Department.

During the previous year, in order to preserve the secrecy of sensitive
military and diplomatic materials, President Washington had introduced
the practice of designating some of the information provided to Congress
as confidential. Since information provided to Congress was generally
open to the public, on July 1 of that same year the very first Congress

passed an act that recognized that some information held by the president should not be made public.[3] As a follow-up, in early 1792, the House adopted a new standing rule that would allow them to strictly protect confidential information from disclosure to the public.[4] It then requested information from the executive branch on the St. Clair case. In response, on March 31 Washington convened a meeting of the heads of all three of his departments (Secretary of War Henry Knox, Secretary of State Jefferson, Secretary of the Treasury Hamilton) and Attorney General Edmund Randolph. According to Jefferson's account of the meeting, while the president did not doubt the propriety of the request, Washington was aware that his response would set a precedent. He also was particularly concerned that "there might be papers of so secret a nature, as that they ought not to be given up."[5]

After a couple of days of careful thought, the committee met again, agreed that the House could rightfully request documents as a part of an "inquest," and recommended that the president "exercise discretion," ought only "to communicate such papers as the public good would permit, and ought to refuse those, the disclosure of which would injure the public." Washington and his colleagues decided to cooperate fully with the House after concluding "in this case, that there was not a paper which might not be properly produced."[6] Washington also thought it appropriate that General St. Clair make himself available to the House in order to explain his conduct. The House committee examined the documents provided, took testimony from executive branch department heads and other witnesses, and received St. Clair's written statement.[7]

Nearly two years later, on January 24, 1794, the Senate passed a resolution requesting that the president provide it with correspondence between Gouverneur Morris, the American minister to France, and the French government, as well as Morris's communications with the office of the Secretary of State. Washington again approached his advisors.[8] Morris, who had an intense dislike for the revolutionary regime in France, "had enraged that government as well as its American sympathizers." Edmund Randolph, who had succeeded Jefferson as secretary of state, reported to the president that a review of the documents revealed that they contained certain passages that would be impolitic to disclose. Secretaries Knox and Hamilton recommended the president exercise discretion and advised against release. Randolph and newly appointed attorney general William Bradford agreed that the president should exercise his discretion and transmit only that information he deemed appropriate. Bradford contended that the president had the authority to do so, grounding his argument on constitutional principles, the rights of the executive, and the nature of diplomacy and strongly suggesting a separation of powers rationale. He further reasoned that despite the fact that the Senate resolution called for all correspondence, it did not "exclude, in the construction of it" the authority of the executive to withhold material that "any circumstances may render improper to be communicated,"[9] a practice better known today as executive privilege. On February 26, Washington provided the Senate with a confidential redacted version of the requested correspondence, removing "particulars," which in his judgment "for public considerations, ought not to be communicated."[10]

Hamilton and the Mishandling of Funds

In early1793 Congress once again requested information from the president during its investigation of the possible mishandling of funds by Secretary of the Treasury Alexander Hamilton. At the same time the House modified its standing rule on the disclosure of confidential materials, claiming it could choose to disclose or not on its own authority. While such a rule might complicate presidential decisions on turning over sensitive intelligence materials in the future, it apparently had little if any effect on Washington's decision in this case. Hamilton claimed "that his communications with the president were privileged from disclosure to the House." The House disagreed. The President found no impropriety and the requested documents were provided to the House.[11]

The historical origins of Hamilton's claim of privilege perhaps can be traced to reactions to the 1701 Act of Settlement. The British Parliament wanted to know who was deciding policies of the king. Sometimes resolutions emanating from the king's council of advisors (Privy Council) did not bear the signatures of those who had given their advice or consent. So in section 3 of the act, Parliament required that "all resolutions taken thereupon shall be signed by such of the Privy Council as shall advise and consent to the same." As a consequence, many advisors ceased to offer advice and some stopped attending meetings altogether. The offending provision of the act was repealed early in Queen Anne's reign.[12]

Jay's Treaty

The case most often cited as an early example of the president's use of executive privilege occurred in 1796 when President Washington refused to comply with a House request for documents relating to the Treaty of Amity, Commerce, and Navigation with Great Britain. The treaty, often referred to as Jay's Treaty after John Jay, who had negotiated the treaty for the United States, among other things expanded trade between the two countries and secured a withdrawal of British forces from forts they occupied in the Northwest Territory in violation of the 1783 Treaty of Paris ending the Revolutionary War.[13]

Jay's Treaty was the subject of intense controversy in the United States. Jeffersonian Democratic-Republicans hotly contested the treaty, arguing inter alia that the 1778 Treaty of Alliance with France was still in effect and that Jay's Treaty could not take effect without the approval of the House of Representatives because it regulated commerce and exercised powers granted to Congress. On March 2, 1796, two days after the treaty went into effect and the day following Washington's message to Congress so stating, Congressman Edward Livingston introduced a resolution requesting that the president provide the House a copy of the instructions initially given to Jay upon entering into negotiations with Britain, "together with the correspondence and other documents relative to the Treaty." Since negotiations with Britain were ongoing, Livingston some days later added to the resolution the phrase "excepting such of said papers as any existing negotiation may render improper to be disclosed." Thus, Congress itself had opened the door for the president, at his discretion, to withhold information. The House approved the resolution 62–37.[14]

Nonetheless, Washington denied the House request, claiming the need for secrecy and contending that "full disclosure of all measures, demands, or eventual concessions...proposed or contemplated, would be extremely impolitic" with a possible "pernicious influence on future negotiations," and "perhaps danger and mischief, in relations to other powers." Moreover, Washington concluded that since he had provided all papers to the Senate for their advice and consent and the treaty had been duly ratified, it had become the law of the land. As such the duties under the treaty become obligatory.[15]

Some have argued that Washington's refusal to provide the House correspondence associated with Jay's Treaty set an early precedent for the right of the president, at his discretion, to withhold documents from Congress. On the other hand, Louis Fisher cautioned: "It would be incorrect to regard Washington's decision to withhold documents from the House as an exercise in executive privilege to keep documents from Congress." In seeking its advice and consent, he had provided the papers affecting the negotiations to the Senate, the body constitutionally charged with the co-powers of treaty making.[16] Nonetheless, the case raised an important question as to whether in the making and ratification of a treaty, which by the Constitution, once ratified, is the supreme law of the land, the president and the Senate have ipso facto appropriated the right of the House to decide on the provision of any laws or funds required for treaty implementation.

Adams and the X, Y, Z Affair

During the administration of John Adams (1797–1803), relations among the United States, Great Britain, and France became a key issue. The British and the French were once again involved in one of their perennial wars. France, having aided the United States in its war with Britain, was upset over Washington's proclamation of neutrality and the Jay's Treaty with Britain, both of which appeared to the French to be a breach of the 1778 U.S.–French Treaty of Alliance and Treaty of Amity and Commerce.

In response, French warships and privateers began seizing American merchant vessels in the West Indies. The Federalists clamored for war.

To calm the situation and avert war, Adams sent Elbridge Gerry, John Marshall, and Charles C. Pinckney to Paris to reach an accommodation. Adams's emissaries were met by three French representatives sent by the ever-wily French foreign minister, Talleyrand. The French representatives made it clear that if the Americans were to expect serious and fruitful negotiations, the United States would have to pay a bribe to Talleyrand and arrange for a large loan to the French government. The Americans refused. France then issued harsher decrees on American shipping.

When the first official dispatches reached Adams, he went before Congress and asked for the authority to arm merchant ships and to take other defensive measures. The Jeffersonian Democratic-Republicans, who favored France, smelled a Federalist plot to drive the United States toward war with France. The House of Representatives demanded the president provide it with all relevant diplomatic correspondence, believing Adams had exaggerated the affair. Initially, Adams refused. Later, encouraged by Federalist supporters, he forwarded all dispatches to the House, substituting the initials X, Y, and Z in place of the real names of Talleyrand's representatives.[17]

Thomas Jefferson and James Monroe

Thomas Jefferson, prior to the trial of Aaron Burr for treason, was confronted with a request from Congress for "any information in possession of the Executive, except as he may deem the public welfare require not be disclosed"[18] that was related to Burr's supposed conspiracy to overthrow the government.

In the year or so following Aaron Burr's 1805 departure from the vice presidency, Jefferson had received a number of warnings that Burr was engaged in a conspiracy against the state. Jefferson mentioned the conspiracy in his annual message to Congress, prompting the House to issue its request. The president responded that the material was "voluminous," "little of it had been given under oath so as to constitute formal and legal evidence," it contained "rumors, conjectures, and suspicions" that rendered it "difficult to sift out the real facts," and some of it had been delivered in "private confidence." Thus "neither safety nor justice will permit the exposing of names." Jefferson did provide the House with at least 13 different documents but apparently withheld over 50, many of which fit the categories he had described. [19]

In a related case involving the trial of Burr, Jefferson boldly claimed executive privilege. He had been subpoenaed by the U.S. Circuit Court at Richmond, Virginia, *deuces tecum* (a writ requiring him to appear in person with the requested documents). Jefferson refused, responding that while "all persons owe obedience to subpoenas," the president has still higher obligations to the "particular set of duties imposed on him." As such the courts could not command the president to respond to every subpoena, keeping him "constantly trudging from north and south and east and west, and withdrawing him entirely from his constitutional duties." This would be an infringement on the doctrine of separation of powers. He further declared it was the president's right to decide "what papers coming to him as President, the public interest permits to be communicated [and] to whom." Marshall disagreed and issued the subpoena. Jefferson did not formally reply to the subpoena. Nonetheless, he did provide some if not all of the documents and offered to testify by deposition.[20]

In 1825 Congress requested that President James Monroe provide documents relating to charges against naval officers in the Pacific. In its request, Congress acquiesced to presidential discretion, asking only for documents that the president "may deem compatible with the public interest." Monroe exercised the discretion granted and withheld the documents, reasoning that since "a thorough and impartial investigation" had yet to take place and the accused officers had not yet been provided an opportunity to defend themselves, the release of the documents would violate their rights.[21]

Andrew Jackson to Grover Cleveland

Successive presidents of the 19th century occasionally chose to withhold information from Congress, though they sometimes added new reasons for declining to provide the information. For example, Jackson refused to provide the Senate with documents containing information about discussions with his cabinet. He believed that the Senate was engaged in petty partisan politics and that in making the request for documents containing information on the private conversations with members of his cabinet pursuant to his duties as the nation's chief executive, the Senate had transgressed its authority, encroaching on executive domain. The Senate acquiesced.[22]

In 1843 the House of Representatives called on President John Tyler to provide it with all information related to army reports on Cherokee land frauds. Tyler initially refused, reiterating reasons advanced by previous presidents for the exercise of discretion and adding to the list yet a new category—the protection of active investigation and litigation.[23] However, when the House challenged Tyler's assertions, declaring that whereas in private litigation "public safety requires that particular evidence to be suppressed," in legislative investigation, where the object was to expose abuses in the administration itself, "the public safety requires that it should be disclosed."[24] In the face of the House's determined stand, Tyler sent the House the requested papers.[25]

Also in 1843 Tyler had come out in favor of the annexation of Texas. He secretly sought to assure Texans that they would be protected by American forces should Mexico renew hostilities. In early 1844 Tyler deployed military forces along America's southern frontier and in the Gulf of Mexico. Later that year, when Tyler submitted the treaty of annexation to the Senate, the Senate demanded information about U.S. troop deployments to the border with Mexico and other incriminating matters. Tyler provided the requested materials.

In 1846 James Polk refused a House request for a presidential accounting of $5,460 spent for "contingency purposes" during the Tyler administration, when negotiations were under way with Great Britain to settle the northeast boundary of the United States.

Since the early days of the Republic, Congress had provided funds for the president's use for intelligence purposes. Responding to a request by Washington during his first state of the Union message, Congress had passed a law on July 1, 1790, setting up the Contingency Fund of Foreign Intercourse, better known as the Secret Service Fund or fund for spies as was later acknowledged in the Senate. By 1794 the fund had grown to over $1 million and represented about 12 percent of the federal budget.[26] A subsequent law later regularized the fund and made the president the sole judge as to whether expenditures should be made public.

Polk, in declining to provide the information, remarked:

The experience of every nation on earth has demonstrated that emergencies may arise in which it becomes absolutely necessary for the public safety or the public good to make expenditures the very object of which would be defeated by publicity. . . . In no nation is the application of such sums ever made public.[27]

Though Polk recognized the House as "the grand inquest of the nation," he made it clear that short of impeachment proceedings, which would open the doors of the executive branch to an examination of all available information, he would decide what might be furnished the House. Thus, Polk significantly raised the threshold for the provision of papers to Congress.

Just two years later the House asked Polk for the papers detailing his instructions to the American minister to Mexico. This time Congress deviated from its time-honored approach of *requesting* that the president supply the information "if not incompatible with the public interest." Rather the House issued an "unconditional" call for all papers. Polk condemned the House for failing to provide "the customary and usual reservation contained in calls of either House of Congress upon the Executive for information relating to our intercourse with foreign nations" and rebuked the House for its "unconstitutional" request.[28]

A few years later, during the administration of Franklin Pierce, a particularly pernicious practice evolved. President Franklin Pierce and the southern Democrats wanted Cuba. In April 1854 Secretary of State William L. Marcy instructed U.S. minister to Spain Pierre Soulé to try to buy

Cuba for $130 million or, failing that, to "detach the island from the Spanish Dominion and from all dependence on any European Power." In August Marcy instructed Soulé to meet with the U.S. ministers to Britain and France to discuss annexation. The three ministers met in Ostend, Belgium, and drafted a confidential document known as the Ostend Manifesto in which they recommended the purchase of Cuba for no more than $120 million. But if Spain refused to sell, they concluded: "We shall be justified in wresting it from Spain." When the manifest became known in Washington, D.C., opponents accused the Pierce administration of attempting to advance the cause of slavery by annexing Cuba.[29] The House demanded a copy of the Ostend Manifesto and documents related to expansion from President Pierce. The State Department furnished the documents, removing an inflammatory page in which the Secretary of State had instructed Soulé to detach Cuba from Spain.[30] Though this was vaguely reminiscent of redactions in the Morris case during the Washington administration, it would be difficult to characterize this omission as anything other than a blatant attempt to deceive Congress to the benefit of not the public, but rather the private welfare of the presidential administration. Regretfully, this would not be the last time the executive branch would attempt to deceive Congress.

In the years following the 1868 impeachment and narrow acquittal of President Andrew Johnson, with the presidency on the defensive, most of the nation's chief executives deferred to congressional requests for information. President Grant turned down one request that was a clear case of harassment. In 1886 President Cleveland rejected a request for papers relating to the removal of a federal attorney, promoting Senate Judiciary Committee chairman George Edmunds to remark that this was the first time in 40 years that either House had failed "on its call to get information that it has asked for from the public departments of Government." The Senate responded by censuring the attorney general for not delivering the papers.[31]

Thus as the first century of the new republic was drawing to a close, the power of Congress to seek and receive information from the executive branch for the effective conduct of its constitutionally mandated duties was largely intact, with presidents usually deferring to congressional requests, including the testimony of senior executive branch officials. Justice Joseph Story in his famous *Commentaries on the Constitution of the United States* summed up the rationale for such an approach in his commentaries on executive duties.

From the nature and duties of the executive department, he must possess more extensive sources of information, as well in regard to domestic as foreign affairs, than can belong to congress. The true workings of the laws; the defects in the nature or arrangements of the general systems of trade, finance, and justice; and the military, naval, and civil establishments of the Union, are more readily seen, and more constantly under the view of the executive, than they can possibly be of any other department. There is great wisdom, therefore, in not merely allowing, but in requiring, the president to lay before congress all facts and information, which may assist their deliberations.[32]

On the other hand, presidents had often laid down markers that under certain conditions—caution, secrecy, ongoing litigation or negotiations, protection of innocents, and so forth—America's chief executive had the right to withhold information for the public good, though not for the private benefit of the president or his administration. For its part, Congress, in general, recognized a limited right of the president to withhold information, almost always preemptively acquiescing by the inclusion in its requests a phrase that the president need not provide information that *he* may deem the public welfare require not be disclosed. Indeed, a strong measure of comity characterized relations between the two branches. The balance of power between the legislative and executive branches that had been sought by the framers apparently had been achieved. The separation of powers was preserved. Checks on executive branch, short of the unlikely use of the heavy-handed impeachment processes, also were preserved, as were checks on unfair demands or excessive intrusion on the executive domain by Congress.

ON FOREIGN POLICY AND WAR POWERS

In the late 18th century and in the 19th century, presidents often took actions in foreign affairs and conflict or potential conflict situations that infringed on or usurped congressional powers. Usually such actions were taken in the absence of constitutional clarity or in response to what they perceived as a crisis or opportunity that demanded quick or secret action. Usually, they recognized that they had gone beyond the charges permitted their office and reported their actions to Congress in acknowledgement of congressional authority.

The relationship between Congress and the president on such issues was tested early in the administration of George Washington. For instance, the Constitution allocates to the American president authority to "receive Ambassadors and other public ministers." However, the Constitution is silent on whether that authority conveys to the executive the right of diplomatic recognition of those countries. Washington was quick to seize the initiative.

After the French Revolution that overthrew the government of King Louis XVI, France dispatched Citizen Edmond Charles Genet to represent France in the United States. In accepting the credentials of the new French minister, Washington thereby conveyed recognition on the new government of France. Pro-French members of Congress, despite what could be taken as an executive branch appropriation of congressional power in foreign affairs, were grateful for the result and did not protest the means. As a result, Congress acquiesced.

Similarly, the Constitution conveys to the president the power "with the Advice and Consent of the Senate, to make Treaties." It is silent on the nature of the manner in which that advice is to be provided. But while Washington was willing to appear before the Senate to discuss treaty issues involving Jay's Treaty of Amity, Commerce, and Navigation with Britain, the Senate, concerned that the president was interfering in its business, rejected his offer. Washington then proceeded to have the treaty negotiated without prior consultation on details.

The Constitution also is silent on whether the obligation to seek the advice and consent of the Senate extends to the breaking or termination of an existing treaty. Approximately one month before receiving Minister Genet, Washington declared the United States neutral in the war between Britain and France. The president had acted unilaterally without congressional authorization. Since the United States had signed a Treaty of Alliance with France in 1778, Washington's decision involved, as a minimum, an interpretation of the treaty and, according to some, a repudiation of assumed treaty obligations. The constitutional question was whether the president had exceeded the authority of his office and infringed on the powers of Congress.

Washington, finding his advisors on opposing sides,[33] took the practical route. Since grand juries were refusing to indict violators of his proclamation of neutrality, particularly those who were assisting the French, because violators had broken no law, his proclamation was without teeth. So Washington turned to Congress, asking it to provide a statutory basis for his proclamation.[34] Congress obliged with the Neutrality Act of 1794.[35]

In general, Washington set the tone for legislative–executive branch relations in the early years of the republic. Although he asserted executive branch authority in the recognition of foreign nations and took the lead in foreign affairs, he was respectful of Congress's war-making authority, and never claimed principal or unilateral or inherent war-making authority.

On the other hand, while Congress itself had established the acceptability of ex post facto consultations on treaties, it also established itself as the body responsible for declarations of neutrality. Additionally, Congress set a precedent that it could, through a broadly worded act, delegate to the president discretion on determining the specifics when it came to the execution of that law. For example, in June 1794 Congress authorized the president to lay and regulate embargoes, "whenever, in his opinion, the public safety shall so require," and to continue or revoke embargoes, "whenever he shall think proper."[36] Similar acts of Congress would continue to reaffirm congressional willingness to delegate such authorities to the president as defined and constrained by the law. Such delegations eventually would be found to be constitutional by the Supreme Court.[37]

WHISKEY REBELLION, 1794

The new federal government had assumed the debts of the states incurred during the Revolutionary War. In 1791 Congress approved a tax on alcohol. The tax imposed a relatively larger burden on small producers (9 cents per gallon) than it did on large producers (6 cents a gallon). Short on cash and frequently using whiskey as a means of exchange, small whiskey producers in western counties from Pennsylvania to Georgia were hard-hit.

By mid-1794 tensions grew into civil protests and civil protests grew into an armed rebellion. Recalling Shays's Rebellion eight years earlier, Washington invoked martial law and called more than 12,000 militiamen to federal service to put down the rebellion.

Congress also opened the door for presidential action during emergencies when it passed the Militia Act of 1792, thus establishing a precedent for presidential emergency powers. The Constitution granted Congress the power "to provide for calling forth the militia to execute the laws of the union, suppress insurrections and repel invasions." In anticipation of emergency situations demanding a quick response, Congress delegated its authority to the president. Such situations included an invasion of the United States or the "imminent danger of invasion from any foreign nation or Indian tribe," as well "insurrections in any state against the government thereof."[38] Thus President Washington was able to act with legal authority in calling militias to service against Indian tribes and to take action during the Whiskey Rebellion (see "Whiskey Rebellion, 1794).[39]

Quasi War and the Supreme Court

In July 1796 France, still at war with the British, was feeling betrayed by American neutrality and outraged by Jay's Treaty of 1795, as well as by the U.S. refusal to pay back loans to Republican France that it previously had incurred to the French Crown. In retaliation, it began seizing U.S. ships trading with Britain.[40] In April 1797, to avoid involving the United States in hostilities, Adams's secretary of the treasury issued a circular restraining the arming of merchant ships sailing from the United States to the West Indies or Europe.[41] By June 1797 the French and their privateers had seized 316 vessels.[42]

In March 1798, after two attempts the previous year to get Congress to authorize the arming of U.S. merchant ships, word reached Adams of the failure of his three envoys to secure an agreement with France and of the insulting manner in which they had been received (see "Adams and the X, Y, Z Affair" earlier in this chapter). Adams then rescinded instructions he had issued prohibiting the arming of merchant ships and urged Congress to promptly adopt his recommended precautionary measures.[43] Congressional opposition to the Adams efforts crumbled and within a year Congress had passed no fewer than 24 acts[44] that provided for the arming of merchant ships, the capturing of French shipping, increasing the size of the regular army, funding the construction of new warships, creation of a Department of the Navy, establishing a Marine Corps, suspending commercial intercourse with France, and abrogating the Treaty of Alliance. The undeclared quasi war with France was on. Adams had neither initiated nor sustained it without the consent of Congress. The war finally ended with the Treaty of Montefontaine, but not before France and the United States had experienced numerous naval engagements and ship seizures.

On the other hand, a truly significant question did emerge from Adams's handling of the quasi war: Had Adams, by suspending his instructions prohibiting the arming of merchants without first seeking congressional approval, exceeded his constitutional authority and usurped Congress's responsibility to declare war?[45] The argument that he had does not appear to be sustainable (see "Had Adams Usurped Congressional Authorities in Suspending His Prohibition on the Arming of U.S. Merchant Ships?").

HAD ADAMS USURPED CONGRESSIONAL AUTHORITIES IN SUSPENDING HIS PROHIBITION ON THE ARMING OF U.S. MERCHANT SHIPS?

According to Professor Dean Alfange Jr., Adams could be seen as indirectly authorizing vessels sailing under the American flag to use force to resist the lawful actions afforded by international law to belligerents to board neutral shipping in order to search for contraband items destined for their enemies. On the other hand, under international law, every merchant ship on the high seas is regarded as part of the territory of the state to which it belongs.* Thus, if Adams's objective was to preclude France not from valid searches under international law, but rather from those searches undertaken as hostile acts "solely for the purpose of demonstrating French discontent with American foreign policy," which seems to have been the case, then Adams carried out his constitutional duty to repel foreign attacks on the United States.

See Alfange, "Quasi-War," 279–80.
*Henry W. Halleck, *International Law* (San Francisco: H. H. Bancroft, 1861), 592, cited by Alfange.

Three Supreme Court cases that emerged from actions taken during the quasi war with France established several important precedents. All three cases involved the seizure of merchant vessels by American ships. The first two cases addressed the nature of war and whether war actually existed, since Congress had not formally declared so. The third addressed the limits of presidential power once war had been authorized.

In *Bas v. Tingy* (1800)[46] a French privateer had captured the American ship *Eliza*, captained by John Bas. Three weeks after its capture, the American ship *Ganges* recaptured the *Eliza*. The captain of the *Ganges* (Tingy) sued for salvage rights equaling half the value. However, the law allowing the salvage value of one-half applies only to states that are at war with the United States. But the American Congress had not formally declared war against France.

The Court, in delivering its opinion, confirmed that Congress is the constitutional body granted the power to *authorize* hostilities either through a formal declaration or by other authorizing acts and that its powers extend to both general, or "perfect," or limited, or "imperfect," wars. In this case, since Congress had authorized hostilities, a state of (imperfect) war existed.

The *Talbot v. Seeman* (1801)[47] case involved the merchant vessel *Amelia*, whose owners were from a country that was neutral in the Franco-American quasi war. The French had seized the vessel and armed and manned it. The American warship USS *Constitution* subsequently captured the ship. Captain Talbot, commander of the USS *Constitution*, asserted salvage rights over the vessel. Seeman and other owners claimed that the vessel should be returned to them, arguing that since there was no declared war, the seizure was illegal. Chief Justice Marshall responded for the Court, reaffirming the Court's decision in *Bas v. Tingy* that Congress may authorize general or partial hostilities, and having done so the laws of war apply.

The third case to emerge from the quasi war, *Little v. Barreme* (1804)[48] involved the seizure of a Danish merchant ship, the *Flying Fish*, by an American frigate. In 1799 Congress had passed a law authorizing the seizure of American ships sailing *to* French ports. President Adams's instructions to the secretary of the navy expanded on the legislation to include ships traveling *to or from* French ports, including those that might have really been American but covered by Danish or other foreign papers. Under such instructions, the USS *Boston* seized the *Flying Fish* after its departure from the French port of Jeremie en route to St. Thomas, then under Danish control. The claimants (Barreme) argued that the seizure was illegal and sued for the vessel's return and damages. Chief Justice Marshall ruled that the task of the president is to "take care that the laws be faithfully executed," and therefore his instructions had exceeded the authority granted him under the law. Thus the Court found in favor of Barreme.

The Court's ruling in these three cases clearly set down important constitutional markers. The Constitution grants to Congress and Congress alone the "whole powers" to "authorize" hostilities, whether they be general or limited/partial. And even in war, be it general or partial, where Congress has legislated, the president cannot exceed the authorities granted him by Congress.

From the Shores of Tripoli

Presidents from Thomas Jefferson to John Tyler, with a few exceptions, characteristically followed the precedents set by Washington and Adams in foreign affairs. They also comported with Supreme Court cases that had defined the role of Congress and limits of executive power in war and peace.

Jefferson

After assuming the presidency in 1801 President Thomas Jefferson refused to pay the customary tribute to rulers of the Barbary States (see "Jefferson and the Barbary Pirates"). He then sent a small squadron of frigates into the Mediterranean to protect American commerce from attack. Jefferson's "military operations received advanced authority from Congress in ten separate statutes."[49] Indeed, although the pasha of Tripoli had declared war on the United States, Jefferson resisted the temptation to interpret this act by the pasha as a justification for unlimited military activity. Rather, he sent a small squadron of frigates to the Mediterranean to protect American merchant vessels from attack. He then asked Congress for further guidance. When a Tripolitan cruiser attacked one of the U.S. frigates, the U.S. ship returned fire in defense and captured the ship.

Jefferson, in reporting the incident in his first annual message to Congress in December 1801, noted that since only Congress had the right to license hostilities, beyond responding to the attack, the U.S. frigate took no further offensive action. Jefferson told Congress: "Unauthorized by the Constitution, without the sanction of Congress, to go beyond the line of defense, the vessel, being disabled from committing further hostilities, was liberated with its crew." Thus Jefferson had resisted the temptation to go beyond defense and wage an offensive war. Congress responded by passing a law authorizing the navy to wage limited war against Tripoli.[50]

When faced with incursions into Louisiana by the Spanish in Florida, Jefferson exhibited the same reluctance to move beyond strict constitutionality that he had demonstrated in the case of the Barbary pirates. In a special message to Congress in December 1805 he said: "Congress alone is constitutionally invested with the power of changing our condition from

JEFFERSON AND THE BARBARY PIRATES

Ottoman Corsairs, or Barbary pirates, operating from North Africa, had been attacking ships, raiding coastal towns, and enslaving captives in the Mediterranean and along the western coasts of Africa and Europe since the 11th century. European powers were either forced to defend their merchant shipping or pay tribute to the rulers of the Barbary States.

When U.S. shipping lost the protection of the British navy at the end of the Revolutionary War, America followed the custom of paying tribute. Jefferson had long opposed such payments, contending that payment only invited more demands. Rather, arguing for a "strong navy that can reach the pirates," he asserted: "It would be best to effect peace through war." When he became president in 1801, he refused to accede to Tripoli's demand for money. The pasha of Tripoli responded by declaring war.

For greater detail, see Gerard W. Gawalt, "America and the Barbary Pirates: An International Battle Against an Unconventional Foe," The Library of Congress American Memory Series at http://memory.loc.gov/ammem/collections/jefferson_papers/mtjprece.html.

peace to war, I have thought it my duty to await their authority for using force."[51]

On the occasion of the unprovoked attack on the American frigate USS *Chesapeake* in June 1807 by the British ship HMS *Leopard* (see "The Chesapeake Affair, 1807"),[52] Jefferson did, however, spend unappropriated money for munitions and undertook major initiatives to strengthen America's defenses. "Uncertain how far hostilities were intended, and the town of Norfolk, indeed, being threatened with immediate attack,"[53] Jefferson readied America's defenses.

With Congress out of session until later in the year, Jefferson "called all naval vessels and merchant vessels home, ordered naval gunboats readied, armed seven coastal fortresses, sent field guns to state militia, gave warnings to all frontier posts, and informed state governors that he might call 100,000 militia members to federal service."[54] Jefferson had exercised prerogative powers well within the responsibilities accorded his office by the framers of the Constitution. An American ship had been attacked, suddenly and without warning.

Recognizing the prerogatives of Congress, he did reconvene that body early, carefully explained his actions, and sought post facto blessing.[55] Jefferson claimed no inherent powers. Rather, he undertook the activities that he later acknowledged were done "at his own peril," throwing himself on the justice of the country to decide whether he had acted for the good or hurt of the people.[56]

THE CHESAPEAKE AFFAIR, 1807*

The *Chesapeake* had departed Hampton Roads, Virginia, on the morning of June 22 en route to the Mediterranean to protect American merchant vessels from the Barbary States. Midafternoon, 10 miles southeast of Cape Henry, the captain of the *Leopard*, after signaling he wished to send dispatches to the Mediterranean through the courtesy of the *Chesapeake*, boarded the American ship and demanded to search the ship for deserters. When denied, the *Leopard*, in an unprecedented surprise attack, a virtual act of war, opened fire on the *Chesapeake*, killing three and wounding 18. After the American ship struck its colors to avoid additional casualties, the British boarded the ship and took four sailors they claimed were deserters. The American public was outraged. Jefferson closed U.S. ports and coastal waters to British ships, only to find that British commanders haughtily remained anchored in Chesapeake Bay, endangering Norfolk and other nearby ports.

*Paterson et al., *American Foreign Relations*, vol. 1, 38–42.

Madison and Monroe and the Monroe Doctrine

James Madison, as a framer of the Constitution, was a strong proponent of limiting the power of the chief executive. As president, he continued the practices of his predecessors in foreign affairs. When it came to war, he was careful not to tread on congressional prerogatives. For example, in 1815, during what is often called the Second Barbary War, he sought and obtained congressional authorizations for limited hostilities against Algeria.

President James Monroe, on the other hand, was in some ways an exception to the general approach to legislative–executive branch relations taken by the first four presidents. Monroe, on occasion, was prepared to undertake formidable diplomatic initiatives on his own. The most notable example was what later became known as the Monroe Doctrine, in which, among other things, he declared that henceforth the American continents should "not be considered as subjects for future colonization by European powers" and "any attempt on their part to extend their system to any portion of this hemisphere, as dangerous to our peace and safety" and "unfriendly" toward the United States.[57]

Though prior to that announcement Monroe had consulted with members of his cabinet and other senior statesmen, he did not consult but rather informed Congress. Congress, for its part, did little. Some of its members expressed their concern that the president was "assuming unwarranted power." But for the most part, the president's promulgation of a doctrine that if implemented could lead to war went largely unchallenged by Congress.[58]

Despite the grand assertions of Monroe's Doctrine, however, it was apparently not his administration's intention to trample the war power prerogatives of Congress in pursuit of the doctrine's objectives. When his secretary of state, John Quincy Adams, was asked by the government of Colombia how the United States intended to resist the interference of the Holy Alliance in Latin American affairs, he replied that the Constitution confided "the ultimate decision...to the Legislative Department."[59]

On the other hand, Monroe was unable to resist the temptation to go beyond the concept of defense adhered to by Jefferson during the Barbary war. Rather, without prior consultations with Congress or prior agreement with Spain, he ordered General Andrew Jackson to take the offensive and pursue raiding Seminole Indians, if necessary, into Spanish Florida, claiming the right to take offensive action "on the principle of self-defense."[60] In late March 1818 Jackson crossed into Florida, chasing Indians, fighting Spaniards, and hanging Englishmen. Such activities might well have involved the United States in a war with Spain.

Congress investigated. But public praise for Jackson's boldness and success, as well as politics, trumped constitutional responsibility. Congress failed to repudiate either Jackson or Monroe.[61] Congress thus permitted an aggrandizement of presidential power. Heretofore, the concept that had been tacitly, though not explicitly, agreed to at the Constitutional Convention—that the president has the right to repel attacks—was allowed, without formal congressional objection, to expand to include the right to take offensive action in self-defense.

It would be wrong, however, to conclude that Monroe differed greatly from his predecessors. As Madison had written in *Federalist 51:* "In a republican government, the legislative authority necessarily predominates." Monroe agreed. In a message delivered to the House of Representatives in May 1822, he acknowledged that in examining the powers of the three branches of national government:

Of these the legislative,...is by far the most important. The whole system of the National Government may be said to rest essentially on the powers granted to this branch.[62]

John Quincy Adams

John Quincy Adams, when serving as Monroe's secretary of state, had defended General Jackson on his incursion into Florida and was "unique among the statesmen of the first half-century of the republic in objecting to the assignment of war power to Congress," which he considered better placed with the executive.[63] Nonetheless, when president, he was careful not to usurp congressional war-making powers. Reiterating the same point Adams himself had made a few years earlier, Adams's secretary of state, Henry Clay, told the Argentines:

When the case shall arrive,...and it becomes consequently necessary to decide whether this country will or will not engage in war, Congress alone, you well know, is competent, by our Constitution, to decide that question.[64]

During Adams's tenure, the Supreme Court, in the *Martin v. Mott* (1827) case, attempted to clarify the prerogative powers of the president in emergencies and to define what might constitute an emergency in which such powers might be executed. The case involved a dispute between the governors of the New England states and the federal government, which arose during the War of 1812. Though the Militia Act of 1795, which had replaced the Militia Act of 1792, had granted the president the right to call forth the militia when the United States was in imminent danger of invasion, the governors of the New England states refused to do so. They claimed that the right to determine the danger of invasion rested with each of them as commanders in chief of their respective state militias. State supreme courts had supported the governors' assertions.

When the case finally reached the Supreme Court in 1827, Justice Story, delivering the opinion of the Court, held that "the authority to decide whether the exigency has arisen, belongs exclusively to the President, and that his decision is conclusive upon all other persons." Importantly, Story further concluded that though this power belongs to the president, it is "limited" and "to be exercised upon sudden emergencies, upon great occasions of state, and under circumstances which may be vital to the existence of the Union."[65] Thus, the Court recognized a prerogative power of the executive but carefully circumscribed that power.

Old Hickory

General Andrew Jackson had earned the name "Old Hickory" for his strict discipline as he marched his troops back to Tennessee following his decisive defeat of the British in the Battle of New Orleans, the final major battle of the War of 1812. The same toughness characterized his presidency. He was an assertive president, particularly in domestic politics.

However assertive Jackson was on domestic issues, he generally deferred to Congress on issues that might involve war. Though he had taken it upon himself to order a U.S. warship to Latin America to protect American merchant shipping from attacks by raiders from Argentina, he sought ex post facto congressional support for his actions. And while Congress had largely acquiesced and presidents had come to freely exercise the power of diplomatic recognition, when it came to recognizing the independence of Texas, which was still claimed by Mexico, Jackson deferred to Congress.

A major issue did arise during Jackson's presidency: Could Congress delegate its war-making authority to the president? France had failed to pay long-standing claims for damages to American merchant shipping during its war with England earlier in the century. Jackson recommended "that a law be passed authorizing reprisals upon French property in case provision shall not be made for the payment of the debt at the approaching session of the French Chambers."[66] Such legislation, if passed, would have granted Jackson authority to seize French vessels, which could be seen as an act of war.

This was not the first time the issue of congressional delegation of its authority had arisen. In 1799 Hamilton had proposed, but to no avail, that the war-making authority be delegated to President Adams during America's quasi war with France should negotiations fail. In 1810 President Madison had objected to a Senate resolution authorizing him, should he deem it expedient, to order the navy to protect American shipping against British and French raiders. He considered it an unconstitutional delegation to the President of Congress's war-making authority.[67]

Following a similar line of reasoning Congress rejected the resolution that would grant Jackson his request. One of those who led the fight against the resolution asked his colleagues whether when it was Congress's duty "to decide on our great relations with foreign nations, we would shrink from the task and throw the responsibility... on other departments of Government."[68]

John Tyler

John Tyler was an unpopular president who succeeded to the presidency following the death of William Henry Harrison, who had served only 32 days in office. Tyler spouted constitutionalism. Nevertheless, he sought annexation of Texas to the Union "as a vehicle for lifting his political fortunes."[69] Texas, however, had withdrawn its annexation request in 1838 and feared that any renewed effort at annexation would jeopardize efforts to gain Mexican recognition of Texas independence and possibility invite renewed efforts by Mexico to resecure Texas to Mexico. In 1843, to reassure Texans that they would be safe from Mexican attack, Tyler instructed his secretary of state to assure Texans orally that, once a treaty was signed, American forces would protect them. Unfortunately the American chargé in Austin put the oral assurance in writing. Tyler, fearing Congress might demand all papers relating to his policies toward Texas, divorced himself from the promise and publicly declared: "The employment of the army or navy against a foreign power, with which the United States are at peace, is not within the competency of the President."[70]

Tyler, however, had not given up. His administration entered into negotiations with Texas and signed a treaty of annexation on April 12, 1844. Since Mexico had announced that it would consider a ratification of the treaty a declaration of war, Tyler, unilaterally, without congressional authorization, deployed military forces to the border between Texas and Mexico and to the Gulf of Mexico to protect Texas from Mexico pending Senate approval of a treaty.[71] Though perhaps a prudent action, this was hardly a defensive act, since Texas was not yet a member of the federal union. The Senate, for its part, demanded an accounting of American actions and on June 8, 1844, unwilling to take a controversial step during an election year, rejected the treaty. But Congress did not sanction Tyler for the deployment of forces without its approval.

With much of the country in favor of annexation and the elections over, Tyler decided to bypass the requirement for a two-thirds vote in the Senate for ratification. After consulting president-elect James Polk, he proposed annexation a House–Senate joint resolution, which would require only a majority vote. Nowhere does the Constitution suggest House participation in the treaty-making process.

Once again politics trumped the exercise by Congress of its constitutional responsibilities, and Texas was annexed. "Congress, by annexing Texas through joint resolution, placed another weapon in the hands of the Presidency."[72]

To the Halls of Montezuma and Beyond

James K. Polk

On September 14, 1847, army and marine forces under the command of General Winfield Scott entered the heart of Mexico City and captured the Mexican National Plaza, where before had stood the Halls of Montezuma.

The war with Mexico had begun nearly a year and a half earlier when President James Polk ordered "Old Rough and Ready" General Zachary Taylor across the Nueces River, previously the commonly accepted boundary between the United Sates and Mexico, into territory claimed by Texas since its independence from Mexico. Some assumed that Polk wanted war with Mexico not only in order to gain the territory between the Nueces and Rio Grande rivers, but also as a pretext to capture California.

Taylor had headed south into territory claimed by Mexico and after reaching the north bank of the Rio Grande blockaded the Mexican town of Matamoras, an act of war under international law. Following some weeks of tension and negotiations, the Mexican military responded to Taylor's transgressions and attacked his forces. When word reached Washington, Polk sent a war message to Congress. "The cup of forbearance has been exhausted," Polk wrote. "Mexico...has invaded our territory and shed American blood upon American soil."[73] Polk requested that Congress recognize that a state of war existed between the United States and Mexico.

Congress had no independent source of intelligence. There were no formal intelligence structures. Intelligence, or what there was of it, was in the hands of the executive departments. Congress, accepting at face value the president's word, did not choose to probe further. Debate in the House was limited to two hours. Those who sought additional time to examine the 144 pages of documents that Polk had sent to Congress along with his war message were denied. The Speaker of the House repeatedly failed to recognize those who wished to ask detailed questions about how the war got started. Some argued there was insufficient information to determine whether the government of Mexico intended war. Some wondered whether it might have been an errant commander who had undertaken the attack on American forces. Some wondered whether, in fact, the U.S. president had the authority to blockade the port of Matamoras in the first place.[74] Those who supported the president's call may well have remembered the political fate that befell the Federalist Party, many of whose members opposed the War of 1812.[75] Many had considered those who opposed that war treasonous and their opposition contributed to the demise of the party as a political movement.

Demonstrating the kind of patriotism that suffocates responsibility, Congressman Brinkerhoff declared:

For myself I hold it no part of my duty to inquire how this war originated, not wherefore; whether it was the fault of any one here, or any one connected with the government. It is enough for me, as a man professing an ordinary share of patriotism and representing a patriotic constituency, to know it exists; and from this state of things, to arrive at the conclusion (necessarily, it seems to me) that our only course is to conquer peace by a vigorous prosecution of the war just commenced.[76]

On May 11, 1846, the House voted 174 to 14 in favor of the resolution. The following day the Senate followed suit, voting 40 to 2. Legislation had been stampeded through Congress and the war was on.

As the war was approaching its end, the House of Representatives debated a joint resolution honoring Major General Taylor. Congressman Ashmun moved to amend the resolution praising Taylor's successes, adding "in a war unnecessarily and unconstitutionally begun by the President of the United States."[77] Ignoring the role that Congress itself had played in recognizing the existence of a state of war two years earlier, the House passed the amendment 85 to 81. The war finally ended with the signing of a peace treaty at Guadalupe Hidalgo in February 1848.

Had a pattern been set for future actions by Congress such as the Tonkin Gulf Resolution of 1964 or perhaps the 2003 Iraq War, especially in light of the fate that met those who opposed the Gulf War of 1990–1991? John Quincy Adams, an expansionist himself, decried the war, declaring Polk's claim of Mexican aggression "in direct and notorious violation of the truth." Abraham Lincoln, at that time a representative from Illinois, commented in a letter to his partner, W. H. Herndon, "Allow the President to invade a neighboring nation, whenever *he* shall deem it necessary to repel an invasion...and you allow him to make war at pleasure. Study to see if you can fix *any limit* to his power in this respect." Lincoln further commented:

Suppose a President "should choose to say he thinks it necessary to invade Canada, to prevent the British from invading us, how could you stop him? You may say to him, "I see no probability of the British invading us" but he will say to you "be silent: I see it, if you don't."[78]

The reason the Constitution granted the war-making power to Congress, Lincoln continued, was because kings had always been involving and impoverishing their people in wars. "This, our [constitutional] convention understood to be the most oppressive of all Kingly oppressions; and they resolved to so frame the Constitution that no one man should hold the power of bringing this oppression upon us."[79]

An important Supreme Court ruling emerged from the war. The 1850 *Fleming v. Page* case was brought to recover duties paid to Page, collector at the port of Philadelphia, by Fleming and Marshal on goods shipped from Tampico, Mexico, at that time conquered and under the control of the U.S. military. Fleming contended that once conquered Tampico had become part of the Union. Therefore goods shipped from there should not be subjected to foreign duties. In delivering the opinion of the Court, Chief Justice Roger B. Taney denied the claim, maintaining that the boundaries of the United States had not been extended by conquest. More importantly, Taney went on to clarify and circumscribe the duties of the president when acting as commander in chief, asserting that once war is declared, the duties and power of the president acting in the capacity of commander in chief "are purely military."

He is authorized to direct the movement of...military forces...employ them in the manner he may deem most effectual....He may invade the hostile country, and subject it to the sovereignty and authority of the United States. But his conquests do not enlarge the boundaries of this Union, nor extend the operation of our institutions and laws beyond the limits before assigned to them by the legislative power.[80]

Thus, the Court, building on the *Little v. Barreme* case, set forth the principle that in times of war or other authorized hostilities the office of the president accrues no political functions in conquered and occupied lands beyond those granted by Congress.

Millard Fillmore, Franklin Pierce, and James Buchanan

Following the short presidency and untimely death in office of President Zachary Taylor, both presidents Milliard Fillmore and Franklin

Pierce exercised what they considered their prerogative to send a military force into situations that might lead to war. But both men, unlike Polk, respected the prerogative of Congress to authorize hostilities. In 1852 under Fillmore and in 1854 under Pierce, Commodore Matthew Perry was ordered to Japan to seek protection for shipwrecked American seamen who heretofore had often been captured and treated brutally and to open Japan to trade. Though in both instances Perry arrived in Japan in command of a fleet of warships, both presidents recognized that only Congress had the right to declare war.

President James Buchanan recognized that Congress had the sole and exclusive power under the Constitution to authorize hostilities whether general or limited in nature.[81] However, he was concerned about the limits on executive branch authority in the field of foreign affairs. In his second annual message to Congress in December 1858 he wrote: "The executive government of this country in its intercourse with foreign nations is limited to the employment of diplomacy alone." Buchanan further noted that once having employed diplomacy, the executive branch "can proceed no further. It can not legitimately resort to force without the direct authority of Congress, except in resisting and repelling hostile attacks."[82] Lamenting the fact that the powers of the president were limited, Buchanan expressed his concern that the executive branch "can do no more than remonstrate" when outrages are committed.[83] To resolve this problem, he often asked Congress for a pre-delegation of authority to act in situations where the local authorities in foreign countries "do not possess the physical power, even if they possess the will, to protect" American lives and property.[84] Congress consistently refused to pre-delegate such authority to Buchanan.

Another important court case, *Durand v. Hollins* (1860),[85] emerged during this period. In 1854 an American warship under the command of Lieutenant Hollins bombarded the town of Greytown, Nicaragua, because the local authorities refused to pay reparations for an attack on the U.S. consul in that city. Durand, an American citizen whose property had been destroyed in the bombardment, sued Hollins in federal court for damages. Hollins contended that he was acting lawfully under the orders of the president and secretary of the navy and that no damages should be paid. Justice Samuel Nelson, on circuit, concurred. Nelson went on to note that the president was "the only legitimate Organ of the General Government, to open and carry on correspondence or negotiations with foreign nations...For this purpose, the whole Executive power of the country is placed in his hands," and that the president may exercise that power through the "departments of government...by negotiation or by force." Nelson further concluded that since "acts of lawless violence, or of threatened violence to the citizen or his property, cannot be anticipated...to be effectual...may...require the most prompt and decided action."[86] He also acknowledged that it was the duty of the president to use those powers under certain circumstances in the defense of American citizens or property abroad. Thus, on the one hand Nelson advanced the cause of presidential prerogative powers. On the other hand, in a view consistent with previous Supreme Court decisions, Nelson limited the use of those powers to times of emergency, leaving undefined just what those "certain circumstances" were when the president could act to protect American citizens and property. The case would become the focus of national controversy a century later, with some arguing that the president has not only the duty but also the responsibility to use American military forces abroad to protect American lives, property, and interests without seeking prior approval from Congress.

Lincoln and Locke

The presidency of Abraham Lincoln tested the limits of John Locke's theories on prerogative powers in the American context. On April 12, 1861, Confederate forces opened fire on the federal garrison at Fort Sumter in the harbor of Charleston, South Carolina. The Southern states had risen in rebellion. The president faced stark choices—the destruction of the Federal Union or its preservation through the use of force. No doubt, Congress's unwillingness to grant Buchanan his request for authority to protect American lives and property led Lincoln to delay calling Congress into special session until the war had already been under way for nearly three months. No doubt, he believed the situation was dire. No doubt it met the requirements set forth by Justice Story for the exercise of prerogative in the *Martin v. Mott* case—in "sudden emergencies, upon great occasions of state, and under circumstances which may be vital to the existence of the Union."

In meeting the emergency with force, "Lincoln ignored one law and constitutional provision after another."[87] Among other things, without congressional authorization, he called 75,000 militia to federal service, blockaded Southern ports, called into the service of the infantry and cavalry more than 40,000 volunteers, increased the size of the regular army and navy, spent public money, and authorized the suspension of the privilege of the writ of habeas corpus and ordered the arrest and detention of individuals who might be "dangerous to the public safety."[88] However, in so doing, Lincoln was exercising not Blackstone's nearly absolute prerogatives of kings (see chapter 2), but rather Locke's more temporary and thus limited prerogatives to be judged by the people's representatives in terms of whether the prerogatives exercised served the "good of society."

Lincoln recognized he had exceeded his authority under Article II of the Constitution and had tread on the authorities constitutionally granted to the people's representatives. He believed he had done so in an extraordinary emergency for the public good. In near perfect Lockean form, Lincoln made use of the power available to him for the good of society until such time as the legislature assembled and sanctioned his efforts. On July 4,

1861, during their first session following the commencement of hostilities, Lincoln informed Congress:

These measures, whether strictly legal or not, were ventured upon under what appeared to be a popular demand and a public necessity, trusting then, as now, that Congress would readily ratify them. It is believed that nothing has been done beyond the constitutional competency of Congress.[89]

Of course Lincoln can be faulted for not having called Congress into session earlier. Though in responding to the most desperate of emergencies since the Revolutionary War, he may well have felt that speed of response and unity of effort were essential if the Union was to be preserved. Yet, it is important to keep in mind that though Lincoln justified his actions based on the need to respond in an emergency, his solemn obligation to "preserve, protect, and defend the Constitution" and his role as commander in chief, Lincoln made no claims of inherent power but rather conceded that he had exceeded his authority and sought retroactive congressional approval for his actions, albeit after significant steps had been taken to respond to the situation.

Congress debated at length Lincoln's request and on August 6, 1861, declared: "All acts, proclamations, and orders of the President of the United States after the fourth of March...are hereby approved and in all respects legalized and made valid, to the same intent and effect as if they had been issued and done under the previous express authority and direction of the Congress of the United States."[90] The exception was Lincoln's suspension of writs of habeas corpus. Lincoln had argued that such a suspension was constitutionally authorized during times of rebellion or invasion, when the public safety may so require, that the Constitution was silent on which branch or who had the authority to exercise such a power, and that confronted with a dangerous emergency it was the president's to exercise, by virtue of his duty to take care that the laws be faithfully executed.[91] Congress apparently disagreed.

From a practical point of view, Lincoln's suspension of habeas corpus may have seemed justified. However, his argument that the Constitution was silent on which branch had the authority to authorize a suspension of such a basic right of citizens was hollow. Nowhere else in the Constitution but in Article I, which among other things defines the powers of Congress and the limitations thereto, is the issue of habeas corpus raised. It is not unreasonable to presume that the framers considered the suspension of such a right a congressional, not a presidential, prerogative. Congress could have held its ground. However, once again, Congress unnecessarily conceded power to the executive branch.

Lincoln also can be faulted for continuing to exercise unilateral power until war's end. Again, since Congress acquiesced, it bears a lion's share of the responsibility for the expansion of presidential power during the Civil War.

For its part, the Supreme Court in the *Prize Cases* in 1863 affirmed the *limited* right of the president to respond to sudden attacks. The question before the Court had to do with the seizure of ships. President Lincoln had not sought a declaration of war but proceeded to blockade Southern ports and seize Southern shipping. Under international law, in the absence of war such seizures were an act of piracy. Justice Robert C. Grier delivered the opinion of the Court, holding that if the United States is invaded by a foreign nation "or States organized in rebellion," the president is "not only authorized but bound to resist force, by force....without waiting for special legislative authority." Thus the Court supported the presidential use of emergency powers. Nevertheless, Grier reiterated: "Congress alone has the power to declare...war." The president, he said, "has no power to initiate or declare a war either against a foreign nation or a domestic State."[92]

Of greater concern are the initiatives undertaken without congressional authorization after Congress had reconvened. Throughout the war Lincoln exercised a wide variety of powers, which, if legal at all, were heretofore generally understood to be within the purview of Congress. For example, he asserted the right to proclaim martial law behind the lines, arrest people without a warrant, seize property, suppress newspapers, and emancipate the slaves.[93] Such actions led historian Arthur Schlesinger to remark: "No President had ever undertaken such sweeping action in the absence of congressional authorization. No President had ever challenged Congress with such a massive collection of faits accomplis."[94]

Though in peacetime Lincoln recognized that the powers of the presidency would be limited,[95] he believed that in wartime, under his powers as commander in chief, he had the authority to undertake actions that might not be constitutional in times of peace. "I conceive that I may in an emergency do things on military grounds which cannot constitutionally be done by Congress," Lincoln speculated, adding: "As commander-in-chief...I suppose I have the right to take any measure which may best subdue the enemy."[96]

Congress Resurgent

With the end of the war, as Lincoln had noted, the powers adhering to the presidency during a desperate emergency began to wane. First, the Supreme Court, perhaps reluctant to act firmly in time of war, stepped in. In *Ex-parte Milligan* (1866) the Court went beyond the confines of a decision solely relevant to the issue of habeas corpus and military courts that had been placed before it. Echoing concerns so often expressed by the framers, the Court repudiated the idea that in times of emergency there might be a higher law than the Constitution.[97]

Four years later the Supreme Court clarified the role of the president vis-à-vis Congress. In *Miller v. U.S.* the Court held that while "presidential war powers derived from congressional authorization, those of Congress were limited only by the 'law of nations.'"[98]

Congress also was prepared to clip the wings of the presidency. When President Andrew Johnson was seen to be working against congressional efforts during Reconstruction following the war, Congress mulled ideas of impeachment. When Congress overrode the president's veto and passed the Tenure of Office Act, Johnson chose to ignore the act and its requirement of obtaining Senate consent to remove an executive branch official whose appointment required confirmation by the Senate. The House responded by impeaching him. Nearly three months later, he was acquitted by a one-vote margin in the Senate. The impeachment of the president was a turbulent and disruptive process not to be repeated for more than a century.

The impeachment of Johnson, however, may have calmed subsequent presidents' ardor for challenging the powers of Congress. For 30 years following the Civil War, in the absence of any great crises that might propel the executive branch to the forefront, power shifted back toward Congress.

Nevertheless, presidents as well as American military commanders continued to involve the United States in military adventures, sometimes acting with the implied or expressed approval of Congress (e.g., interdicting slave vessels involved in African slave trading, 1920–1923) and often authorizing the use of force against non-sovereign entities (pirates, privateers, slave traders, etc.) without first seeking congressional authorization. And sometimes the use of force by military commanders exceeded the authority granted to them by Congress or the president. On occasion presidents also used force without specific congressional authority, though sometimes acting under a general authorization such as that provided by the 1792 and 1795 Militia Acts. Usually the use of force involved trivial incidents, such as those that emerged when, during periods of insurrections or civil disturbances, foreign governments were unable to provide protection to Americans or their interests (e.g., Sumatra, 1832, 1838–1839; Fiji Islands, 1840, 1855, 1858; Africa, seven times from 1820 to 1859; Korea, 1871, 1888; Mexico, 1876; Egypt, 1882; Samoa, 1888–1889).[99]

Congress did, however, step squarely into its responsibilities in treaty making, reasserting its power at every opportunity. In 1868 the Senate changed its rules to make it easier to amend treaties, requiring only a simple majority to do so. In 1870, when Grant attempted to annex the Dominican Republic by treaty, the Senate rejected it. Indeed, the Senate exercised its power over treaties "with relish, freely rewriting, amending and rejecting treaties negotiated by the executive."[100] Between 1871 and 1898 it ratified no important treaties.[101]

THE FIRST HUNDRED YEARS

During a century following the departure of the framers of the Constitution from Philadelphia, America's chief executives did, for the most part, just what the founders expected. They attempted to accrue power to their office. Nevertheless, with few exceptions they generally provided Congress information it requested. Though there were no formal intelligence structures aside from the short-lived Bureau of Military Intelligence created during the Civil War and the Office of Naval Intelligence and the Military Intelligence Division created in 1882 and 1885, respectively, throughout the 18th and 19th centuries Congress was generally content to leave intelligence matters to the president and his advisors.[102] Presidents also generally were respectful of the Senate's shared responsibility in the making of treaties with foreign nations and the congressional prerogative to authorize hostilities against "sovereign powers."

Those who advance the theory of unilateral executive powers often cite such early presidents as Washington, Adams, Jefferson, Monroe, Jackson, and Lincoln as having set historical precedents for the exercise of such powers in foreign affairs or war making or both. But, more often than not, as we have seen, the arguments brought to bear are a distortion of the political reality surrounding the events in question. Polk, of course, was perhaps the most notable exception, not only in authorizing the movement of military forces into lands claimed by Mexico, an action that was likely to result in a major war, but also for misleading Congress on the circumstances that led to war.

Presidents, and their military commanders on occasion acting on their own initiative, did, however, continue to involve the United States in military conflicts. Incidents were generally, although not always, minor in nature, varying in length, intensity, and number of casualties. None of these events posed grave dangers to America. Many were of such insignificance so as to barely warrant the attention of a busy Congress.

Congress, for its part, generally resisted the temptation to delegate its war-making authority to the president, though it had granted the president authority to exercise his discretion on the details of broad enabling legislation and to act in certain emergencies. On the other hand Congress passed up opportunities to hold the executive in check. The result was a general acceptance of executive predominance in foreign relations; tacit acceptance of the concept that the president can wage an offensive war in defense; implicit acceptance that the president, under certain circumstances, can use U.S. military forces against non-sovereign entities; an endorsement of the idea that the president can seek a joint resolution of Congress as a means of bypassing the treaty requirement of a two-thirds vote of the Senate; and an egregious willingness to allow the president to engage in war on the face value of statements by the president and on the barest threads of intelligence about the actual course of events. Thus, any erosion of congressional authority in both foreign affairs and war making during this period finds its roots as much in congressional acquiescence as it does in presidential assertion.

CHAPTER 4

Gathering Clouds

As the 19th century was drawing to a close, storm clouds began to appear. Power that had moved in the direction of Congress following the Civil War began to swing back in favor of the president. Global imperial competition conspired with events in the Western Hemisphere and around the globe to propel the United States onto the world scene. As global issues began to cast the presidency into the foreground, presidents were increasingly willing to take a more strident approach in addressing events that threatened burgeoning U.S. interests at home and abroad. The Great War and ensuing depression thrust additional power into the hands of the president and added an aura to the office that even infected Congress. Court rulings and congressional acquiescence further pushed the pendulum of power in the direction of the presidency.

IN RE NEAGLE

While the Constitution grants power to Congress "to make all laws which shall be necessary and proper for carrying into execution" those other powers specifically assigned Congress, it is silent on whether the president has such so-called implied powers. The *In re Neagle* (1890) case erased that doubt. The Court held that the Constitution requires the president to take an oath in which he solemnly swears to "faithfully execute the office of President of the United States, and will to the best of [his] ability, preserve, protect and defend the Constitution of the United States." According to the Court, as a consequence of this oath the president "is invested" with those powers that are "necessary and implied" in order to carry out his charge to protect and defend the Constitution.[1] The Court further concluded that the President's duty was not "limited to the enforcement of acts of Congress or of treaties of the United States according to their *express terms* [emphasis in original]." Rather it includes "the rights, duties and obligations growing out of the Constitution itself, our international relations, and all the protection implied by the nature of the government under the Constitution."[2] Thus, by its ruling the Court, in further advancing presidential power, built upon the *Durand v. Hollins* case, which recognized the right of the president to act to protect American lives and property, and further opened the door to unilateral presidential action in international affairs. If not forbidden by the Constitution or the laws of the nation, the president may have the power to act. Hence foreign and domestic urgencies, including the need to pull the country from the economic depression of the 1890s and the abetting belief that expanding foreign trade could cure it, worked to place power back in the hands of the president.

WAR ADVANCES PRESIDENTIAL POWER

Oddly enough, however, it was Congress itself that in no small way helped impel the pendulum back in the direction of executive power. Following an explosion that resulted in the sinking of the battleship USS *Maine* and the loss of 266 American lives in Havana Harbor on February 15, 1898, and the ensuing pro-war hysteria driven by a "yellow press," it was the people and members of Congress who clamored for war. With few outside sources of intelligence on the sinking and an apparent willingness to accept newspaper accounts that fixed the blame for the explosion on a Spanish mine despite conflicting reports on the cause of the explosion,[3] Congress permitted itself to be caught up in a war fever. A declaration of war was issued on April 25, 1898.

War, however, always enlarges the power of the executive. Recalling Madison's concerns, presidents derive much power and importance from war.[4] Moreover, by the end of the war the United States had emerged as a world power. It had defeated Spain, and its troops now occupied the Spanish colonies of Cuba, Puerto Rico, and part of the Philippines. America was feeling its oats.

Captain Alfred Thayer Mahan's lectures at the naval war college (1886–1889) had attracted wide attention. His thesis: "Victory in war and a vigorous foreign trade, two measures of greatness," depend on sea power. "Ships of war require fueling stations and colonies, which further enhance foreign commerce and national power."[5] American imperialists and businessmen now had markets and geostrategic considerations on their mind. The United States had acquired the Philippines. Only a stone's throw away lay rich Chinese markets and the strategically positioned Chinese ports for America's expanding navy.

MCKINLEY DISPATCHES TROOPS

In June 1900, pursuant to an agreement with other nations in the wake of the Boxer Rebellion (see "Boxer Rebellion, 1900"), President McKinley ordered 5,000 U.S. troops to China as part of an international contingent of forces to restore order and to protect European legations and American lives and property.[6] Historian Arthur Schlesinger Jr. has written: "The intervention in China marked the start of a crucial shift in the presidential employment of armed force overseas. In the nineteenth century, military force committed without congressional authorization had been typically used against nongovernmental organizations. Now it was beginning to be used against sovereign states."[7] Though the Chinese had declared war on the United States, McKinley neither sought a declaration of war nor consulted Congress on the agreement he had made to dispatch troops. Nor did he seek Senate approval for the1901 Boxer Protocol, signed between China and the United States and other European powers engaged in the conflict that ended the war.

ROOSEVELT AND THE ABSENCE OF CRISES

Like Andrew Jackson, Theodore Roosevelt was an assertive president. He expanded the powers of the president in domestic politics as well as in foreign affairs. He had an expansive approach to presidential prerogatives, believing that by virtue of his election by the people, he had a broad mandate to do good, even if his actions lacked constitutional authority.[8]

BOXER REBELLION, 1900

China, rendered helpless following the first Sino-Japanese war (1894–1894), was being carved up by European powers into spheres of influence, with discriminatory trading privileges. American traders had long sought to expand their trade with China. Now American trading interests seemed threatened by European policies. Seeking to secure the future for American commercial interests, in September 1899 the United States sent a note to five European powers and Japan requesting an "open door" in trade policy in which they would respect the trade opportunity for all nations in their respective spheres. In the meantime, resentful Chinese nationalists rose in rebellion against the European imperialist intruders. Led by a secret society called *Yihwquan* (Boxers), they murdered hundreds of Christian missionaries and their Chinese converts and laid siege to foreign legations in Beijing.

See Paterson et al., *American Foreign Relations,* vol. 1, 225–26.

For example, in domestic affairs he had his secretary of war, Elihu Root, place 10,000 soldiers on alert in case they were needed to run the coal mines in Pennsylvania during a miners' strike.[9] He also helped to initiate the modern practice of rule by executive order, issuing 1,006 such orders, more than all prior or subsequent presidents combined, save for Woodrow Wilson and Franklin Roosevelt.[10]

Roosevelt's tussles with Congress over information, interestingly enough, began on a domestic issue. Though known as a "trust buster," Roosevelt failed to take action against U.S. Steel. Prior to joining the Roosevelt administration, Attorney General Philander Chase Knox had arranged for the merger of railroad, oil, coal, iron, and steel interests of Carnegie, J. P. Morgan, Rockefeller, and others into the largest conglomerate in history—U.S. Steel. During the Banker's Panic of 1907, Roosevelt himself had tacitly approved the merger of Tennessee Coal and Iron Company as a part of the conglomerate. When Knox's replacement, Joseph Bonaparte, was "directed" by a Senate resolution to inform the Senate on the steps taken by the Department of Justice toward the prosecution of U.S. Steel under the Sherman Act for its acquisition of Tennessee Coal and Steel, Roosevelt was furious. He demanded the Senate call a halt to the practice of directing his cabinet officials to answer resolutions of inquiry, contending that the only manner in which Congress can direct a cabinet office or the president is by law or by joint resolution, either of which must be signed by the president in order to have force. Roosevelt also reportedly provided the relevant information to the Senate, but instructed Bonaparte not to respond to the portion of the resolution that called for a statement of his reasons for nonaction.[11] The Senate threatened to imprison the head of the Bureau of Corporations for contempt if the requested information was not provided. Roosevelt then ordered the papers be delivered to the White House, challenging the Senate to come and get them. Reminiscent of Polk, Roosevelt told a friend: "The only way the Senate or the committee can get those papers is through my impeachment,"[12] thus challenging Congress's methods as well as its right to information from the executive branch. Congress acquiesced.

In foreign affairs, Roosevelt was equally assertive, though, as he personally lamented, the absence of crises denied him his proper opportunity for greatness: "If there is no war, you don't get the great general; if there is no great occasion, you don't get the great statesman."[13] Nevertheless, when confronted with an opportunity, Roosevelt did not hesitate to act. For example, following the collapse of negotiations with Colombia in 1903 on securing rights to build a canal across the Isthmus of Panama, the United States became involved in a plot by Panamanian revolutionaries in a revolt against Colombia. Assured that a new government in Panama would quickly grant the United States rights to build the proposed canal, Roosevelt, on the eve of the rebellion, dispatched several warships to Panama, under the pretext of maintaining free and uninterrupted transit to and from the ports and maintaining order along the line of the cross-isthmus railroad.[14] Commanders had further instructions to prevent any landing of armed force, either government or insurgent.

Though this had the sound of a balanced order, its effect was to prevent the government of Colombia from landing forces to put down the rebellion. This was in violation of the 1846 treaty guaranteeing the sovereignty of Colombia (then New Granada) and in violation of international law.[15] Three days after the revolt began, Roosevelt recognized the new government of Panama. Roosevelt boasted: "I took the canal zone and let Congress debate, and while the debate goes on the canal does also."[16] In his autobiography written in 1913, Roosevelt revealed his view of the prerogatives of the president. In a comment reflective of the Supreme Court's *In re Neagle* decision, Roosevelt wrote: "My belief was that it was not only his right but his duty to do anything that the needs of a nation demand unless such action was forbidden by the Constitution or the laws."

In January 1904, when the Panama Canal treaty was laid before the Senate for ratification, a resolution was introduced declaring that the president's action in Panama had been in violation of a treaty with Colombia as well as in violation of international law. During the debate, Senator John T. Morgan indignantly asserted: "The President has paused in his usurpation of the war power.... To obtain ratification of his excessive adventure he comes to the Senate ... to join him in giving sanction to a war he had begun."[17] Nevertheless, the Senate ratified the treaty.

Roosevelt's "adventures" in Panama were not his only challenges to the American constitutional system. Theodore Roosevelt undertook the use of military force against sovereign states without congressional authorization and "with less consultation than ever."[18] Moreover, he seemed to take pride in defying Congress. In 1907 Roosevelt decided to send all 16 U.S. battleships around the world in a display of American naval might. He informed skeptical congressmen that he had enough funds to get them halfway; the choice was theirs as to whether to provide funding for the return of America's "Great White Fleet."[19]

In his annual message to Congress in December 1904, Roosevelt introduced what became known as the Roosevelt Corollary to the Monroe Doctrine. He asserted that the United States has the right to intervene to stabilize the economic affairs of small states in the Caribbean and Central America if they were unable to pay their international debts. Using this presidentially declared power to intervene in this region, "Troops would be sent abroad not to protect American lives and property but to promote American foreign policy."[20]

In 1905 Roosevelt put teeth in his corollary. The Dominican Republic had been unable to pay its $32 million worth of debts.[21] Roosevelt negotiated a treaty with the Dominican Republic, which would put the customs houses of that nation under American control to forestall attempts by European creditors to seize them. When the Senate failed to approve the treaty, Roosevelt issued an executive order guaranteeing the territorial integrity of the Dominican Republic and declaring that the United States would assume responsibility for its customs house collections.[22] The Senate, still miffed over Roosevelt's handling of the Panamanian affair, reacted angrily when it learned about Roosevelt's efforts to bypass Congress once again. Roosevelt reworked his executive order into a treaty. The Senate initially rejected the reworked treaty, but eventually agreed.[23]

William Howard Taft continued the precedents set by his predecessor, issuing executive orders and intervening twice in Nicaragua, and once each in Cuba and Honduras.[24] Indeed, Taft contended that the president as commander in chief could "order the Army and Navy anywhere he will, if appropriations furnish the means of transportation."[25]

Shortly after assuming the presidency, Taft issued an executive order instructing department heads to refer congressional requests to the president when they believed them to be incompatible with the national interest. After leaving office he contended that the Constitution did not require the president to provide Congress "confidential information which he has acquired for the purpose of enabling him to discharge his constitutional duties, if he does not deem the disclosure of such information prudent or in the public interest."[26] While this formulation was not entirely new to exceptions claimed by previous presidents, it begged the question of what might be meant by the word "prudent." It also made clear that in his view the withholding of information did not require the customary deference paid to the president in congressional requests granting him the right to decide what was in the public interest. Thus, for all practical purposes, according to Taft, what might be released to Congress was entirely up to presidential discretion. Confronted with such usurpations of congressional prerogatives, Congress as a body usually acquiesced.

WILSON AND THE WAR

When it came to foreign affairs, President Woodrow Wilson harbored a broad view of presidential power. Five years before assuming the presidency he wrote:

One of the greatest of the President's powers... [is] his control, which is very absolute, in foreign affairs... The President can not conclude a treaty with a foreign power without the consent of the Senate, but he may guide every step of diplomacy, and to guide diplomacy is to determine what treaties must be made.[27]

Nonetheless, once president, Wilson generally recognized the prerogatives of Congress, particularly on issues involving the potential for conflict. On the other hand, World War I had the effect of greatly increasing the power of the presidency.[28] The president and Congress had to adapt to the needs of a "total war." Information about potential foreign adversaries and their activities in the United States was sorely lacking. Wilson, as a champion of open diplomacy, disdained the use of spies and was generally suspicious of intelligence.[29]

Wilson's views on intelligence began to change, however, as a result of the close association developed with the British intelligence chief in Washington. Wilson soon recognized a need for additional information on immediate dangers at home. Immediately after the United States entered the war in April 1917, Wilson tasked the fledgling Federal Bureau of Investigation to identify and neutralize threats to U.S. national security from foreign intelligence operatives. That same month the first U.S. signals intelligence agency was formed within the army. The agency's task, among other things, was to decode foreign military communications. After the end of the war, the agency was transferred to the State Department, where it was known as the "Black Chamber" and focused on foreign diplomatic rather than military communications.[30]

Congress, as in the past, remained generally content to leave the gathering of information on foreign governments and their intelligence operations in the United States, to the extent that they existed, to the executive branch, strangely cutting itself off from the very information that was needed to exercise its prerogatives on foreign policy and on issues of war and peace. Like the president, Congress also had to deal with a vast range of complex issues in a fast-moving and fluid environment. By delegating its powers to the president, the problem would be solved. And so Congress did just that. It delegated to the president "the broadest discretion in dealing with broadly defined subject matter in the furtherance of objectives equally broadly defined."[31] Thus the president was granted powers under a variety of acts to regulate such activities as the importation, manufacture, storage, mining, and distribution of necessities; the requisitioning of food, fuel, feeds, and other necessities; and the power to raise an army by conscription and to censor mail, cable, and radio communications with foreign countries.[32] Though perhaps necessitated by exigencies, such powers granted to the president during wartime enhanced the stature of the presidency in ways that would carry over following the war.

Still, once the war ended, Congress demonstrated that if it had the willpower it could preserve its prerogative power. Wilson had made a fatal mistake following the armistice of November 11, 1918, that ended the actual fighting. He failed to involve the Senate in his efforts to construct a better world order at the Versailles peace conference. After spending almost six months in Europe negotiating a postwar peace, he found the Senate unwilling to endorse the Versailles Treaty and its planned League of Nations.

COOLIDGE AND THE AMERICAN POLICEMAN

Unfortunately, though members of Congress denied Wilson his vision of a postwar world, they themselves remained divided over the limits of presidential authority. After Calvin Coolidge assumed the presidency, the Senate took no action when Coolidge refused its request for information on companies under investigation by the Bureau of Internal Revenue. Coolidge contended that the information was confidential and not germane to Congress's constitutional duties,[33] presumably believing that it was within the prerogative of the president to decide what was and what was not within the scope of the Senate's constitutional responsibilities.

When Coolidge decided to send 5,000 marines back into Nicaragua in 1927 without seeking congressional authorization, some members of Congress objected. Most criticisms, however, were about policy, not constitutionality. Moreover, when in 1928 Senator Blaine introduced an amendment to cut off funds for the marines, Senator Norris asserted that if Congress remained silent, "The power of declaring war . . . will be entirely taken away by the executive." In contrast, Senator Hiram Bingham maintained that presidential war was constitutional.[34]

When Coolidge dispatched troops to Nicaragua, he chillingly introduced a novel idea that would resurface in a somewhat different form some 20-odd years later. Coolidge said: "We are not making war on Nicaragua any more than a policeman on the street is making war on a passerby."[35]

By the 1930s, having observed since the turn of the century increasing unilateral presidential decision making in war and peace and "determined that no one man should again seize control of foreign policy,"[36] Congress finally began to reassert itself.

ROOSEVELT, THE SUPREME COURT, AND WAR

Perhaps mindful of Congress's new assertive mood, Franklin Delano Roosevelt, in his inaugural address in March 1933, set a tone of both determination and conciliation. Faced with the dire emergency of the Great Depression, he warned that while "the normal balance of Executive and legislative authority may be wholly adequate to meet the unprecedented task before us . . . an unprecedented demand and need for undelayed action may call for temporary departure from that normal balance of public procedure." He further declared:

I am prepared under my constitutional duty to recommend the measures that a stricken Nation . . . may require. These measures, or such other measures as the Congress may build out of its experience and wisdom, I shall seek, within my constitutional authority, to bring to speedy adoption. But in the event . . . that the national emergency is still critical, I shall not evade the clear course of duty that will then confront me. I shall ask the Congress for the one remaining instrument to meet the crisis—broad Executive power to wage a war against the emergency.[37]

Thus in few words Roosevelt alerted Congress that there might be a need to stretch constitutional norms to meet the challenges that were confronting the nation. Nevertheless, during the 12-plus years of Franklin Delano Roosevelt's presidency, though information was withheld from Congress on several occasions, Roosevelt usually did so for much the same reasons advanced by Jefferson and Monroe, contending that files too often contained a mixture of rumor, conjecture, and suspicion, the disclose of which might do damage to innocent persons and impede investigative processes[38] or that the release of materials might endanger the public interest or involved privileged discussions.

But in 1943 and 1944 the Roosevelt administration appeared to step beyond the boundaries of the precedents established early in the republic. In 1943 the director of the Bureau of the Budget refused a House committee subpoena to testify because the president had instructed that the files remain confidential. Also that year the acting secretary of war received instructions from the president not to provide documents pertaining to the Departments of War and Navy.[39] Even more troubling, in 1944 FBI director J. Edgar Hoover, supported by Attorney General Francis Biddle, refused a subpoena to testify before a House committee. Biddle also refused to provide the committee with the president's directive, which had served as the basis for Hoover's refusal. Raising an argument first advanced by Hamilton, when Congress was seeking information on his alleged mishandling of funds—an argument that had been rejected by Washington—Biddle declared: "As a matter of law and of long-established constitutional practice, communications between the President and the Attorney General are confidential and privileged, and are not subject to inquiry by a committee of one of the houses of Congress." A few months later, the director of the Office of Censorship refused to transmit to a Senate committee requested information unless subpoenaed to do so. No subpoena was issued.[40]

As for information relevant to foreign relations, in the years immediately preceding World War II the United States was largely limited to the information it received from its foreign missions. President Herbert Hoover had decided that the interception of diplomatic cables and correspondence by the State Department was inappropriate. Henry Stimson, Hoover's secretary of state, blithely announced, "Gentlemen do not read each other's mail." Intelligence on diplomatic issues that had been initiated following World War I had ended a decade later without much more than a whimper from Congress.

As war approached, the president himself had to rely heavily on American and British friends traveling abroad to provide him with information on the intentions of foreign leaders. In July 1941 Roosevelt appointed William Donovan coordinator of information and tasked him to form a nonmilitary intelligence organization to "collect and analyze all information and data which may bear upon the national security" for the president and those he designated.[41] Following the attack on Pearl Harbor, U.S. intelligence efforts began to expand. The Office of Strategic Services

(OSS) was formed under the Joint Chiefs of Staff in June of the following year. Donovan was placed in charge and his organization folded into the OSS, which assumed the additional duties of carrying out clandestine operations against the Axis powers. Congress remained content to leave information-gathering efforts largely in the hands of the president.

In dealing with the depression, Roosevelt also sought greater authority than had been historically customary. Congress responded by granting Roosevelt broad discretionary powers. On the other hand, Congress was not willing to grant the president such discretion on foreign political or military policies. As war clouds gathered in Europe and Asia, isolationists in Congress constrained Roosevelt's ability to act by passing strict neutrality laws in 1935 and again in 1936. Among the restrictions that were legislated, once the president declared that a state of war existed, Americans could not ship arms to or provide loans or credits to any nation at war.[42]

The president, concerned about Nazi and Japanese aggression, was granted some leeway when Congress passed the Neutrality Act of 1937, which extended the provision of the previous acts to include civil wars but also permitted the sale of arms on a "cash and carry" basis. In Europe, Britain, with its large fleet of surface ships, would be the principal beneficiary. Interestingly, in the Pacific the president chose to use this new authority in the negative. After war broke out between Japan and China in 1937, Roosevelt declined to recognize that war existed, since he feared that the Japanese would benefit because they had the cash to buy arms.[43]

On September 1, 1939, Germany attacked Poland. War in Europe had begun. Two days later England, France, Australia, and New Zealand declared war on Germany. On September 5 the United States proclaimed neutrality. On September 8, Roosevelt declared a "limited national emergency" existed and increased the strength of the armed forces. However, even after war broke out in Europe, Roosevelt, under the tight leash of legislative constraint, felt it necessary to go to Congress to seek a repeal of the arms embargo provisions of the Neutrality Acts so that England and France could obtain weapons and ammunition from the United States.[44] His efforts were successful. Congress repealed those provisions on November 4, 1939.

As the war in Europe and Asia progressed, Roosevelt expanded the powers of the presidency. In 1940 and 1941 Roosevelt had seized the initiative in proposing legislation. During those two years the isolationists were unable to kill a single major foreign policy proposal.[45] Following his overwhelming victory over Wendell Willkie in the 1940 presidential elections and convinced that the United States needed to assist the British, Roosevelt grew bolder. In January 1941 he proposed a plan to Congress in which the United States would "lend-lease or otherwise dispose of arms" and other supplies needed by any country whose security was vital to the defense of the United States. In March Congress passed the Lend-Lease Act.

Though not engaged in the war in Europe, the United States had taken sides. In April 1941 German submarines sank nearly half of a 22-ship

British convoy. Following an agreement he had reached earlier that year with Britain, Roosevelt, under the umbrella of his role as commander in chief, ordered U.S. warships to patrol for German submarines halfway across the Atlantic. He sought neither prior approval of nor consultations with Congress.[46] That same month Roosevelt entered into an executive agreement with Denmark to send U.S. troops to Greenland. There was little objection from Congress.[47] In late May Roosevelt upgraded the state of "limited" emergency he had announced in 1939, by declaring a state of "unlimited national emergency."

On July 7, 1941, he informed Congress that he had dispatched naval forces to Iceland "to supplement and eventually replace" those of Britain in order to protect that country from attack. He also informed Congress that he had issued orders to the navy to take "all necessary steps... to insure the safety of communications in the approaches between Iceland and the United States as well as on the seas between the United States and all other strategic outposts."[48]

Senator Robert A. Taft of Ohio protested that Roosevelt had "no legal or constitutional right to send American troops to Iceland" without congressional authorization, arguing that there had been no attack on the United States, and there was no threat of an attack. Hence if the Senate acquiesced in such presidential actions it might "nullify for all time the constitutional authority distinctly reserved to Congress to declare war." Only a single senator supported Taft's protest.[49]

On August 12, 1941, Roosevelt and British prime minister Winston Churchill met secretly in Placentia Bay off the coast of Newfoundland to craft war and postwar plans. Following this meeting, Roosevelt told Churchill that "he would wage war, but not declare it, and that he would become more and more provocative. If the Germans did not like it, they could attack American forces."[50] In September, following an attack by a German submarine on the U.S. destroyer *Greer*, which was carrying mail and passengers to Iceland, Roosevelt ordered naval convoys as far as Iceland and issued a "shoot-on-sight" command to the navy.[51] And so Roosevelt, without congressional authority, took it upon himself to deliberately move American forces into harm's way, even encouraging attack.

In the Pacific in July 1940 Roosevelt withheld aviation fuel and top-grade scrap iron from Japan. In September he extended the embargo to all scrap metals. In July the following year he froze all Japanese funds, and his administration stopped all trade, including oil, with Japan.[52]

Nevertheless, Roosevelt's assumption of authority in crisis, for the most part, had been sanctioned by two critical Supreme Court cases. The first was the 1936 *United States v. Curtiss-Wright Export Corporation* case. The Curtiss-Wright Corporation had been accused of violating the law. In 1934 Congress had passed a joint resolution authorizing the president to place an embargo on arms to Bolivia and Paraguay, who were then engaged in a war over the Chaco region bordering both countries.

The president immediately proclaimed an embargo. Attorneys for Curtiss-Wright argued that Congress had unlawfully delegated its authority to the president. Though the district court ruled in favor of the corporation, contending that the joint resolution indeed was an attempt on the part of Congress to abdicate its responsibilities, the Supreme Court reversed the decision.

Justice Douglas Sutherland in delivering the Court's opinion suggested that had Congress's 1934 joint resolution "related solely to internal affairs," it might have "constituted an unlawful delegation of legislative power," as the Court had found in the *Schechter Poultry Corporation v. United States* case one year earlier.[53] However, according to Sutherland, there are "fundamental" differences between the realms of domestic and foreign affairs. In foreign affairs different standards apply. Those standards, as "practically every volume of the United States Statutes" demonstrates, do permit Congress to authorize the president to exercise discretion in taking action on issues affecting foreign relations.[54] By this ruling, the Court had freed Congress of a principle that served as a constraint on its behavior and that of the executive dating back to the ideas advanced by John Locke.

Locke wrote:

The Legislative cannot transfer the power of making laws to any other hands, for it being but a delegated power from the people, they, who have it cannot pass it over to others.... And when the people have said, "We will submit, and be governed by laws made by such men, and in such forms," nobody else can say other men shall make laws for them; nor can they be bound by any laws but such as are enacted by those whom they have chosen and authorised to make laws for them.[55]

The idea behind Locke's contention as applied to republican governance was straightforward. If the legislative can delegate its powers to the executive, then the two powers are conjoined and the doctrine of separation of powers ceases to exist. The Court's ruling would appear to have done just that. When it came to foreign affairs the non-delegation principle would be seen to have a different applicability and be subject to lesser constraints.

Sutherland also went beyond the demands of the case and in a rather torturous manner asserted powers for the president not previously claimed by America's chief executives, acknowledged by Congress, or in the author's view substantiated either by the Constitution or by the evident intent of the framers. While it is beyond the scope of this effort to examine in detail all the errors of judgment in the historical landscape of presidential power that were advanced by Sutherland—others have done so admirably—[56] the picture finally painted by Sutherland has had the effect of providing argument for the aggrandizement of presidential power to the level of virtual dictator in foreign affairs. This was certainly not an outcome that would have been welcomed by those who labored in Philadelphia the summer of 1787.

In the name of the Court, Sutherland declared that this case was dealing not just with the authority vested in the president by Congress, "but with such an authority plus the very delicate, plenary and exclusive power of the President as the sole organ of the federal government in the field of international relations—a power which does not require as a basis for its exercise an act of Congress but which, of course, like every other governmental power, must be exercised in subordination to the applicable provisions of the Constitution."[57]

The second case, *United States v. Belmont*, arose from Roosevelt's efforts to settle affairs with the Soviet Union in conjunction with his formal recognition of that country. Roosevelt had entered into an agreement with the USSR, assigning to the United States all claims by Soviet citizens on Americans that had arisen since the communist government came to power. When the U.S. government requested that the Belmont Bank of New York turn over assets deposited by a Russian company that was subsequently nationalized as the communists came to power, the bank refused, arguing that the government's action was based on an executive agreement that, unlike a treaty, did not have the force of law. Justice Sutherland rendered the Court's ruling, reiterating that the executive had authority to speak as the sole organ of that government, noting that negotiations, agreements, and understandings "were within the competence of the president" and that not all international compacts require Senate approval,[58] and concluding that the President's power to negotiate agreements without Senate approval for all intents and purposes has the same effect as a treaty.[59]

Still, while Roosevelt kept tight reins on the military and diplomatic aspects of the war and increasingly seized on his role as commander in chief and on powers to act in an emergency following the Japanese attack on Pearl Harbor in December 1941, he also paid deference to the prerogatives of Congress. Above all, Roosevelt was determined to seek congressional support for America's postwar policies.[60]

THE ERODING POWERS OF CONGRESS

The early part of the 20th century witnessed an accelerating erosion of congressional power as a result of presidential assertion, Supreme Court rulings, and perhaps above all congressional acquiescence. In disregard of congressional prerogatives, McKinley sent troops abroad to engage in hostilities and signed a protocol, perhaps more rightfully called a treaty, ending the war in China. Theodore Roosevelt's extensive use of executive orders; his categorical refusal to provide papers to the Senate pursuant to its investigations; his dispatch of warships to Panama to support Panamanian revolutionaries in violation of the U.S. treaty with Colombia; his open defiance of Congress as he dispatched the "Great White Fleet" around the world; and his issuance of a "corollary" to the Monroe Doctrine that signaled the United States was prepared not only to send troops abroad to protect American lives and property, but also now to do so in order to advance American interests were a reflection of his belief that the president has the right to do anything that the nation demands unless forbidden by the Constitution or the laws as the president so interprets. Taft reinforced the idea that the president could refuse to provide information requested by Congress as a part of its investigative powers, as well as the notion that if funds were available, the president had the authority in his own right to send troops anywhere in the world.

Two world wars and the Great Depression served to advance presidential power at the expense of and usually with the consent of Congress. Meanwhile, Coolidge had advanced the idea that American forces could be sent abroad as policemen, a concept pernicious in its subtlety and dangerous in its implications.

The Supreme Court aided and abetted this trend. The Court had opened the door widely for Congress to pass laws delegating its powers to the "broad discretion" of the president, thus providing Congress an easy way to avoid tough decisions and escape blame for policy failures. As one observer concluded: "By the postwar era, Congress had long been out of practice when it came to taking responsibility for the laws Americans lived under."[61] Furthermore, the assertion that the president has "plenary and exclusive" power as the "sole organ" of government in the field of international relations opened the door for claims by future presidents of an "inherent" power to act in foreign affairs, war, and peace.

It would appear that Sutherland as well as others have oft failed to recognize the inherent contradiction that exists between the assertion of the president's plenary (i.e., absolute and unqualified) power in foreign affairs and the fact that the president cannot send one ambassador abroad or culminate one treaty with a foreign nation without the consent of the Senate. Moreover, the entire operation of the executive branch, whether in domestic or foreign affairs, is completely dependent on appropriations from Congress. Furthermore, those who rest their case on the inherent power of the president to act unilaterally in foreign affairs and in war on Sutherland's ill-conceived notion that the president enjoys plenary authority on such matters choose to ignore the caveat so slightly placed at the end of his grand assertion that "like every other governmental power, must be exercised in subordination to the applicable provisions of the Constitution."[62]

When the Supreme Court linked the "sole organ" theory to compacts, agreements, and understandings, it left the door open to an expansive view of executive powers, which might well include unbounded presidential authority to enter into agreements that commit the nation without having to seek Senate approval. Such an approach would largely void an important check on executive power that had been envisaged by those who wrote and ratified the Constitution.

In the *Ex parte Quirin* (1942) case, the Court, in a process that has been questioned by some, including justices who participated in the decision,[63] upheld the authority of the president to convene military commissions to try unlawful combatants for attempts to commit sabotage. On the other hand, in a part of the ruling that is most often ignored, the Court reiterated the limits of the powers of the president in his role as commander in chief. Chief Justice Harlan Stone, delivering the Court's opinion, stated:

The Constitution thus invests the President as Commander in Chief with the power to wage war which Congress has declared, and to carry into effect all laws passed by Congress for the conduct of war and for the government and regulation of the Armed Forces, and all laws defining and punishing offences against the law of nations, including those which pertain to the conduct of war.[64]

For its part, Congress mostly acquiesced. Its failure to object to the usurpation of power served to erode congressional prerogatives in war and treaty making. When confronted with presidential encroachments on congressional powers, Congress usually capitulated. Had Congress been cowed by Supreme Court decisions? Did Congress understand the full implications of those decisions? Was Congress overwhelmed by the tasks of dealing with two world wars and the Great Depression? Was it over-awed by the persona of presidents or was it too weak, too divided, and too befuddled to stand firm on its constitutional responsibilities? What-ever the answer to those questions, the clouds that were gathering were endangering the system of checks and balances so desperately sought by the framers of the Constitution as a means of ensuring wise republican governance.

CHAPTER 5

A Rise and Fall in Presidential Power

In 1835 Alexis de Tocqueville in his *Democracy in America* observed that in the United States, "Executive power is limited and exceptional." The president is "the executor of the laws, but he has no real part in making them.... [H]e is not part of the sovereign power, but its agent." Juxtaposed to the legislature, "The President is an inferior and dependant power.... In the exercise of executive power the President is constantly subject to jealous supervision. He prepares treaties, but he does not make them; he suggests officials for appointments, but he does not appoint them." His power "is exercised only within the sphere of restricted authority." Nevertheless, de Tocqueville reasoned that the president has sufficient powers that should America be "constantly menaced, and its great interests were continually interwoven with those of other powerful nations, one could see the prestige of the executive growing."[1]

By late 1940s the Cold War was well under way. Soviet troops had remained in Eastern Europe following the end of World War II. Governments in that part of the world had come under communist control. The USSR had provided clandestine support for strikes in France and Italy, supported the Communists in the Greek civil war, pressured Turkey for revisions to the 1936 Montreux Convention governing access to the Bosporus and Dardanelles, sought concessions in Turkish Armenia and bases from which they could dominate the straits, and had refused to leave Iran in violation of wartime agreements. In April 1949, 10 western European nations joined the United States and Canada to form the North Atlantic Treaty Organization. By October of that year, China had fallen to the communists under Mao and communism was becoming a worldwide menace. The security of the United States was threatened, and as predicted by de Tocqueville over a century earlier, power flowed toward America's chief magistrate. Americans seemed to accept the secrecy and clandestine behavior of the executive branch of government. Armed with Supreme Court rulings that had opened the door for an aggrandizement of presidential power and a Congress that had grown accustomed to acquiescence, if not abdication, in the face of presidential challenges, postwar presidents seldom hesitated in exercising prerogatives beyond those specifically delegated by the Constitution or envisaged by the framers.

TRUMAN

Aware of the intelligence failures that preceded the Japanese attack on Pearl Harbor and confronted with the growing dangers of the Cold War, President Harry S. Truman was dissatisfied with the United States's haphazard and uncoordinated approach to the gathering of information on foreign powers. To rectify the situation Truman sought an intelligence organization that would serve the president effectively during times of peace and war that was less haphazard, more centralized, and better coordinated and that would bring order and priority to the information that he received.

When Congress passed the National Security Act of 1947, creating a postwar national security structure, it also had in mind the need for a peacetime centralized intelligence apparatus that would operate within the executive branch of government but independent of the other executive departments and agencies. So as part of the National Security Act of 1947, Congress created the Central Intelligence Agency. The CIA was to be headed by a director who was to correlate, evaluate, and disseminate intelligence obtained by the intelligence elements of other departments and agencies. Thus, for all practical purposes, while other intelligence organizations (e.g., military service intelligence elements) retained their responsibilities for producing intelligence related to their department's specific mission, the CIA became the focal point for national-level intelligence on foreign countries.

Shortly after the passage of the National Security Act, the CIA was given an additional responsibility for covert actions[2] and with the coming of the Korean War was charged with the task of providing its own independent analysis.[3] Similarly, the rest of the American intelligence apparatus maintained and operated by the newly created Department of Defense, individual military services or by the Department of State, was expanding dramatically to meet the needs of the Cold War.

Congress was to have a significant role in this. It not only was the legislative branch responsible for appropriating funds for the new intelligence apparatus, but also assumed the task of overseeing the activities of the CIA. Responsibility for approving CIA appropriations fell to the

defense subcommittees of the House and Senate appropriations committees, while oversight was assigned to special intelligence subcommittees
of the armed services of both chambers. Presumably Congress, as well as
the executive branch, would now have information at its disposal that
would assist in making critical foreign policy and defense decisions.

However, as both external and internal security issues proliferated,
Truman clamped down on the data flow to Congress, issuing a sweeping secrecy order blocking congressional efforts to acquire information
from executive branch offices related to security issues.[4] Truman's action
seemed to have little effect on Congress. As far as foreign intelligence was
concerned, Congress, for the most part, was content to defer to the executive branch. Only a few members of Congress were actually involved in
monitoring the activities of the intelligence community. Intelligence subcommittees usually included the chairman and ranking minority member
of the full committee and two or three other committee members deemed
trustworthy and responsible.[5] Staff was kept to a minimum. When briefed
by the intelligence community, committee members frequently asked no
questions. One former CIA legislative counsel observed: "One of the problems was you couldn't get Congress to get interested."[6] In a similar vein,
Clark Clifford, who served as general counsel under Truman and helped
write the National Security Act of 1947, is reported to have remarked,
"Congress chose not to be involved and preferred to be uninformed."[7]
Indeed, throughout the entire period from 1947 until 1974, the Senate
committees responsible for monitoring the intelligence committees were
dominated by members who firmly endorsed executive leadership in foreign affairs.[8]

Truman also was the first president to claim "inherent" powers in both
domestic and foreign affairs. After seizing the steel mills in early April
1952, following a rejection by the steel industry of the Wage Stabilization
Board recommendations on wages and prices during the Korean War, Truman proclaimed: "The President of the United States has very great inherent powers to meet great national emergencies."[9]

This was not the first time Truman had exercised what he considered to
be his "inherent" power to act in an emergency. On June 25, 1950, North
Korean forces crossed the 38th Parallel and attacked South Korea. That
same day the United Nation's Security Council condemned the attack as
"a breach of the peace" and called for "the immediate cessation of hostilities" and for "Member States to render every assistance to the United Nations in the execution of this resolution." North Korea continued its attack.
Two days later the Security Council passed Resolution 83, stating that
"urgent military measures were required to restore international peace
and security" and recommended that UN members "furnish such assistance…as may be necessary to repel the armed attack." However, a day
earlier, without consulting Congress, Truman had decided to deploy U.S.
air and sea forces to assist South Korean forces. He announced his decision

the following day and added that he had ordered the Seventh Fleet to prevent any Chinese attack on Formosa (Taiwan),[10] effectively putting the Chinese Nationalists under U.S. protection. Three days after the attack, Senator Robert A. Taft, while supporting Truman's dispatch of forces to Korea and announcing that he would vote for a joint resolution authorizing American intervention, declared that the president had acted without "legal authority." On June 29 the president ordered U.S. ground forces into action. Acting with the advice of Secretary of State Dean Acheson, Truman decided not to seek congressional approval but rather rely on his powers as commander in chief.[11]

Truman's actions were unprecedented. Never before had a president committed American military forces to a major foreign war without first seeking the approval of Congress. There is little doubt that with the Cold War well under way, Truman felt he was confronting a genuine emergency. Under such circumstances, presidents had often placed U.S. troops in harm's way. As early as the *Martin v. Mott* case of 1827 the Supreme Court had sustained presidential prerogatives in times of emergency. However, his failure to seek ex post facto approval set a dangerous precedent, one that threatened to undermine the very foundations of republican governance and its systems of checks and balances.

In a further attack on the constitutional processes, Truman, when asked during a press conference about a previous statement in which he contended that the United States was not at war, responded: "We are not at war." Later in that same press conference, when asked if it would be correct to call U.S. efforts in Korea a "police action," the president answered, "Yes. That is exactly what it amounts to." The dangerous conclusion that could be drawn from his response, which was reminiscent of Coolidge's comment after sending troops to Nicaragua in 1927, was that presidents could completely bypass the constitutional authority granted solely to Congress and initiate hostilities by simply declaring a major war a "police action."

Some in Congress objected to Truman's failure to seek approval for the war. Others contended the president did not need congressional authorization to commit U.S. forces to combat,[12] arguing as Truman had that the sufficient authority existed under the UN charter[13] and under his powers as commander in chief. Ultimately, Congress ratified the president's actions by appropriating money for the war effort and extending the draft.[14] But it had denied itself the opportunity to examine in depth such a commitment of American forces on the continent of Asia, undermined its constitutional authority in the realm of war making, and denied to the American public a careful examination of America's strategy for dealing with such Cold War challenges, the very essence of the responsibility of the legislative body in a democracy.

Later that same year Truman announced that he intended to send four more divisions to reinforce the two American divisions already in Europe in order to strengthen defenses against a possible Soviet attack. Once again, this action represented a dangerous expansion of presidential prerogative. Never before had a president committed such a vast number of troops to a theater of potential conflict. When asked at a news conference in early January whether he believed he needed the approval of Congress to send additional troops to Europe, Truman answered, "No, I do not."[15] Seven days later he added: "Under the President's constitutional powers as Commander in Chief of the Armed Forces he has the authority to send troops anywhere in the world."[16] Truman did not seek congressional approval.

This time the Senate did react. Though after a lengthy debate the Senate endorsed Truman's plans, it tacked on an amendment that required the president to return to Congress for approval should he wish to send additional troops to Europe in the future. The amendment initially was rejected 44–46, with some Senators claiming the president had the power to send armed forces anywhere he felt U.S. security interests demanded. The amendment finally carried 49–43.[17]

A little over a year later presidential prerogative was dealt a blow. In the *Youngstown Sheet & Tube Co. et al. v. Sawyer* case brought on by Truman's seizure of the steel mills, the Supreme Court ruled the seizure unconstitutional.[18] This strongly undercut Truman's contention that in times of national emergency the president had "very great inherent powers." However, that case pertained to the president's actions in the domestic arena. It did not address the question of the inherent powers of the president in foreign affairs or war making.

EISENHOWER

President Dwight D. Eisenhower generally continued the practices established by Truman concerning the release of foreign intelligence information, while launching a new and potentially dangerous approach to the general provision of information to Congress. With the Cold War now in full bloom, Americans seemed to accept, and in some ways Congress seemed to prefer a level of secrecy previously tolerated only during "hot" wars. In the past, though presidents often claimed one or another reason for exercising discretion in the release of materials to Congress, usually under the rubric of protecting the public interest, they nearly always conceded the general principle that Congress has a right to information and more often than not provided almost everything, if not all, that Congress requested. The window for rejection was generally narrowly defined, and presidents had generally complied with congressional requests.

In contrast, under Eisenhower the purview of the president was greatly expanded. In 1954 the communist witch hunt by Senator Joseph McCarthy was in full swing, lashing out at nearly every government agency thought to be harboring communists. In an effort to shield the executive branch from McCarthy's reckless investigative tactics, Eisenhower "made the most absolute assertion of presidential right to withhold information from Congress ever uttered to that day."[19] In May he declared: "It is essential to efficient and effective administration that employees of the Executive Branch be in a position to be completely candid in advising each other on official matters." Therefore, "It is not in the public interest that any of their conversations or communications, or any documents or reproductions, concerning such advice be disclosed."[20]

Though in the case of Alexander Hamilton, Washington had rejected such a claim, other presidents had claimed a right to hold privileged discussions with their top aides. None, however, had claimed that the privilege extended to the entire executive branch on all conversations, communications, documents, and so forth. This was a very significant expansion of the presidential claims of executive privilege. "The historic rule had been disclosure, with exceptions; the new rule was denial, with exception."[21] Distaste for McCarthy had so permeated the public and Congress that few noted or reacted to Eisenhower's directive and its grand expansion of presidential prerogative. Congress, unable to separate its displeasure of McCarthy from the need to protect its constitutional powers, abdicated its responsibility to do so. As a result, during the last five years of Eisenhower's term, administration officials, following Eisenhower's directive, refused well over 40 requests for information—more than all previous presidential administrations combined.[22]

Two court cases during this time contributed to the debate over executive privilege. In 1953 in *United States v. Reynolds,* the Supreme Court in a 5–3 decision ruled that the military may refuse to divulge requested information when national security is at stake.[23] Nonetheless, in the 1958 case of *Kaiser Aluminum & Chemical Corp. v. United States,* the Court ruled that there is no absolute privilege to refuse to provide information, that it was ultimately up to the courts "to determine executive privilege in litigation." The Court, however, went on to note that the assertion of "privilege by the Executive vis-à-vis Congress is a judicially undecided issue."[24]

Nevertheless, throughout this period, beyond seeing to intelligence agency appropriations, congressional involvement in U.S. foreign intelligence activities remained minimal. The director of Central Intelligence and his representatives usually interacted directly with the chairmen and ranking minority members of the armed services or appropriations committees, who for the most part were strong supporters of intelligence and saw little need for or benefit from intrusive oversight by Congress.[25] Staff involvement also was limited to one or two senior members of the staff of each of these committees who made certain that the needs of the intelligence community were adequately funded.[26] Formal hearings and testimony were rare, intelligence subcommittees met only a few times each year, and virtually all oversight was conducted behind closed doors. Thus, oversight, as during the Truman years, remained tightly circumscribed.[27]

On the other hand, Congress was able to play a greater role than it had played during the Truman years on issues involving the movement of forces and their possible deployment into harm's way. Eisenhower, apparently recognizing that Truman had committed a serious error both politically and constitutionally,[28] sought congressional approval when deployed forces might face hostilities. In 1954 when pressured to assist the French in Indochina, he told reporters that he would not involve the United States in a war unless it was one in which Congress declared.[29] In January 1955, following an August 1954 announcement by communist China that Chinese Nationalist Taiwan must be liberated and China's January 1955 attack on offshore islands held by the Nationalists, Eisenhower sought and received a joint resolution authorizing him to take military action in defense of the Nationalist Chinese. Two years later he sought approval to use force in the Middle East, if necessary. Congress, in responding, unfortunately legislated away its constitutional responsibilities, granting the president general authority to decide when, where, why, and against whom U.S. military forces would be used in the Middle East.

While Eisenhower was careful to involve Congress in the overt deployment of U.S. forces into harm's way, he did not seek congressional approval for covert operations by CIA operatives. Impressed with the successes of clandestine operations behind enemy lines during World War II, Eisenhower placed a high priority on covert operations, whether in assisting in the overthrow or attempted overthrow of governments as in Iran in 1953, Guatemala in 1954, and Indonesia in 1958, or supporting the invasion of Cuba in 1960–1961 by anti-Castro Cuban exiles. Congress, however, was left largely in the dark.

KENNEDY

Even before his election as president, Senator John F. Kennedy believed in the power of the presidency in the field of foreign relations. Early in 1960, Kennedy remarked that however large the role of Congress was in domestic policy, "It is the President alone who must make major decisions of our foreign policy."[30] Kennedy was riding a wave of enthusiasm for presidential power that crossed party lines and in many ways characterized the thinking among intellectuals. With the Cold War at hand and cataclysm a mere hours or minutes away, there seemed to be no room for checks on presidential power and the niceties of constitutional governance as envisaged by the framers. As historian Arthur M. Schlesinger Jr. has written, "In foreign affairs Congress and the executive alike, as if under hypnosis, unquestionably accepted the thesis of executive supremacy."[31]

Nonetheless, Kennedy did not follow Eisenhower's restrictive approach to providing information requested by Congress. Rather, Kennedy, irritated while serving as a Senator by the abuse of executive privilege under Eisenhower, established the principle that only he, and he alone, would invoke executive privilege. As a result, the Kennedy administration was much more forthcoming. According to Morton Rosenberg there appeared to be only two instances when Kennedy failed to provide Congress with requested information.[32] Nevertheless, upon entering office, he was no more willing than Eisenhower to keep Congress informed of covert activities undertaken by the CIA.

Less than three months after assuming office Kennedy authorized the ill-fated "Bay of Pigs" attempt to invade Cuba and overthrow the government of Fidel Castro that had been initially planned during the Eisenhower administration. Apparently, it never dawned on Eisenhower even to discuss the project informally with members of Congress.[33] So Congress was largely in the dark, as final preparations for an attack by a CIA-trained force of Cuban exiles got under way. Kennedy ordered the invasion of Cuba without consulting Congress, though he did seek the opinion of Senator Fulbright, chairman of the Foreign Relations Committee.[34]

Similarly, when Soviet missiles were discovered in Cuba in mid-October 1962, Kennedy neither consulted with nor sought the approval of Congress to use military force to prevent additional missiles from arriving in Cuba. In the Bay of Pigs case, the counsel of Congress might have resulted in the avoidance of the disaster. In the 1962 missile case, it could be argued that the situation was so acute, the crisis so severe, the time frame for decision so short, and the need for secrecy so critical to success that perhaps Kennedy could be excused for exercising prerogative power in such an emergency. Furthermore, shortly before the crisis, Congress passed a resolution expressing the determination of the United States, "by whatever means may be necessary, including the use of arms," to prevent the Marxist-Leninist regime in Cuba from "extending...its aggressive or subversive activities to any part of the hemisphere."[35]

Unfortunately, in debating the resolution, the "Senators deferred broadly to the President's supposed authority in foreign affairs and the war power."[36] One senator, apparently expressing what he believed to be the view of the Senate, remarked: "We all recognize that the final decision is left to the President of the United States by the Constitution." To this assertion, Louis Fisher, a senior specialist in separation of powers with the Congressional Research Service of the Library of Congress, responded that the Senator had failed to say "precisely when and how the Constitution had been amended."[37]

JOHNSON

Though President Lyndon B. Johnson, like Kennedy, was more open to the sharing of information with Congress than either Truman or Eisenhower, Congress continued its practice of deference to the president on foreign policy.[38] On August 5, 1964, Johnson appealed to Congress "for a resolution expressing the unity and determination of the United States in supporting freedom and in protecting peace in southeast Asia." The United States had been involved in Vietnam since the early days of the Cold War. Between 1950 and 1954, the United States had spent over $4 million to support French efforts to defeat Vietnamese communists (Vietminh) under Ho Chi Minh.[39] After easing the French out, following their defeat at Dien Bien Phu and the subsequent partitioned Vietnam at the 17th parallel, with the communists in the north and France's Vietnamese allies in the south, the United States committed itself to strengthening the south against possible aggression from the north. To accomplish this Eisenhower sent over about 700 military advisors. That number grew to about 16,000 during the Kennedy administration.

To assist South Vietnam in its efforts to slow the flow of military support from North Vietnam to communist forces in the south, the United States dispatched destroyers to gather intelligence on the disposition of key targets in the north that might be attacked by South Vietnamese patrol boats or commandos. On the afternoon of August 2, 1964, while operating in international waters, the destroyer USS *Maddox* was attacked by three North Vietnamese patrol boats. Torpedoes missed their mark and the *Maddox* was unharmed in the attack. Two days later, the Maddox, reinforced by the destroyer USS *Turner Joy*, was back on station gathering intelligence. That night the warships reported that they were attacked by several fast craft, though the circumstances at the time were murky. The next day, after investigating the matter thoroughly, the commander of the *Maddox* communicated to his superiors his doubts about whether an attack had actually occurred. His superiors then relayed the information to Washington. Even President Johnson, a few days after the second attack, expressed doubts about the incident, confiding in an aide, "Hell, those dumb stupid sailors were just shooting at flying fish." Later official and unofficial investigations revealed, with near certainty, that North Vietnamese naval forces did not attack *Maddox* and *Turner Joy* on August 4.[40]

Nevertheless, a resolution requested by the president was hastened through Congress with little debate. As one observer put it, the resolution had been "rushed through Congress... in a stampede of misinformation and misconception, if not of deliberate deception."[41] Without seeking additional confirming information, Congress overwhelmingly passed what became known as the Tonkin Gulf Resolution. The House vote was unanimous, 416–0. The Senate voted 88–2. The resolution authorized the president "to take all necessary measures to repel any armed attack against the forces of the United States and to prevent further aggression." Congress further declared, "The United States is... prepared, *as the President determines* [italics added], to take all necessary steps, including the use of armed force, to assist any member or protocol state of the Southeast Asia Collective Defense Treaty requesting assistance in defense of its freedom." With such a broad mandate, Congress had granted the president the authority to determine the circumstances under which the United States would go to war nearly anywhere in southeast Asia. Johnson is reported to have remarked that the resolution was "like grandma's nightshirt—it covered everything."[42]

In the House, while no one opposed the legislation, in committee discussions concern was raised that if the resolution was passed it would signal that legislators were "abdicating [their] congressional rights and congressional responsibilities with respect to the declaration of war and with respect to foreign affairs generally." However, legislators were apparently satisfied that this would not be the case when assured that "it was the attitude of the executive that such would not be the case."[43] And so the fox was given rule of the henhouse.

Once again the din of a false patriotism overshadowed the constitutional responsibility to clearly ascertain the facts and act accordingly. As one Senator from Georgia put it "Our national honor is at stake. We cannot and we will not shrink from defending it."[44] By its own action Congress had delivered to the president a blank check. The concentration of such powers in the hands of the America's chief executive is just what the framers of the Constitution were seeking to avoid. And this was a concentration without historical parallel. The Union was not threatened. The United States had not been attacked nor was it under the threat of imminent attack. No country had declared war against the United States.

Johnson wasted no time. Like Kennedy, he had an expansive view of presidential prerogative in foreign policy. While he never believed he needed congressional authority to act in southeast Asia, he considered it useful politically.[45] Though his request for authority gave the appearance of having been cast in the urgency of the moment, it had been conceived in February and a resolution had been readied for presentation to Congress two months before the alleged incident.[46]

In early 1965, armed with his resolution and without seeking congressional authority, Johnson greatly expanded the war. Those in Congress who strongly opposed military intervention refused to speak out publicly.[47] At the height of the war there were over a half million American fighting men engaged in the conflict. Johnson, to the irritation of some members of Congress, could wave the resolution in their faces. It was Congress that had set the president free to engage in a conflict that would last longer than any previous war in which the United States had become engaged; would result in more casualties that any other of America's wars except the Civil War and the two World Wars; would cost more in constant dollars than all major wars in which the United States fought to that date except for World War II; and, despite such costs, would be lost.

It was with similar panache grounded in his confidence in presidential prerogatives that Johnson acted during a crisis in the Dominican Republic. In 1965 when a rebellion broke out in an attempt to reinstall Juan Bosch, the democratically elected though left-leaning president who had been removed in a coup 19 months earlier, Johnson did not hesitate to send in

American troops, claiming the need to protect American lives.[48] Though he informed congressional leaders of his actions, he did not seek congressional authorization.

Subsequent contingents of marines and other military forces raised the total number of U.S. military forces to 22,000, a number far in excess of what was needed to quell rioting and to protect American lives and property. Over the days and weeks following the initial deployments the underlying reason for such a large deployment became evident. Troubled by communist gains in Vietnam and the possible spread of communism in the hemisphere, though he had not consulted the CIA, Johnson believed communist Cuba had a hand in the rebellion and feared a communist takeover of the Dominican government. Given the turmoil in Santo Domingo, no doubt the safety of an estimated 3,500 American citizens living in the city was a great concern. Thus the urgency of the situation might have warranted the exercise of presidential prerogative, since the exercise of emergency powers to protect American lives had long been a recognized principle of constitutional law (e.g., *Durand v. Hollins*, 1860). In this situation, however, the emergency prerogatives doctrine could be challenged. The situation had been developing for days. American military forces had been dispatched to the area and were in a standby mode. Surely the president had time, if he had cared to take it, to consult with and seek congressional approval to use U.S. military forces to extricate American citizens and others who might be endangered should the situation further deteriorate.

Such an "armed intervention for political purposes clearly raised questions which under the Constitution,...called for congressional participation."[49] Congress, though, having grown accustomed to deference to presidential unilateral use of military force, did not even object to the president's failure to return to Congress after the immediate crisis to seek ex post facto approval. Nor did Congress object to Johnson's failure to seek congressional authority to maintain forces in the Dominican Republic for another 16 months. Though congressional approval undoubtedly would have been forthcoming, Congress, once again, abdicated its constitutional responsibilities.

Congress, of course, was not alone in its deference to the president. Following the Korean War, the nation itself had been caught up in a frenzy of presidential adoration. Leading figures, both Democratic and Republican, the press, and even some historians flocked to the side of unadulterated adulation of presidential powers. In 1960 Dean Rusk, then at the Rockefeller Foundation, claimed the commander in chief clause provided the president with "an independent source of constitutional authority."[50]

Later in the decade two leading Republican Senators made absurd claims for presidential power. Senator Everett Dirksen declared, "I have run down many legal cases before the Supreme Court...I have found as yet no delimitation on the power of the Commander in Chief under the

Constitution." Similarly, Senator Barry Goldwater asserted: "The Constitution gives the President, not the Congress the primary war-making powers."[51]

NIXON

Though shortly after entering into office President Richard M. Nixon declared his intent "to comply to the fullest extent possible with congressional requests for information,"[52] he and officials in his administration often refused to provide Congress with documents or testimony.[53] The General Accounting Office, the audit, evaluation, and investigative arm of Congress, found it "far more difficult ever than in the Eisenhower years to gain access to pertinent records."[54] Additionally, there were numerous instances when delaying tactics and outright evasion served to deny Congress the information it sought just as well as would have the claim of executive privilege. Senator Stuart Symington of Missouri, chairman of the Senate Foreign Relations Committee and member of the Armed Services and Atomic Energy Committees, with access to more secret information than anyone else in the Senate, said that he found himself "often in ignorance" about what the United States had promised to foreign countries.[55]

Nixon had adopted Eisenhower's thesis that the president had "uncontrolled discretion" to withhold information in the possession of the executive branch if he believed disclosure "would impair the proper exercise of his constitutional functions." When Senators inquired of Attorney General Richard Kleindienst whether the president was saying that Congress now had no power to compel testimony over presidential objection, Kleindienst replied that that is exactly what he was saying. The president's judgment is final. If it didn't like it, then Congress could cut off funds or impeach the president.[56] In 1972, counsel to the president John Dean, in a letter to Jeremy J. Stone, wrote: "No recent President has ever claimed a 'blanket immunity' that would prevent his assistants from testifying before Congress on any subject," but this was what his own president was claiming.[57]

Nixon justified his position, declaring it a "practical necessity...staff members must not be inhibited by the possibility that their advice and assistance will ever become a matter of public debate, either during their tenure in Government or at a later date. Otherwise, the candor with which advice is rendered and the quality of such assistance will inevitably be compromised and weakened."[58]

Thus, Nixon further shut the door on congressional access to information. This closing off of the White House staff from Congress was particularly problematical, since much of Nixon's foreign policy was fashioned not so much in the Department of State as it was in the basement of the White House by H. R. Haldeman, John Ehrlichman, and Henry Kissinger. Nixon's draconian approach was without precedent. He was claiming absolute power over the flow of materials and/or testimony to Congress.

The comity that generally had characterized relations between the legislative and executive branches had broken down. The balance envisaged by the framers had shifted dramatically toward the executive. The checks on executive power were now dangerously thin. For some the imperial presidency was at hand. However, Newton's third law of motion was already at work.

When Congress and Special Prosecutor Archibald Cox, in their investigation of the Watergate scandal involving Nixon and his associates, sought the White House tapes containing Oval Office conversations, Nixon refused, claiming absolute executive privilege. Cox responded:

Any blanket claim of privilege to withhold this evidence from the grand jury is without legal foundation. It therefore becomes my duty promptly to seek subpoenas and other available legal procedures for obtaining the evidence for the grand jury. The effort to obtain these tapes and other documentary evidence is the impartial pursuit of justice according to law.[59]

The dispute reached the Supreme Court, and in *United States v. Nixon,* the Court, in an 8–0 decision, ruled against Nixon. The Court, however, did not reject completely the presidential claim of executive privilege. Rather, it accepted the argument of the president's counsel that to ensure "complete candor and objectivity from advisors,"[60] there existed a "valid need for protection of communications between high government officials and those who advise and assist them in the performance of their manifold duties." Nevertheless, the Court concluded:

Neither the doctrine of separation of powers, nor the need for confidentiality of high-level communications, *without more,* can sustain an absolute, unqualified Presidential privilege of immunity from *judicial process* under *all* circumstances.[61] [emphases added]

Thus, in this case, the Court recognized the president's authority to assert executive privilege, but that authority was limited, not absolute, and pertained only to communications among high-level officials. The Court also concluded that to the extent that the claim to confidentiality "relates to the effective discharge of a President's powers, it is constitutionally based" and therefore can be considered "presumptively privileged." However, the claim of privilege "without more" may be unsustainable. The Court noted that the so-called "more" might be the need to protect "military, diplomatic, or sensitive national security secrets."[62]

Though one might infer from the Court's opinion a more expansive interpretation of presidential privilege, it is important to note that the Court's ruling pertained to the exercise of executive privilege in judicial proceedings. The Court did not directly address questions of privilege when exercise thereof might infringe on the public welfare through the denial of information essential to the constitutionally derived legislative functions of Congress. Indeed, the Court specifically noted: "We are not here concerned with the balance between the President's generalized interest in confidentiality.... and congressional demands for information, nor with the President's interest in preserving state secrets."[63]

The decisions of the Supreme Court were further reaffirmed in 1977. In the *Nixon v. Administrator of General Services* case, the Court reiterated that exercise of executive privilege was a qualified, not absolute, right of the president. It is narrow in scope, limited to communications "in performance of [a president's] responsibilities...of his office...and made in the process of shaping policies and making decisions." Finally the Court, once again, recognized "Congress' broad investigative power."[64]

Thus, while the Court had rebuked presidential claims of absolute executive privilege, the Court also recognized the general principle of executive privilege, as constitutionally derived from the concept of separation of powers. Nevertheless, a considerable number of uncertainties remained concerning the exact extent of the privilege.

It was in foreign affairs and on issues of war and peace, however, that Congress found its constitutional role so often limited by the president's assumption of congressional prerogatives. Though Johnson believed he had the power to act in foreign affairs and war making by virtue of presidential prerogative and consulted Congress and sought its blessing for political purposes, President Richard M. Nixon discarded all pretenses and sought to rule as czar.

The office of the president provides a variety of venues for governing without congressional interference. Among the many tools available to presidents are executive agreements, executive orders, presidential proclamations and directives, military orders, and National Security Council policy papers and decision memoranda. Presidents have used one or more of these tools since the early days of the Republic.[65] Nixon made full use of such tools to limit congressional interference in what he considered executive branch business. Schlesinger lamented that Nixon had created an "imperial presidency." Since he was convinced that the republic was in mortal danger, he "had produced an unprecedented concentration of power in the White House."[66]

In foreign affairs, particularly in pursuing the war in Vietnam, Nixon seldom sought congressional approval and often acted without so much as informing Congress in advance. So it was as the Nixon administration engaged in a number of executive agreements with foreign nations promising assistance of some sort, often in exchange for basing rights or use of facilities. The administration also frequently avowed its intent to assist countries should their security be threatened.

When in 1969 a subcommittee was formed in the Senate to look into executive agreements that had been made by the executive branch in lieu of treaties, committee members were surprised at how often their constitutional prerogatives had been circumvented and how often the Senate had been kept in the dark. Opening the first session, subcommittee chairman Sam J. Ervin remarked: "The use of executive agreements as a substitute for treaties has spiraled in recent years." He further noted:

Although a majority of the ever-increasing number of executive agreements deal with routine technical matters, it is obvious, to my mind, that in recent years the so-called executive agreement has been used to deal with problems formerly dealt with only by treaty, compelling the conclusion that executive agreements are being used to circumvent the treatymaking provisions of the Constitution. Such a development is contrary to the constitutional principles envisioned by the Founding Fathers as well as a clear violation of the doctrine of separation of powers.[67]

Similarly, Senator Stuart Symington in a statement to the subcommittee expressed his concerns:

When executive agreements rather than treaties are utilized, the tendency is to keep the Congress in ignorance of the very facts the Congress must know in order to sensibly exercise its responsibilities about foreign affairs.[68]

Despite such expressed concerns on the part of Congress, one of Nixon's most significant foreign policy initiatives, the 1972 opening to China, was initiated in secrecy without congressional involvement.[69]

Secrecy also became a key feature of Nixon's policies in southeast Asia. From March 1969 until May 1970 American bombers were engaged in bombing Vietcong sanctuaries inside Cambodia. Nixon had approved the plan, but only a few U.S. officials were aware of the bombings.[70] The entire exercise was to ensure that the American public was not made aware of the effort. On April 30, 1970, after a coup brought pro-American Lon Nol to power, Nixon ordered U.S. troops into Cambodia to interdict communist forces using the eastern part of that country for attacks into South Vietnam. He argued that the invasion was necessary "to protect our men who are in Vietnam and to guarantee the continued success of our withdrawal and Vietnamization programs."[71] This was a blatant attack on a sovereign neutral country, an action the framers of the Constitution would have clearly seen as within the purview of Congress. Nixon neither sought the approval of nor consulted with Congress before taking action, later claiming, "There were times when the Commander in Chief...will have to act quickly."[72]

Congress, angered for having, once again, been kept in the dark, responded by repealing the Gulf of Tonkin Resolution. However, Nixon continued to refuse to accept congressional declarations on southeast Asian policy.[73] In early 1971 Nixon approved a South Vietnamese invasion of Laos. In May 1972 he announced a naval blockade of North Vietnam and the mining of Haiphong Harbor. In 1973, once again, he acted unilaterally, resuming the bombing of Cambodia. This was a presidency unbridled by constitutional constraints, leading Schlesinger to assert: "By the early 1970s the American president had become on issues of war and peace the most absolute monarch (with the possible exception of Mao Tse-tung of China) among the great powers of the world."[74]

The courts largely sidestepped cases brought by those who claimed the president had acted without constitutional authority. Although Congress finally began to discuss legislation that would end the war, the signing of the Paris Peace Accords in late January 1973 made further action seem unnecessary. In an attempt to limit future unilateral decisions on the use of military forces, Congress did pass the War Powers Resolution midyear. The resolution attempted to clarify the conditions under which the president as commander in chief could constitutionally "introduce U.S. Armed Forces into hostilities, or into situations where imminent involvement in hostilities is clearly indicated by the circumstances." The resolution indicated three such conditions: "only pursuant to (1) a declaration of war, (2) specific statutory authorization, or (3) a national emergency created by an attack upon the United States, its territories or possessions, or armed forces." The resolution also mandated that the "the President in every possible instance shall consult with Congress, before introducing United States Armed Forces into situations where imminent involvement in hostilities is clearly indicated." Further, in the absence of a congressional declaration of war, the resolution required the president to report any introduction of U.S. armed forces into hostilities or situations of imminent hostilities, into a foreign country's territory, airspace, or waters, while equipped for combat or in numbers that substantially enlarge the numbers of U.S. armed forces equipped for combat already stationed in a foreign country within 48 hours of having done so. Additionally, the resolution required the president to terminate any use of armed forces "within sixty calendar days after a report is submitted or is required to be submitted" unless Congress "(1) has declared war or enacted a specific authorization for such use of United States Armed Forces, (2) has extended by law such sixty-day period, or (3) is physically unable to meet as a result of an armed attack upon the United States." Finally, any time U.S. armed forces are engaged in hostilities without a declaration of war or specific statutory authorization, Congress by concurrent resolution can direct the president to remove those forces from combat.[75]

Whether that law has had any effect on limiting presidential prerogatives has been a matter of debate ever since it was passed over the president's veto. Some have argued that the language of the resolution is too vague to have much of an effect on the president. For example, the resolution authorizes the president to act unilaterally in an emergency created by an attack on the United States. Yet it fails to define what constitutes an emergency, or an attack, or even what is meant by United States. Thus it provides the president wide leeway to define an emergency. It also raises the question of whether an attack on the "United States" might be construed to include an attack on American government personnel or U.S. citizens and their property abroad or an attack on America's vital or other worldwide interests.[76]

Others contend that the resolution had the effect, among other things, of granting the president what that office had heretofore lacked—unilateral authority to use force anywhere in the world under conditions that he decides for 60 or 90 days.[77]

Moreover, the Court threw a monkey wrench into the section of the War Powers Resolution that permits Congress to direct the president to remove U.S. armed forces from hostilities in the absence of a declaration of war or specific statutory authorization. In the 1983 *INS v. Chadha* case[78] the Supreme Court invalidated the legislative veto, an action in which the Congress through joint or concurrent resolution attempts to repeal a previously authorized act. The Court held that such resolutions are not law until signed by the president, thus throwing into doubt Congress's ability to force the president to terminate hostilities by such resolutions.

In July 1974 Nixon chose to ignore the resolution and ordered military forces to evacuate American civilians from Cyprus in the midst of hostilities following Turkish intervention in a Greek government–sponsored coup that removed President Makarios from power. Nixon did not seek congressional approval, inform Congress, or report in accordance with the requirements of the War Powers Resolution. Indeed, presidents have consistently denied the constitutionality of the War Powers Resolution. Though usually reporting their activity to Congress, they have refused explicit adherence to its provisions.[79]

PUTTING THE GENIE BACK IN THE BOTTLE

When Nixon left, the presidency was in a weakened state. By the mid-1970s the congressional laissez-faire attitude toward acquiring information from the executive branch, particularly on intelligence activities, changed. The U.S. intelligence agencies' abuses in the 1960s and 70s, which included activities that seriously infringed upon the basic rights of Americans as well as covert activities against foreign leaders and governments, caused an uproar. They also brought to an end, albeit too briefly, the postwar period marked by congressional acquiescence.

Congress had become troubled by findings that surfaced during Senate Armed Service Committee hearings about U.S. covert activities in Cambodia, Laos, and North Vietnam during the Vietnam War and by disquieting information concerning U.S. covert activities elsewhere. In an attempt to get its hands on an aspect of American foreign policy that had eluded it since the days of Eisenhower, Congress passed the 1974 Hughes-Ryan amendment to the Foreign Assistance Act of 1961. The amendment prohibited the use of appropriated funds by or on behalf of the CIA for "operations in foreign countries, other than activities intended solely for obtaining necessary intelligence unless and until the President issued a *Finding* that each such operation is important to the national security of the United States." The amendment also required the president to report "in a timely fashion, a description and scope of such operation[s] to the appropriate committees of Congress." This was interpreted to mean the six congressional committees with intelligence oversight responsibilities—the Armed Services and Appropriations Committees of both houses of Congress and now the Senate Foreign Relations and House Foreign Affairs Committees.[80] The following year, Congress put teeth into its determination to rein in covert activities undertaken by U.S. intelligence agencies, by passing, for the first time, legislation that terminated funding for covert activities in Angola.

Then came the findings of the committees chaired by Senator Frank Church in the Senate and Congressman Otis Pike in the House that had been formed to investigate the serious, numerous, and widely spread intelligence agency abuses, including attempted assassinations of such foreign leaders as Patrice Lumumba of the Congo, presidents Trujillo of the Dominican Republic, Diem of South Vietnam, and Castro of Cuba. Soon after, both houses of Congress established new intelligence oversight structures.

In May 1976 the Senate by a 72–22 majority passed Resolution 400, which established the Senate Select Committee on Intelligence. It was the task of this new committee to "make every effort to assure that the departments and agencies of the United States provide *informed and timely* [emphasis added] intelligence necessary for the executive and legislative branches to make sound decisions affecting the security and vital interests of the Nation." In addition, the new committee was "to provide vigilant legislative oversight over intelligence activities of the United States to assure that such activities are in conformity with the Constitution and the laws of the United States."

The resolution also included the nonbinding statement that it was "the sense of the Senate" that intelligence agencies keep the Senate "fully and currently informed with respect to intelligence activities, including significant anticipated activities."[81]

In July of the following year by a vote of 227–171 the House followed suit, passing House Resolution 658, which established the House Permanent Select Committee on Intelligence. The Resolution mandated that all matters relating to intelligence or intelligence-related activities undertaken by the CIA and other departments and agencies be referred to this new select committee. Now both houses of Congress would, at least in theory, have timely information to make sound decisions affecting foreign and national security policy. The combined effect of closer oversight of

U.S. intelligence efforts and the War Powers Resolution was to serve as a limitation on the further aggrandizement of presidential power.

Ford and Carter

Despite Nixon's decision to ignore the requirements set forth in the War Powers Resolution, future presidents, having been granted by Congress statutory authority to engage in hostilities, could now be seen to be acting in compliance with congressional wishes by reporting their actions, while still proclaiming presidential prerogative and taking advantage of a lack of clarity in the provisions of the War Powers Resolution. In the nearly two and a half years of the presidency of Gerald Ford and the four years of that of Jimmy Carter, there were six cases involving the use of military forces. Five of these were reported to Congress pursuant to the War Powers Resolution.

Three of the four reported cases and the one unreported case during the Ford administration involved the evacuation of American citizens and foreign nationals. The three reported cases were associated with the April 1975 U.S. withdrawals from Asia—Vietnam, Cambodia, and South Vietnam. Though in all three cases the president probably had time to go to Congress to seek authorization, he could lean on the *Durand v. Hollins* 1860 ruling for legal justification for acting unilaterally in the rescue of endangered American citizens. The major issue in all three cases was the rescue of foreign nationals, which was not covered by *Durand v. Hollins*. President Ford did seek a clarification from Congress. However, he took action before Congress responded.[82] The one unreported case involved the evacuation of American and Europeans from Lebanon in July 1976 during fighting between Lebanese factions. The evacuation was neither authorized nor later approved by Congress.

The remaining case was the use of force to free the crew of the *Mayaguez*, a U.S. merchant ship seized by the communist government that had recently taken over in Cambodia. Recalling the North Korean seizure of the USS *Pueblo* in 1968, when the American crew members were held for more than a year, and fearing that the crew would be moved from the more remote location they were initially being held to a location that might have made any rescue attempt exceedingly difficult, Ford, "pursuant to the President's constitutional Executive power and his authority as Commander-in-Chief,"[83] chose to act immediately without seeking Congress's approval. Little effort had been expended on diplomatic efforts to solve the crisis. Forty-one marines were killed in the action to rescue 39 crewmen. Ford, however, did formally report his actions to Congress as required by the War Powers Resolution.

In this situation no amount of second-guessing is likely to bear fruit. Surely Ford might have benefited from discussions with members of Congress. But the president believed time was critical. Under such

POLITICAL QUESTIONS DOCTRINE

The Supreme Court formulated the political questions doctrine in the early 1800s. Political questions are those questions that usually, though not exclusively, involve constitutional questions between the legislative and executive branches,* which the Court has deemed inappropriate for the Court to address, considering it within the powers of the two branches to settle politically. Since the 1960s the Court has become slightly more willing to address such matters, as was evidenced by the *United States v. Nixon* 1974 case.

* See *Luther v. Borden*, 48 U.S. 1 (1849).

circumstances, he exercised his prerogative powers, now well-established in law and practice, to respond. After the rescue was completed, "Legislators expressed pride in their country and their President."[84] Later a *Mayaguez* crew member sought damages, arguing, among other things, that the military operation was executed in a negligent manner. The federal district court judge ruled that Ford's action was immune from judicial review under the political questions doctrine (see "Political Questions Doctrine").[85]

President Carter used military force without congressional approval in the April 1980 attempted rescue of 52 American hostages held in Iran since November 1979. Though Carter later reported to Congress "consistent with the reporting provisions of the War Powers Resolution,"[86] stating the "operation was ordered and conducted pursuant to the President's powers under the Constitution as Chief Executive and as Commander-in-Chief of the United States Armed Forces,"[87] he did not consult with Congress and chose to inform members of Congress only after the mission was well under way.

Secretary of State Cyrus Vance, who believed there were still political options that should have been considered before opting for the use of military force, resigned over the action. In keeping Congress in the dark, undoubtedly secrecy was paramount in Carter's mind. The mission was a complete failure. In a slight recognition of the value of the constitutional processes that he had failed to engage, Carter later mused that had he informed Senate Majority Leader Robert C. Byrd, with whom he met the evening before the operation commenced, "His advice would have been valuable."[88]

Carter also extended the power of the presidency when he abrogated the 1954 Mutual Defense Treaty with Taiwan, which opened the way for the recognition of the People's Republic of China. His action raised the same question that President Washington's declaration of neutrality had in the war between France and England—namely, can the president abrogate a treaty made with the advice and consent of the Senate? Senator Barry Goldwater and other members of Congress sued Carter, contending he had exceeded his constitutional authority in abrogating the treaty without the advice and consent of the Senate. The Supreme Court dismissed the case, ruling that "a dispute between Congress and the President is not ready for judicial review unless and until each branch has taken action asserting its constitutional authority." Congress had not done so. Thus the case was a nonjusticiable political question and was remanded back to the District Court with directions to dismiss the complaint.[89]

Characteristic of both the Ford and Carter administrations was a greater willingness, sometimes more declared than real, to provide to Congress information it had requested. As Nixon's vice president, Ford had become sensitized to the unfavorable connotations appended to the term "executive privilege" during the Watergate era. To avoid potential criticism, his administration often attempted to conceal the use of executive privilege by using other terms or citing statutory authority as a basis for keeping secrets or by seeking a compromise with Congress that would preclude the necessity of invoking privilege.[90] Nevertheless, in 1975 during a Senate Judiciary subcommittee investigation on promises of aid to South Vietnam in case North Vietnam did not honor the Paris Peace Accords, Ford refused to release requested documents.[91] On the other hand, Ford generally accommodated Congress on its requests. He personally appeared before a House subcommittee to respond to questions about the pardon he had granted to Nixon. He was willing to furnish Congress with information in areas where previous presidents had been unwilling or reluctant to cooperate with congressional inquiries. He agreed to provide Congress with information about the CIA and FBI. President Ford, however, "never conceded that the legislature had a right of access to sensitive executive branch information."[92]

President Carter, like his predecessor, was cautious in his approach to withholding information from Congress. Though he never issued formal guidelines on the subject, several procedures did evolve. In November 1980, an interdepartmental memorandum noted that while no official procedures had been established, the administration had adopted de facto the procedures issued by the Nixon administration. Presidential Counsel Lloyd Cutler further cautioned that presidential advisors could not waive executive privilege without presidential approval.[93] Though the Carter administration did not frequently invoke executive privilege, Carter, like Ford, accepted in principle the concept that under certain circumstances the president would be justified in exercising his prerogative to withhold information and indeed he did so. For example, in 1975, Carter instructed Energy Secretary Charles Duncan to claim executive privilege in response to a congressional demand for documents relating to the development and implementation of a policy to impose a petroleum import fee.[94]

Several important contributions to the body of jurisprudence on executive privilege were made in 1977. In the *Nixon v. Administrator of General Services* case, mentioned earlier, the Court held that exercise of executive privilege by the president was a qualified, not absolute, right. In *United States v. AT&T*, the U.S. Court of Appeals, D.C. Circuit, went further, noting that since the Constitution assigns both Congress and the president powers relating to national security, the executive branch has no absolute claim of executive privilege against Congress, even in the area of national security. The Court also suggested that it would not intervene between Congress and the president in executive privilege disputes, unless the two branches themselves failed to reach an accommodation.[95]

Meanwhile, with the establishment of the House and Senate intelligence committees, Congress began to streamline its oversight activities as well as play a more active role in overseeing U.S. intelligence efforts.[96] Oversight of intelligence activities during this period, however, was primarily aimed at ensuring that intelligence agencies operated within the law and were adequately funded. They were not centrally focused on the quality of the intelligence effort, nor were they ever 100 percent effective. Thus, while Congress had a greater assurance that the intelligence community's covert and other activities were in accordance with its wishes, it seemed less interested in ensuring that the information gathered met the standards for effective decision making on foreign policy and war.

Nevertheless, the increase in oversight led to an increase in the materials made available to congressional intelligence committees by the intelligence community. This led both committees to adopt informal ground rules with the CIA to govern the sharing of intelligence, permitting the intelligence committees to have access to a great variety of classified data and information. Still, the rules permitted the agency or the president or his advisors to limit access to information it deemed sensitive—a loophole that could and would be used to limit the flow of information to Congress.

In 1978, reflecting concerns of the times and intent on demonstrating that the new arrangement for the flow of information to Congress could work,[97] President Carter issued Executive Order 12036. Among other things, the executive order established restrictions on intelligence activities, including restrictions designed to protect individual privacy and civil liberties and a prohibition of assassination. It also established the requirement that intelligence officials comply with the "sense of the Senate" language embodied in the Senate resolution establishing the Senate Select Committee on Intelligence, requiring intelligence community officials to keep the congressional intelligence committees "fully and currently informed" of their intelligence activities, "including any significant anticipated activities." Additionally, Carter's executive order mandated that intelligence agencies provide congressional intelligence committees any information or document in their possession, custody, or control that the committees might request, as well as report to both committees "in a timely fashion...intelligence activities that are illegal or improper and the corrective actions...taken or planned." Again, this did not guarantee the unfettered provision of information to Congress or fully impede intelligence community activities that might have been of a questionable nature, since the executive order bore the standard caveat that whatever was done had to be consistent with any procedures the president might establish, as well as consistent with authorities and duties conferred on the executive and legislative branches by the Constitution. In short, the president could establish procedures or could claim executive privilege and thus limit information passed to the committees.

Unsatisfied with the Carter administration's failure to "fully inform" Congress of CIA activities relating to the rescue attempt during the Iranian hostage crisis of 1979–1980 and determined to strengthen the oversight processes, Congress passed and the president signed the Intelligence Oversight Act of 1980. This act established in law many of the features of Carter's executive order. Moreover, where the 1974 Hughes-Ryan amendment obliged the CIA to provide notice to Congress of its covert activities "in a timely fashion," the Intelligence Oversight Act of 1980 extended the reporting obligation to any agency conducting intelligence operations. The act required the director of Central Intelligence and heads of *all* (emphasis added) departments, agencies, and other U.S. entities involved in intelligence activities to furnish any information or material concerning intelligence activities in their possession that is requested by either of the intelligence committees and to keep the intelligence committees fully and currently informed of all intelligence activities, including any "significant anticipated intelligence" activities and report in "a timely fashion...any illegal intelligence activity or any significant intelligence failure and the corrective action" taken or planned.

Should the executive branch departments or agencies fail to provide prior notice to the intelligence committees of intelligence operations in foreign countries, other than activities intended solely for obtaining necessary intelligence (i.e., covert actions), the act required the president "in a timely fashion" to "fully inform" the committees of such activities and to provide a statement explaining the reasons for not giving prior notice.

To close another possible loophole in the oversight process regarding withholding information based on security concerns from Congress, the act further noted:

Nothing in this Act shall be construed as authority to withhold information from the intelligence committees on the grounds that providing the information to the intelligence committees would constitute the unauthorized disclosure of classified information or information relating to intelligence sources and methods.

In a concession to the executive branch, the act limited the number of congressional committees receiving notice of covert actions from the previous six to just the two intelligence committees. Congress also recognized that under extraordinary circumstances affecting the vital interests of the United States, the president might find it essential to limit the number of those receiving prior notice. Under such circumstances, he could opt to limit notice to the chairman and ranking minority members of the intelligence committees, the Speaker and minority leader of the House of Representatives, and the majority and minority leaders of the Senate. This group became known as the "Gang of Eight."

The act also carefully noted that the act shouldn't be construed as requiring approval of the intelligence committees as a condition precedent to the initiation of any significant anticipated intelligence activity.[98]

Reagan

Though President Ronald Reagan reasserted claims to unconditional executive privilege,[99] he never followed through with such claims. Reagan directed the assertion of privilege only three times,[100] none of which involved foreign policy or security issues and after all of which Reagan administration officials ultimately turned over all or most of the materials requested by Congress. Indeed, by the time Ronald Reagan assumed office, relationships between executive branch intelligence agencies and Congress and particularly the congressional intelligence committees were reasonably well established.[101] In principle, the committees recognized no limit on their right to obtain information or documentation from the intelligence community. In practice, they recognized that they might be denied access to certain highly classified information, such as the identity of clandestine agents, or access might be limited to the committee chairman and ranking minority member and perhaps certain selected staff.[102] With such an accommodation in place, the sharing of classified information by intelligence agencies with Congress increased, including the sharing of such materials with non-oversight committees.[103] In return, congressional intelligence committees, though carefully scrutinizing intelligence community budgets, were supportive of increases.

On the other hand, it would appear that the War Powers Resolution, crafted to provide Congress a role in the deployment of U.S. military forces abroad, posed no constraint on President Ronald Reagan's use of military forces. A believer in the inherent powers of the president acting as commander in chief, he intervened in eight conflicts, deploying military forces ranging from a few soldiers to thousands of army, naval, and air personnel.[104] In 1981 he sent military personnel to the Sinai to support the UN-sponsored Multinational Force whose task it was to supervise the implementation of the security provisions of the Egyptian-Israeli peace treaty. That same year he also sent advisors to El Salvador to assist in that country's civil war, and from 1982 to 1990 he sent thousands of naval and air forces and ground troops to Honduras. Many were there to assist the Contras in their fight to overthrow the government of Nicaragua. In 1982 he sent 2,000 marines to Lebanon as part of a three-nation peacekeeping force, only to find American forces entangled in Lebanon's sectarian strife. Reagan sent two AWACS electronic surveillance planes and eight F-15 fighter planes and ground logistical support forces to Sudan in August 1983 to assist Chad against Libyan and rebel forces. In October he attacked Grenada, ostensibly to protect the lives of nearly 1,000 Americans on the island following an internecine struggle among competing communist groups that resulted in a coup that ousted Prime Minister Maurice Bishop. In 1986 he dispatched air and naval forces to attack Libya in retaliation for the bombing of a discotheque in West Berlin that killed American servicemen. A German court that later tried one of the individuals involved in the bombing concluded that it wasn't clear that the Libyan government or its intelligence services actually ordered the attack. Though in what may be considered tacit recognition of Libya's responsibility for the bombing, Libya signaled its willingness to compensate the bombing victims. And in 1987, when the USS. *Stark* was attacked in the Persian Gulf by an Iraqi aircraft, killing 37 American sailors during Iraq's war with Iran, Reagan became concerned that the flow of Middle East oil would be impeded by the threat of further attacks. He then reflagged and provided military escorts for Kuwaiti tankers transiting the Gulf.[105]

On only one occasion, the Sinai deployment, did he seek or receive congressional approval. Only in one instance (Lebanon) did Congress later authorize his dispatch of U.S. military forces. Over a year later Congress passed a resolution authorizing U.S. troops to participate in the multinational operation in Lebanon for 18 months. Despite the magnitude of some of the operations and their international implications, members of Congress were seldom consulted or informed beforehand. However, Reagan, often though not always, and not immediately, reported his actions to Congress, though without recognizing the constitutionality of the War Powers Resolution requirements. On three occasions—El Salvador, Grenada, and the Persian Gulf—members of Congress filed suit against one or more aspects of the president's actions. All suits were unsuccessful.[106] Congress seemed singularly unable or unwilling to control the president in his use of military forces abroad.

However, in the early 1980s Congress became increasingly concerned over U.S. intelligence agencies' activities in Central America. Allegations that the CIA may have been involved in political violence in El Salvador and Guatemala and the agency's role in the civil war in Nicaragua were of particular concern.[107]

In Nicaragua, Congress was aware that President Reagan had authorized the CIA to provide assistance, including military assistance to an insurgent group known as the Contras. The Contras opposed rule by the pro-communist Sandinista government that had led the revolution against Nicaraguan dictator Anastasio Somoza and taken over control of the Nicaraguan government in 1979. Concerned that Nicaragua might become another Vietnam, congressional intelligence committees became involved in limiting covert assistance to the Contras. These restrictions, collectively known as the Boland amendments,[108] culminated in the passing of Public Law 98–215 in December 1982, which prohibited covert assistance to the Contras for the purpose of overthrowing the government of Nicaragua.

When Senate intelligence committee members learned in April 1984 that CIA operatives had covertly assisted the Contras in the mining of Nicaraguan harbors, many were notably upset. The mining of Nicaragua's harbors was a violation of international law. Moreover, it had resulted in explosions that damaged ships from several foreign countries, including those of the Netherlands and Japan, both U.S. allies, as well as the Soviet Union. Once again, the Senate committee had not been fully and currently informed of a major CIA covert operation. Not one to mince words, Senator Barry Goldwater, chairman of the Senate's Select Committee on Intelligence, wrote director of Central Intelligence William Casey a pointed letter colorfully noting that he was "pissed off" over the turn of events. Senate committee members were further dismayed over the dissembling by Reagan administrations officials who contended that Goldwater had been fully informed.[109] An informal agreement known as the Casey Accord was reached in June 1984, with the executive branch once again promising to keep congressional intelligence committees informed of significant changes or developments in ongoing covert operations.[110] The Casey Accord, which was approved by the president, also further refined the definition of "significant anticipated activities" as outlined in the Intelligence Oversight Act of 1980, obligating the president to approve in advance such covert activity.[111]

To further strengthen intelligence oversight, the National Security of 1947 was amended, requiring Congress to specifically authorize and appropriate all monies to be spent on intelligence or intelligence-related activities. In addition, the director of Central Intelligence had to give prior notice of any release of funds from the CIA reserve contingencies and any reprogramming or transfer of funds for purposes other than those for which they had been authorized and appropriated by Congress. Moreover, the executive branch was to give notice whenever a covert arms transfer of a single article or service exceeded $1 million in value.[112]

Despite such arrangements, congressional intelligence committees were confronted with what many regarded as the most serious breach of oversight arrangements since the committees were created—the so-called Iran-Contra affair.[113] In October and November 1986, the two closely linked covert operations were publicly exposed. The first involved the sale of arms to Iran. Hezbollah, a radical Islamic group based in Lebanon, had taken a number of Americans hostage. Since Iran was a strong supporter and was thought to be able to influence Hezbollah, Reagan administration officials thought by selling Iran arms, the Iranians might be able to gain the release of the hostages. However, such an action was in contravention of U.S. policy and in possible violation of U.S. arms export controls.

The second covert activity involved providing the funds from the sale of arms to Iran to the Nicaraguan Contra rebels, which had been prohibited by the Boland amendments. Both activities were undertaken with CIA involvement, and in neither case were congressional intelligence committees informed.[114] As a result, Senate and House intelligence committees immediately undertook intensive investigations of the events. On December 1, 1986, President Reagan also took action, with the creation of a special review board, chaired by former Senator John Tower and known as the Tower Commission. In January 1987, the Senate and House established select committees to undertake further investigations. The chairman of the committees agreed to a joint effort. In the course of joint committee investigations 40 days of public hearings were held, more than 500 witnesses were interviewed, and more than 300,000 documents were reviewed.[115]

What became clear from these investigations was that the Reagan administration had largely ignored the accountability structures that had been set in place since the Church and Pike committee reports. The president had not given prior approval to all covert actions that had been undertaken. Not all approvals given had been in writing. And in at least one case, the president had approved a covert action and deliberately ordered the director of Central Intelligence not to inform Congress.[116] Indeed, when asked why two covert arms sales to Iran that exceeded $10 million had not been reported, the reply from the executive branch was that no one item exceeded the $1 million limit that had been previously stipulated by Congress.[117] As one keen observer put it: "Such contempt for the American constitutional form of government was unprecedented."[118]

Once again, to improve the flow of information to Congress, as well as Congress's ability to oversee other activities of the intelligence community, the executive branch recommitted itself to procedures that would permit effective congressional oversight. Following CIA director Casey's death in May 1987, the new director, Judge William Webster, pledged to restore a cooperative relationship between the CIA and congressional intelligence committees. In October, President Reagan signed National Security Decision Directive 286, prohibiting retroactive approval of special activities in foreign countries (i.e., covert actions). Moreover, in all but the "rarest circumstances," no such activity was to take place prior to the president's having signed a written statement, or finding, as it was called, that such activity was important to the national security of the United States.

However, since the president could revise or revoke any national security decision directive without congressional consent, in the spring of 1988 the Senate, in an attempt to emphasize, once again, the need for the executive branch to comply with the law and previous agreements, overwhelmingly passed a bill requiring notice of covert activities within 48 hours. The House failed to act and the legislation never became law.

CHAPTER 6

A Season for Abdication

In March 1985, following the deaths in rapid succession of Yuri Andropov and Konstantin Chernenko, who had recently replaced longtime party leader Leonid Brezhnev, Mikhail Gorbachev was named General Secretary of the Communist Party of the Soviet Union. At age 54, Gorbachev was the youngest leader of the Soviet Union since Joseph Stalin took the reins following Lenin's death. Aware of the systemic weaknesses of communism, Gorbachev soon embarked on a path toward economic restructuring (perestroika) and encouraged greater discussion (glasnost).

By the end of 1991, a 69-year odyssey had come to an end and with it a definitive end to a struggle between East and West that had been the principal focus of Congress's foreign policy and security concerns. Yet new concerns had already begun to emerge. The need for information on and the ability to deal effectively with such issues as drug and human trafficking and counternarcotics, terrorism, and the proliferation of chemical, biological, and nuclear weapons were increasingly on the radar of Congress and the president.

G.H.W. BUSH

President George H. W. Bush, like his predecessor, had an expansive view of presidential prerogatives. He left in place the Reagan guidelines on executive privilege and hence the implication of an unconditional right to deny information to Congress. Yet he pledged to keep Congress informed on covert actions. He also insisted on what he called "the President's constitutional authority to use the armed forces to defend vital U.S. interests."[1]

The Bush administration contended that recommendations made to senior department officials as well as communications between and among senior policy makers throughout the executive branch were protected by executive privilege, whether or not they involved information intended to go to the president.[2] However, like all post-Watergate presidents, George H. W. Bush was sensitive to negative connotations associated with the term. Though executive privilege was sometimes claimed, rather than risk a confrontation with Congress, the Bush administration often relented when threatened with or issued subpoenas or confronted with the possibility. Nevertheless, the Bush administration frequently withheld information without actually claiming executive privilege. Among the techniques used were claims of "attorney-client privilege," "deliberative process privilege," "attorney work product," "internal departmental deliberations," "secret opinions policy," "deliberations of another agency," and "missing documents."[3] According to one House Judiciary Committee staffer, the president "knew how to work the system.... In reality, executive privilege was in full force and effective during the Bush years."[4]

When it came to covert action to advance U.S. foreign policy interests, Bush pledged to provide prior notice to Congress. Should that not be possible, he would provide notice "within a few days." However, if notice were to be withheld for a longer period, he would rely on his authorities under the Constitution. These words, uncoded, meant that the president believed that, in certain circumstances, it was within his constitutionally mandated prerogatives to withhold such information. Despite disagreements between the executive branch and Congress over wording,[5] an accommodation was reached and included in the fiscal year 1991 intelligence authorization bill passed later in the year that significantly revised the Intelligence Oversight Act of 1980.[6]

The bill reiterated all essential elements of the 1980 Oversight Act and reaffirmed the 1974 Hughes-Ryan Amendment requirement as amplified by Reagan's National Security Decision Directive 286 that the president provide written approval for covert actions in the form of a finding that the action was necessary to support identifiable foreign policy objectives and important to the security of the United States. If events precluded written prior approval, a subsequent written approval had to be forthcoming within 48 hours. Additionally, it specifically defined covert action as "an activity or activities of the United States Government to influence political, economic, or military conditions abroad, where it is intended that the role of the United States Government will not be apparent or acknowledged publicly."[7]

Once again, the legislation recognized that under extraordinary circumstances affecting vital interests the president might wish to limit the number of people made aware of the covert activity. Under such circumstances his written approval may be reported to the so-called Congressional "Gang of Eight." Additionally, the new legislation prohibited the president from authorizing actions aimed at influencing U.S. political processes, public opinion, policies, or the media, as well as actions that were in violation of the Constitution or any statute of the United States, unless the president determined such an action was necessary to support identifiable foreign policy objectives of the United States and is important to U.S. national security.[8]

In passing this bill, Congress, in a gratuitous concession to presidential power, acknowledged that the president might exercise what he perceived as his prerogatives under the Constitution to withhold information for longer periods than specified in the legislation. Congress then expressed its view that the Constitution did not provide such authority to the president.[9]

When it came to the use of U.S. military forces, however, Bush felt little constraint. During his four years in office, Bush ordered the use of U.S. military forces on six occasions. Three were relatively minor. In September 1989, Bush deployed approximately 100 military advisors and special forces to Colombia, Bolivia, and Peru. Though Congress had appropriated money for narcotics control efforts in the Andean region, including money for military and law enforcement assistance, the law also stipulated that no security assistance could be provided until the secretary of state submitted certain reports to Congress. Bush objected to that restraint on constitutional grounds and deployed the advisors. In December of that year, Bush ordered aircraft from Clark Air Base to provide assistance in the form of combat air patrols to help the Aquino government in the Philippines restore order and to protect American lives. And in September 1991 Bush authorized the U.S. military to airlift 1,000 Belgian troops and equipment to Kinshasa, Zaire, in the midst of widespread looting and rioting and to retrieve American citizens and third-country nationals from potential danger. He also authorized the airlift of 300 French troops to the Central African Republic. In none of these cases did Congress authorized the use of the U.S. military or specifically give its ex post facto approval. The president provided a report "consistent with" the War Powers Resolution only in the Philippines case.[10] As with past presidents, he did so without recognizing the resolution's constitutionality.

More significantly, on December 20, 1989, with Congress in recess, Bush ordered an invasion of Panama. Fourteen thousand military personnel were rushed to join 13,000 already in place in order to protect American citizens in Panama; restore the democratic process; preserve the integrity of the Panama Canal treaties; and apprehend General Manuel Noriega, who had been accused of massive electoral fraud in the Panamanian elections and indicted on drug trafficking charges by two U.S. federal courts.

Congress had been discussing the problem of Noriega for some time before it adjourned and had encouraged Bush to remove General Noriega from power. The Senate had adopted an amendment supporting the president's use of diplomatic, economic, and military options but had defeated an amendment authorizing Bush to use military force to remove Noriega. Despite Congress's clear interest in the issues or because he feared the outcome, Bush did not consult Congress. He did, however, notify members of Congress a few hours before the invasion. He also reported his actions "consistent with" War Powers Resolution requirements. Congress, for its part, did not authorize the operation in advance or grant approval afterward, although Congress did pass a resolution praising Bush for acting "decisively and appropriately in ordering United States forces to intervene in Panama."[11] During the House debate on the resolution, Congressman Robert Kastenmeier declared that in his view it would be wrong to praise Bush for an action that violated international law and had been condemned by 20 of the 21 Latin American countries.[12]

While in early 1991 President Bush sought and received congressional authorization to engage American forces in conflict with Iraq following that country's invasion of Kuwait, he made no effort to seek nor did he receive authorization for his 1990 deployment of about 350,000 military personnel to the region, placing them directly in harm's way. However, both houses of Congress had adopted legislation supporting efforts to end the Iraqi occupation of Kuwait, and Congress appropriated funds for the deployments. In August 1990 the Senate had unanimously adopted a resolution urging the president "to act immediately ... to seek the ... withdrawal of all Iraqi forces from Kuwaiti territory" and if other efforts failed, then actions "involving air, sea, and land forces as may be needed." Nevertheless, according to Senate Foreign Relations Committee chairman Pell, the measure did not authorize unilateral U.S. military actions.[13] Bush did report his actions "consistent with" the War Powers Resolution. On November 29, 1996, the UN Security Council passed Resolution 678, authorizing member states to use "all necessary means" to force Iraq's withdrawal from Kuwait unless it did so by January 15, 1990. On January 8 Bush asked Congress to pass legislation supporting war. Three days before the deadline Congress passed legislation authorizing the use of force. Four days later combat operations began.

Throughout the process Bush repeatedly held that he did not need congressional authorization to go to war. In signing the congressional legislation authorizing him to use force, he declared that his signing did not "constitute any change in the long-standing positions of the executive branch on either the President's constitutional authority to use the Armed Forces to defend vital U.S. interests or the constitutionality of the War Powers Resolution."[14] Even after asking for authorization, he contended that he had "the inherent power to commit U.S. forces to combat after the U.N. resolution."[15] If Bush were correct in a case where the U.S. has over a half million men and women engaged in a major war against the fifth- or sixth-largest army in the world, then there is nothing left to America's constitutional process with respect to war and peace. Fortunately Congress did debate the issue. The authorizing resolution passed the House

(250–183) and by a close vote the Senate (52–47). The larger issue is how Congress might have handled the situation had the president acted without calling for a resolution.

Bush continued to act as if Congress had no role other than to affirm his decisions on troop deployments and continue to provide the necessary funds for their operations. On December 4, 1992, he ordered U.S. forces to Somalia to participate in a UN-sponsored humanitarian relief effort set up to facilitate aid to people trapped by civil war and famine. By mid-January there were 25,000 U.S. military personnel in that country. Bush did not seek congressional approval, but he did brief Congress on December 4. He also reported to Congress consistent with the War Powers Resolution. Congress, on the other hand, did not authorize the Somalia deployments in advance. However, Attorney General Robert Jackson, in justifying Bush's actions, offered a new rationale for the ever expanding war-making powers of the presidency. Where Bush had suggested that the president has inherent powers to use military force "to defend vital U.S. interests," Jackson simply left out the word "vital" and added "missions of good will or rescue"[16] to the precedent set by *Durand v. Hollins* over 130 years earlier, which had recognized the right of the president to act to protect American lives and property.

CLINTON

Under fire during the election campaign for his lack of experience in international affairs, his character, lack of military experience, and accusations of draft dodging,[17] President Bill Clinton responded that he would be an activist president, pursue an interventionist foreign policy, and be willing to use military force.[18] True to his word, Clinton sustained the intervention in Somalia, though by mid-May 1993 he had reduced the size of the U.S. military commitment from the 25,000 deployed under President Bush to approximately 4,000 troops.[19]

However, in addition to dispatching troops regularly to support humanitarian missions or to protect or evacuate American citizens and third-country nationals from troubled countries, Clinton also employed American military forces in four other conflicts—Bosnia-Herzegovina (1992–1999), Iraq (1993–2000), Haiti (1993–1996), and Kosovo (1999), as well as ordered cruise missile strikes against Sudan and Afghanistan (1998) and provided support for the UN multinational force in East Timor.[20] Though he reported his actions to Congress "consistent with" the requirements of the War Powers Resolution, he neither sought nor received congressional authorization for his use of military forces abroad.

Clinton, like his predecessor, believed in the inherent powers of the president to act in foreign policy and in committing American forces abroad. During his presidency he provided new and creative rationale for expanding the powers of the presidency in war making. Where Bush had suggested that the president's inherent powers extended to use military force "to defend vital U.S. interests," Clinton preferred to follow Jackson's approach. In defending his use of force in Bosnia, Clinton left out the word "vital," claiming he had the power to commit troops overseas without the specific approval of Congress if a "clear American interest" exists.[21]

To his responsibilities to preserve, protect, and defend the Constitution and the implied powers recognized by the Courts to protect American lives and property, he added the idea that such a defense could come after the fact, even if no harm to an American citizen had occurred. In April 1993 a car bomb plot to kill former President George H. W. Bush during a visit to Kuwait was foiled. On June 26, after the president had received evidence that Iraqi intelligence agents were involved, U.S. Navy ships launched 23 Tomahawk missiles against the headquarters of the Iraqi Intelligence Service in retaliation. Clinton asserted that the Iraqi *attack* [emphasis added] against President Bush was an attack against our country and against all Americans.[22] Clinton said the retaliatory Tomahawk missile strikes, which occurred over two months after plotters planned to kill President Bush, was an "exercise of our inherent right of self-defense."[23]

In addition to such justifications, Clinton's advisors apparently added less honorable rationale as the situation in Haiti worsened in July 1994. In a memorandum to UN Secretary General Boutros Boutros-Ghali, Dante Caputo, UN special envoy to Haiti, describing the political calculations within the Clinton White House, noted that Clinton's advisors believed that an invasion of Haiti would be "politically desirable" because it would highlight to the American public "the President's decision making capability and the firmness of leadership in international political matters."[24]

The president, in usurping Congress's constitutional role to commit military forces to conflicts abroad, often cited not only the United Nations as an authorizing body as a justification for America's support of multilateral military efforts abroad, but also that of NATO members. As Clinton explained with regard to air strikes in Bosnia against Bosnian Serb military targets, "The authority under which air strikes can proceed, NATO acting out of area pursuant to U.N. authority, requires the common agreement of our allies."[25] To this Louis Fisher commented: "In other words, Clinton would have to obtain approval from England, Italy, and other NATO allies, but not from Congress."[26]

Congress seemed ill equipped to deal with this continuing assault on its constitutional prerogatives. Increasingly uncertain about its role in American foreign policy and in the commitment of American forces abroad, including in situations where conflict was likely, it vacillated in its attempts to impose its will on the president. More often than not Congress was its own worst enemy. For example, when in 1993 both the Senate and the House passed bills authorizing the deployment of American troops to Somalia with slightly different wording, the two branches of Congress could not agree on compromise language.[27]

Unwilling or unable to challenge the president, Congress often passed nonbinding legislation. For example, when Congress debated placing limits on Clinton's power to send troops to Haiti unless specifically authorized by statute, unable to achieve agreement, it settled for a nonbinding "sense of Congress" resolution that appropriated money should not be expended on military operations in Haiti unless authorized in advance by Congress.[28] After considering various restrictions on military initiatives in Bosnia, Congress settled for a nonbinding, "sense of Congress" resolution that funds appropriated for defense should not be available for deploying U.S. forces to participate in the implementation of peace settlement in Bosnia-Herzegovina "unless previously authorized."[29]

These were not the only nonbinding resolutions passed by the houses of Congress during the tenure of President Clinton. What a great cop-out. In essence what Congress was often saying is that they either disagreed with or could not agree on supporting the president's policy, so if he wished to take action, any blame for failure rested with him. Surely those who met in Philadelphia in 1787 never had such an abdication of responsibility in mind when they created the two houses of Congress. Indeed, when the Senate passed what amounted to an "incoherent bill" that on the one hand expressed support for American troops but expressed "reservations" about sending them to Bosnia, Senate Majority Leader Bob Dole explained that among the purposes the bill was to serve, one of them was to shift responsibility from Congress to the president.[30]

Moreover, during the presidency of Bill Clinton, executive privilege also was in full bloom, with members of his administration threatening or claiming privilege over a dozen times. In 1994 Lloyd Cutler, special counsel to the president, issued a memorandum detailing the executive privilege procedures to be followed. Among its provisions, the memorandum described "the very broad view that all White House communications are presumptively privileged,"[31] as well as those between the White House and any federal department or agency[32]—a stance that appears to be in contradistinction to the Supreme Court ruling in *United States v. Nixon*.

Moreover, it was the position of the Clinton administration that congressional requests for information from the executive branch were less valid when conducting oversight than when considering legislation.[33] This, of course, was not a new argument. It has been "a persistent characteristic of the statements of the Reagan, George H. W. Bush and [now] Clinton Administrations."[34] From this perspective, one must make the absurd assumption that congressional requests for information related to waste, fraud, and abuse; poor administration of the laws; failure to carry out the laws; investigations of corruption or unethical conduct; or arbitrary or capricious behavior on the part of administrators in the executive branch are of lesser importance in terms of Congress's constitutionally grounded responsibilities as compared to lawmaking. To so assert is to claim that Congress, as the people's representatives, has less of a constitutional responsibility to ensure, for example, that the will of the people is properly carried out; that the people's money is properly spent, not corruptly usurped; and that the constitutionally guaranteed rights of the people are not being ignored or undermined than it has to simply make the laws. Neither deliberations during the constitutional convention nor the Constitution substantiate such a claim. Indeed, the Supreme Court has regularly reaffirmed the investigative power of Congress.[35]

Morton Rosenberg has recorded 14 cases during the Clinton administration in which executive privilege "may arguably be deemed formal invocations," having been invoked, asserted, or claimed and later withdrawn.[36] From the perspective of questions related to executive privilege, the most important of these cases was the Espy case.

In March 1994 allegations of improprieties by Agriculture Secretary Mike Espy surfaced. President Clinton instructed the Office of the White House Counsel to investigate. An independent counsel was appointed in early September. In mid-October the grand jury issued a subpoena for all documents that had accumulated or been used in preparation of the White House Counsel's report. Clinton withheld 84 documents, claiming executive privilege based on the need to protect presidential communications as well as deliberative processes. The district court upheld Clinton's claim. However, the Appeals Court reversed the decision.[37] In its findings the Court clarified many of the issues left unanswered in the *United States v. Nixon* case of nearly 25 years earlier.

The Court carefully distinguished between the "presidential communication privilege" and the "deliberative process privilege." While the Court noted that both are designed to protect the confidentially of presidential decision making, the latter disappears completely when there is any reason to believe that government misconduct has occurred, which was the issue in this case. With regard to the valid claim of executive privilege to protect presidential communications in order to ensure that presidential advisors remain willing to provide candid advice, the Court ruled that "the privilege could be overcome only by a substantive showing that 'the subpoenaed materials likely contain important evidence' and that 'the evidence is not available with due diligence elsewhere.'" The Court also ruled that the presidential privilege applies to all documents in their entirety and covers communications made or received by presidential advisors pursuant to advising the president, even if those communications were not made directly to the president. The Court further ruled that presidential privilege covers final and postdecisional materials as well as deliberative ones, but applies only to the White House staff, not to staff in other agencies, and only to those on the White House staff who have "operational proximity" to direct presidential decision making.[38]

Perhaps even more significant, Morton Rosenberg contends that a close reading of the Court's opinion appears to limit the president's right to exercise executive privilege to protect presidential communications only when he is acting in his constitutional functions that are, as the Court put it, "quintessential and non-delegable." Thus they would not pertain to functions that can be performed without the president's direct involvement, including the presidential responsibility to ensure that "the laws are faithfully executed."[39] Such an interpretation would tightly constrict exercise of executive privilege by the president. Once again, however, it is important to keep in mind that as in the decision rendered in *United States v. Nixon,* the Court's ruling pertained to the exercise of executive privilege in judicial proceedings. The Court did not directly address questions of privilege when exercised to preclude the flow of information to Congress.

In terms of information from the intelligence community, congressional intelligence committees continued monitoring intelligence, focusing among other things on such post–Cold War challenges as the proliferation of weapons of mass destruction, drugs, small wars and their aftermath, and terrorism and on such important issues as developments in Russia, the newly independent states of the former Soviet Union, central and eastern Europe, and China. To assist their efforts, in 1996 both intelligence committees installed computer terminals linking them to the intelligence community network known as PolicyNet. This network provides the committees electronic access to most finished intelligence, and in some cases to intelligence reports that are not available in hard copy.[40]

G. W. BUSH

Arguably the gold standard for unrestrained executive power in foreign and security affairs may have been set during the administration of President George W. Bush. The Bush administration laid claim to so-called prerogative powers of the presidency beyond those exercised by former presidents. The principal architect of Bush administration policies was Deputy Counsel to the President John Yoo. Longtime advocate of preeminent executive power, Yoo, citing British constitutional tradition, crafted his model of executive power more in tune with Blackstone's prerogative powers of the king than the rejection of the Blackstone model by the framers of the Constitution.

Blackstone asserted that the king's prerogative powers included "the sole power of sending ambassadors to foreign states, and receiving ambassadors at home," the power "to make treaties, leagues, and alliances with foreign states and princes," and "the sole prerogative of making war and peace."[41] The framers of the federal Constitution, on the other hand, explicitly rejected placing such powers in the untrammeled hand of the president. The president was charged with the responsibility of receiving the ambassadors and other public ministers from foreign countries. But he could nominate only U.S. ambassadors and other senior government officials. The advice and consent of the Senate was required for their appointment. Similarly the president could exercise his treaty-making power only in conjunction with the Senate. On issues of war and peace, the president was designated commander in chief of the army and navy, but only Congress was granted the authority to declare war. The framers were adamant in restraining the president's power to make war, except in the sense that the president was to be in charge of the armed forces once war had begun.[42] To come to any other conclusions about the intent of the framers on this issue demands mental contortions of an extraordinary kind. Nevertheless, this is precisely what Yoo did.

Yoo outlined his views in a memorandum to the president shortly after the 9/11 attacks. On an examination of the text and structure of the U.S. Constitution, Yoo concluded: "The Constitution vests the President with the *plenary* [italics added] authority as Commander-in-chief and the sole organ of the Nation in its foreign relations, to use military force abroad—especially in response to grave national emergencies created by sudden, unforeseen attacks on the people and territory of the United States."[43] By his use of the word "plenary," he ascribed to the president absolute, unqualified, unfettered power in foreign affairs and in matters of war and peace. Such a claim would have horrified the framers of the Constitution. As Madison so presciently warned: "The means of defence [sic] against foreign danger, have been always the instruments of tyranny at home."[44] Gene Healy summed it nicely:

The Bush administration has made some of the broadest assertions of executive power in American history: among them, the power to launch wars at will, to tap phones and read e-mail without a warrant, and to seize American citizens on American soil and hold them for the duration of the War on Terror—in other words, perhaps forever—without ever having to answer to a judge.[45]

As we have seen, George W. Bush was not the first president to claim the right to act unilaterally in foreign affairs or engage in conflicts without the expressed approval of Congress. But Bush advanced a trend that had largely begun with the advent of the Cold War—a trend that in many ways differed substantially from the relationship that had been established between the legislative and executive branches for over 150 years.

The attacks of 9/11 provided the opportunity. The next day he announced that the attacks "were more than acts of terror." On September 14, 2001, Bush declared a "state of national emergency." Dazed and perhaps fearful, unwilling to sustain the deliberative processes required in exercising its constitutional responsibilities, not reasoning to think about the long-term constitutional implications, Congress quickly granted the president sweeping powers. On September 18 Congress authorized the president

to use all necessary and appropriate force against those nations, organizations, or persons he determines planned, authorized, committed, or aided the terrorist attacks that occurred on September 11, 2001, or harbored such organizations or persons, in order to prevent any future acts of international terrorism against the United States by such nations, organizations or persons.[46]

The joint resolution did not include language that had appeared in a White House draft, granting the president the additional power "to deter and pre-empt any future acts of terrorism or aggression against the United States," but granted him authority "to deter and prevent acts of international terrorism against the United States." It also specifically stated: "Nothing in this resolution supersedes any requirement of the War Powers Resolution."[47] Nonetheless, by its actions Congress had granted the president enormous discretionary power to act as he saw fit. Even in urging unanimous support for the legislation, Senator Carl Levin contended: "This joint resolution would authorize the use of force even before the President or Congress knows with certainty which nations, organizations, or persons were involved in the September terrorist acts."[48]

With this authorization in hand, Bush went to war in Afghanistan in early October 2001 "to disrupt the use of Afghanistan as a terrorist base of operations and to attack the military capability of the Taliban regime."[49] Soon after, he acted unilaterally, asserting what he considered his independent constitutional authority, and created military tribunals to try any individual "not a United States citizen" who provided assistance to the 9/11 attacks. He did not consult Congress or members of the judiciary. He based his decision on the ruling of the Supreme Court in *Ex Parte Quirin* that had upheld Roosevelt's tribunals. However, even justices who participated in that decision saw it as an unhappy precedent.[50] As a result, any of the 18 million non–U.S. citizens within the U.S. borders could be held and tried for supposed crimes that might include their having unknowingly contributed funds to an organization that provide aid to an organization, some of whose members are believed to engage in terrorist activity.[51]

Moreover, despite Congress's failure to adopt Bush's draft language in its September 18 resolution authorizing a preemptive attack, in June 2002 the president outlined a willingness to act alone and preemptively.[52] The concept of preemptive war was not new. International law has always recognized the right of a state to use force in self-defense, including anticipatory self-defense understood to mean in response to imminent attack, not some future potentiality. By October, claiming Iraq was in noncompliance with UN resolutions, had weapons of mass destruction, and was prepared to use them, Bush, in what appeared to be more of a demand rather than request, sought authority to take any necessary military action. "I want your vote. I am not going to debate it with you," he reportedly told members of Congress.[53] Again they complied, granting him authority "to use the Armed Forces of the United States as he determines to be necessary" to defend against the "threat posed by Iraq" and enforce relevant UN Security Council resolutions.[54] Once again, Congress had transferred its constitutional responsibilities to the president. Once again, the very checks on presidential authority seen as necessary for sound republican governance and the avoidance of tyranny had been discarded. Was there anything left of the framers' intent on issues of war and peace? An honest answer was probably no.

Equally troubling, if not more so, was congressional deference to executive branch interpretations of the intelligence available concerning Saddam Hussein's acquisition of weapons of mass destruction and his supposed collusion with al-Qaeda. Bush and other senior administration officials unrelentingly advanced the theses that Saddam Hussein had stockpiles of weapons of mass destruction, and since he had used them before, he might be prepared to use them again. Furthermore, they asserted that Saddam had ties to terrorists, had cooperated with al-Qaeda, and might provide weapons of mass destruction to terrorists like those who attacked the United States on September 11, 2001.

The problem with all of these pronouncements was that they were wrong. When American forces and inspectors entered Iraq they found nothing—no active arsenal of chemical weapons, only a few old warheads empty of chemical agents, no biological weapons or mobile laboratories designed to manufacture biological weapons, no nuclear weapons. After the conflict was over, top U.S. weapons inspector David Kay and his Iraq survey team were assigned the task of locating and identifying Iraqi weapons of mass destruction. They found none. Testifying before the Senate Armed Services Committee in January 2004, Kay admitted that with regard to Iraq's possession of weapons of mass destruction, "We were all wrong."[55]

How could this have happened? Surely the intelligence community and the director of Central Intelligence bear a fair share of the blame. Intelligence officials knew that many uncertainties existed in the case supporting the contention that Iraq had weapons of mass destruction. For example, the Bush administration had largely staked its claim that Iraq was "reconstituting its nuclear weapons program"[56] based on Iraq's supposed acquisition from Niger of "yellowcake," a uranium concentrate that is used in the preparation of fuel for nuclear reactors and on Iraq's acquisition of "high-strength aluminum tubes" supposedly "needed for gas centrifuges that are used to enrich uranium for nuclear weapons."[57] Yet, as early as March 2002 Ambassador Wilson as well as the U.S. ambassador to Niger and the deputy commander of European Command, who had responsibility for overseeing U.S. security interests in Africa, could find nothing to substantiate rumors that Iraq had sought yellowcake from Niger.[58] As a result both the State Department and the CIA had concluded that the Niger uranium reports were almost certainly not true.[59]

Furthermore, the U.S. intelligence community was divided over the utility of the use of the aluminum tubes as centrifuge rotors. The Department of Energy, a lead agency on such issues, contended that the tubes "were not well-suited for centrifuge application" and were more likely intended for use in Iraq's 81-millimeter multiple rocket launcher program." Officials from the UN International Atomic Energy Agency agreed, concluding after extensive investigations that the much-publicized aluminum tubes Iraq had attempted to import were not likely to have been related to the manufacture of centrifuges for the enrichment of uranium.[60] After the invasion it was determined that indeed the tubes were intended for use as artillery rocket casings.

Similarly, Bush argued that Iraq "possesses and produces chemical and biological weapons." Yet, General Kamal, one of Saddam Hussein's sons-in-law and the minister of industry, had reported after defecting in 1995 that all chemical and biological weapons had been destroyed on his orders in 1991.[61] Subsequent evidence supporting the contention that Iraq had continued to develop biological and chemical weapons was based primarily on either a single source, known to be unreliable, as was the case with biological weapons, or a single collection means, which was unverified by other reliable and unbiased sources, as was the case with chemical weapons.[62] Moreover, UN inspectors using the best intelligence the United States could furnish them could find neither chemical nor biological weapons, other than a few old chemical weapons most likely left over from the 1980–1988 Iran–Iraq war and overlooked when Kamal had ordered their destruction in 1991. Of course, the intelligence community knew all of this. Moreover, intelligence officials had long argued that there was no evidence to support the Bush administration contention that Saddam Hussein was collaborating with al-Qaeda or, as Bush had put it, Saddam was aiding and protecting terrorists, including members of al-Qaeda.[63]

Though this information was available in the National Intelligence Estimate, the executive summary glossed over such uncertainties. On the other hand, Congress bears a fair share of the blame for not having probed deeper. At least three major factors may have played a role in this failure, none of which constitute an excuse for the inexcusable.

First, the information needed for effective decision making is often difficult to acquire. President George W. Bush was even more aggressive than Clinton in keeping information out of legislative hands.[64] While his administration formally claimed executive privilege only six times,[65] it employed many of the techniques to keep information from Congress that his father had employed so successfully. Aware that members of Congress could challenge his preferred policies, limiting information often permitted the president and senior members of his administration to define the issues and limit congressional scrutiny and debate. When members of Congress requested information in the form of documents or testimony, frequently administration officials declared their willingness to comply and subsequently frustrated congressional efforts by either delaying delivery, excising content, or both, or refusing to testify. Such tactics often are highly successful when a Congress is in the hands of the president's party, as was the case as the decision to attack Iraq was looming.

Second, when information is denied congressional committees, if they deem the information critical to their decision-making processes, they can issue a subpoena to acquire the information. However, in the highly politicized and partisan environment that characterized much of Bush's tenure, it is not surprising that congressional subpoenas of administration officials or threats or citations for contempt were unlikely. Only the chairman, vice chairman, or member designated by the chairman of the Senate intelligence committee can issues subpoenas.[66] House intelligence committee subpoenas can be issued by the chairman of the full committee in consultation, but consultation only with the ranking minority member, or by vote of the committee.[67] To take the further step and declare a person in contempt, both committees require a majority decision of committee members to forward the request to their respective houses, which in turn requires a majority decision in those chambers. Such procedures make the use of Congress's subpoena or contempt powers difficult. This is particularly true when the chamber concerned is in the hands of the party that occupies the White House, which was the case as war approached.

Of course the problem is not peculiar to one party. However, as former Congressman Mickey Edwards argued, demanding that the executive branch comply with legitimate congressional requests for information is not just "the obligation only of the party that opposes the policies of the President in power." It is the obligation of every congressman. Members are not sitting in Congress as a representative of their party or as a representative of the President of the United States. They are in Congress with "certain constitutional obligations." "It is not supposed to be the opposition party that holds a President accountable, it is supposed to be the opposition institution of government."[68] Edwards went on to note:

I think what's happened is that too many members of Congress have allowed their party interests...[to dominate], believing that if the president were to have political difficulties it would hurt the party and hurt them and so forth. They have allowed their political and party interests and, quote, "loyalty to the president"...to trump their institutional obligations....[69]

Finally, as we have seen over time, Congress has grown accustomed to deferring to the president on foreign policy and national security. As a consequence, congressional intelligence committees spend much of their time diligently working on intelligence community authorizations, examining their budgets, investigating accusations of intelligence community wrongdoing, and challenging the executive on intelligence efforts that might be contrary to the law. Though the Senate Select Committee on Intelligence is principally tasked to "make every effort to assure that the appropriate departments and agencies of the United States provide informed and timely intelligence necessary for the executive and legislative branches to make sound decisions affecting the security and vital interests of the Nation"[70] and its House counterpart is tasked to receive all intelligence from U.S. intelligence agencies, evidence suggests these committees spend relatively little time ensuring that the quality of the intelligence product meets the demands of effective decision making. This is apparently largely left to the executive branch. Had the congressional intelligence committees been dutifully fulfilling their statutory mandate, carefully probing the intelligence community on the evidence they possessed that might substantiate the Bush administration contentions, they would have been aware of such deficiencies even before the National Intelligence Estimate was made available to Congress in October 2002, more than a week before both houses of Congress voted in favor of the Iraq War Resolution.

Moreover, once the estimate was made available to members of Congress, few members ever read it. According to one report, no more than six Senators and a handful of representatives read beyond the five-page executive summary.[71] Had they done so they would have found ample evidence that the facile conclusions were supported at best by extremely weak intelligence. They also would have better understood exceptions taken to the overall conclusions by many, including intelligence officials from the departments of State and Energy, and perhaps come to realize that the entire executive branch case for going to war based on Iraq's possession of weapons of mass destruction was built on a house of cards. As a result, they would have been in a better position to inform their colleagues in both houses before the decision was made on whether to authorize the president to go to war. However, as one senior intelligence committee member put it to me during an interview, "I don't think most members [of Congress], including myself, doubted the conclusions [of the Intelligence Estimate] that Saddam Hussein had weapons of mass destruction.... I believed he had weapons of mass destruction. I didn't feel the need to challenge that conclusion."[72]

The failure of Congress to probe the quality of the intelligence, in many cases to take time to read the National Intelligence Estimate or even, in some cases, to read the executive summary, may have been driven by a variety of factors—workload, politics, or deference to the executive branch in the area of foreign policy and security. Whatever the excuse in any individual case may have been, it has led to an appalling loss of lives, heavily taxed the American economy, polarized the nation, caused severe damage to America's reputation abroad, and perhaps even undermined rather than strengthened American security. It is clear that for Congress as a whole and for the congressional committees charged with intelligence oversight, there has been an abdication of responsibility.

Conclusions

No one would deny that the world of the 20th century and the first decade of this century differ dramatically from the environment that existed at the time of the writing of the American Constitution. Since the dawn of the nuclear age and the advent of worldwide terrorism with potential access to weapons of mass destruction, the United States has been constantly menaced. And with the globalization of economics and finance, its fortunes are now interwoven with those of many other countries around the globe, not just in terms of its national security, but also in terms of its economic and social welfare.

The vast number of issues, the complexity of events, and the potential consequences of uninformed or delayed decision making lend credibility to the very need for energy, secrecy, and dispatch in government as foreseen by Hamilton over 200 years ago. Such changes serve to fortify claims for presidential supremacy in foreign affairs. The executive branch, with the world's largest, best-equipped intelligence apparatus, affords access to volumes of information about global issues, and its pyramidal structure provides the unity of command demanded by a brewing crisis or an imminent danger requiring instant decisions.

However, efficiency in government was not the only objective of the framers of the Constitution. Their objectives were broader and of potentially greater benefit to the nation and its peoples. Throughout the deliberations at the constitutional conventions, the theme that was so consistently evidenced was the concern of delegates over excessive power in the hands of the executive. To eliminate such an eventuality, as Louis Fisher and David Gray Adler so succinctly put it, "Delegates embraced the principle of collective decision making, the concept of shared power in foreign affairs, and the cardinal tenet of republican ideology that the conjoined wisdom of many is superior to that of one."[1]

Today, that system of collective decision making and shared power is threatened and no more so than in the arena of foreign affairs and war powers. In times of crisis or conflict, presidents have frequently transgressed the constitutional limits on powers granted them, usurping powers that the framers accorded the legislative branch. "It is of the nature of war," Hamilton warned in *Federalist 8*, "to increase the executive at the expense of the legislative authority."[2] Indeed, a pattern of presidential aggrandizement at the expense of Congress "under the spur of international crisis" has been visible from the beginning of the Republic.[3] However, not until the latter part of the last century have presidents claimed an inherent right to act unilaterally in responding to such crises, ignoring or rejecting over 150 years of history in which such responses, absent the need to repel a sudden attack or imminent danger of attack on the territory of the United States or its citizens abroad or rebellion at home, were generally understood to be in the purview of Congress or at a minimum a joint legislative–executive responsibility.

In recent years, presidents have, as a matter of routine, come to ignore Congress, whether in regard to responding to congressional requests for information or the deployment of military forces into harm's way. When employing U.S. military forces in lesser conflicts, presidents often have completely disregarded congressional prerogatives, whether the situation involved invasions of countries (e.g., Grenada in 1983, Libya in 1986, Panama in 1989) or military attacks on countries (e.g., Libya in 1986, Sudan and Afghanistan in 1998), or support of UN or NATO operations (e.g., Somalia in 1992, Bosnia in 1995, Kosovo in 1999), or support of clandestine operations (e.g., Nicaragua in 1984, the Iran-Contra affair in 1985–1986) or the sending of military advisors into harms way (e.g., El Salvador in 1982–1990).

Even in major wars, presidents have often either ignored Congress, or when not ignored Congress too often has failed to carefully examine the evidence at hand, debate the wisdom of various courses of action, and only then make decisions that will thrust this nation into wars that are often costly in lives and national treasure. This, of course, is not new. For example, it was Congress that failed to verify President Polk's claims that Mexico had invaded American territory and "shed American blood upon American soil,"[4] limited debate, and then exuberantly voted for war. It also was Congress that permitted itself to get caught up in war fever following the sinking of the USS *Maine*. In apparently willingness to accept newspaper accounts rather than undertake a serious and intensive investigation of its own, Congress quickly fixed the blame on Spain and voted for war.

However, in recent years as presidents have boldly proclaimed inherent powers, Congress, unwilling to challenge such claims, has increasingly deferred. When President Truman ordered American troops into action following North Korea's invasion of South Korea, acting on what he considered his inherent powers, he never sought ex post facto authority from Congress. Though Congress provided funds for the war effort, it denied to itself the opportunity to examine in depth such a commitment of American forces on the continent of Asia and denied to the American public a careful examination of America's strategy for dealing with such Cold War challenges. Thus it abdicated the very essence of the responsibility of a legislative body in a democracy.

In the wake of a supposed second attack on American warships in the Gulf of Tonkin, without waiting for a thorough examination of intelligence on the incident, it was Congress that allowed legislation to be stampeded through its halls and provided Lyndon Johnson, in a nearly unanimous vote, a blank check to greatly enlarge a conflict on the Asian mainland that would ultimately result in 58,000 American casualties.

As war with Iraq loomed on the horizon in 2002–2003, it was Congress that failed to oversee the quality of intelligence, even to examine in detail the information available in the very National Intelligence Estimate it had called for, before granting President George W. Bush enormous discretionary power to act as he saw fit.

Even when presidents have gone to Congress for approval, they have been quick to contend that they have inherent authority to take action without congressional approval. The most notable example is President George H. W. Bush's comments in seeking congressional authority to go to war against Iraq in 1991.

As a result, today Congress may be at its weakest point in history in terms of serving as a check on the foreign policy or war powers of the president. In *Federalist Paper 48*, James Madison warned: "Power is of an encroaching nature and that it ought to be effactually restrained from passing the limits assigned to it?"[5] It was just this encroaching nature of power that the framers of the American Constitution were determined to restrain. And it is the encroaching nature of power exercised by recent American presidents that dangerously threatens the system of checks and balances established under the Constitution. Power no longer checks power. Ambition no longer checks ambition.

As Dr. Benjamin Franklin emerged from the Constitutional Convention in 1787 he is reported to have been confronted by a lady who asked him: "Well, Doctor, what have we got, a republic or a monarchy?" Franklin replied: "A republic, if you can keep it."[6] The question we confront today is whether the system of government as designed by the framers will survive, particularly in the field of foreign affairs. With the president in command of information, with an ever increasing propensity on the part of the president to skirt Congress and commit the United States to the security of other nations through executive agreements, and with recent presidents claiming inherent powers to use military force anywhere in the world to defend U.S. interests as they interpret them, the Constitution itself is under attack. In such an environment, Congress has often gifted away its powers to the president, preferring to leave decisions and thus the responsibility and blame for failure on his shoulders, rather than accept the responsibility for a comprehensive examination of the issues and the tough decisions and accountability that such efforts might entail.

We cannot look to presidents to solve this problem. They will continue to act just as the framers had anticipated, stretching their powers whenever possible. Nor can we look to the Courts, which are likely to continue to avoid decisions where it is within the power of the Congress to take action. It is Congress that remains the last bulwark against the improper use of power by presidents. It has been congressional default that has largely permitted presidential aggrandizement.[7] Only Congress can restore its prerogatives and it has it within its power to do so. This will require courage and commitment. Indeed, it will require the kind of commitment to the public good that John Stuart Mill was suggesting applied to all those who hold the franchise to vote. Mill wrote that how the voter uses the ballot "has no more to do with his personal wishes than the verdict of a juryman.... He is bound to give it according to his best and most conscientious opinion of the public good."[8] This pertains no less to members of Congress. It is not allegiance to their personal views, or to their reelection, or to their president that should guide their actions, but their allegiance to their constitutional mandate to provide for the public good.

Chronology

1787   Constitution Convention completes work.

Congress granted power to:
- Declare war and grant letters of marque and reprisal and make rules for captures on land and water
- Raise and support armies and provide and maintain a navy
- Provide for calling for the militia to execute the laws of the Union, suppress insurrections and repel invasions
- Provide for the organizing, arming, and disciplining of the militia

President:
- Is designated as commander in chief of the army and navy
- Has the power, with the advice and consent of the Senate, to make treaties
- Shall nominate and, by and with the advice and consent of the Senate, shall appoint ambassadors, other public minister and consuls, judges of the Supreme Court, and other officers

1792   Congress makes provisions to protect from disclosure confidential materials received.

Congress requests confidential information from President Washington. Washington provides all information requested.

Congress passes Militia Act of 1792 granting the president emergency powers to call state militias into action to execute the laws, suppress insurrections, and repel invasions or to protect against imminent invasion.

1793   House requests information from president. Hamilton claims information is privileged from disclosure. House disagrees. Washington provides information.

President Washington accepts credentials of Citizen Genet as French minister to the United States, establishing the right of the president to recognize governments. Congress acquiesces.

Washington declares the United States neutral in conflict between France and England, in possible violation of 1778 Treaty of Alliance with France. Washington asks Congress for a proclamation of neutrality; Congress obliges, establishing principle that Congress has right to declare neutrality.

1794   Congress authorizes president to lay, regulate, and revoke embargoes, setting the precedent that Congress may delegate authority to the president.

1794–1795 Jay's Treaty establishes the principle of presidents seeking advice of Senate ex post facto.

1795   Militia Act of 1795 replaces Militia Act of 1792 but reaffirms authority granted to president to act in times of emergency.

1796   House requests information on Jay's Treaty. Washington denies requests.

1798   House requests diplomatic correspondence from President Adams on events that led to the X, Y, Z Affair. Adams initially refuses, then submits information.

With the United States involved in a quasi war with France, Adams rescinds previous instructions prohibiting the arming of U.S. merchant ships.

1800   *Bas v. Tingy:* Supreme Court rules Constitution granted Congress the power to *authorize* general or limited hostilities either through a formal declaration or by other authorizing acts.

1801   *Talbot v. Seeman:* Supreme Court reaffirms *Bas v. Tingy*—Congress may authorize general or partial hostilities, and, having done so, the laws of war are applicable.

Jefferson acknowledges right of Congress to initiate war after Barbary pirates attack U.S. frigate, reporting to Congress that only defensive steps were taken.

1804   *Little v. Barreme:* Supreme Court rules that once hostilities have been declared by Congress, the president cannot exceed the authority granted him under the law.

1805   Faced with incursions into Louisiana by the Spanish in Florida, Jefferson takes only defensive actions, again recognizing that only Congress can "change our condition from peace to war."

1807	House requests information from President Jefferson on supposed Burr conspiracy. Jefferson contends materials contain rumors, conjectures, and suspicions and some of material provided to Jefferson was in "private confidence." Jefferson delivers some documents.
	In trial of Aaron Burr, District Court requests Jefferson to deliver papers and appear in person. Court subpoenas Jefferson to appear. Jefferson refuses but sends some documents.
	Following the British attack on the USS *Chesapeake*, with Congress out of session, Jefferson mobilizes for war. Once Congress is reconvened, Jefferson carefully explains his actions and seeks congressional blessing.
1815	President Madison seeks and obtains congressional authorization for hostilities against Algeria in the Second Barbary War.
1818	Without seeking congressional authority, Monroe orders General Jackson to take the offensive and pursue raiding Seminole Indians into Spanish Florida. Congress investigates, but fails to repudiate either Jackson or Monroe.
1823	President Monroe consults with members of Congress but does not seek congressional approval before proclaiming the Monroe Doctrine. But when Colombia asks about its implications, Secretary of State John Quincy Adams makes it clear that only Congress can declare war.
1825	Congress requests President Monroe provide documents he "may deem compatible with the public interest" relating to charges against naval officer in Pacific. Monroe withholds documents.
1827	*Martin v. Mott:* Supreme Court rules that the power to decide when an exigency exists resides with the president. But that power is "limited" and "to be exercised upon sudden emergencies...under circumstances which may be vital to the existence of the Union."
1831	Without congressional authority, President Jackson sends a U.S warship to Latin America to protect against Argentine raiders and then seeks ex post facto congressional support.
1834	When Jackson recommends that Congress pass a law authorizing him to resort to force should France fail to make payment on its debt to the United States, Congress refuses to delegate its power to initiate hostilities.
1836	Though Washington had established the precedent that presidents have the right to recognize foreign governments, because a recognition of Texas might mean war with Mexico, Jackson defers to Congress.
1843	House requests President Tyler provide information related to Cherokee land frauds. Tyler initially refuses. House challenges Tyler. Tyler provides requested information.

After secretly assuring Texans they would be protected by American forces once a treaty of annexation was signed, Tyler divorces himself from the promise, stating that the employment of military force against a foreign power "is not within the competency of the President."

1844   Tyler deploys military forces to the border between Texas and Mexico and into the Gulf of Mexico to protect Texas pending approval of a treaty of annexation. The Senate rejects the treaty, but Congress fails to sanction Tyler for deploying forces without its approval.

1846   House requests President Polk provide an accounting of monies spent for "contingency purposes" during Tyler administration. Polk refuses.

Polk sends General Taylor into territory claimed by Mexico, without seeking congressional approval. Taylor blockades Matamoras. Mexico retaliates. Without verifying the facts, Congress limits debate on the issue, accepts at face value Polk's explanation of events, passes resolution recognizing a state of war exists, and engages in a war with Mexico.

1848   House issues "unconditional" call for papers from Polk detailing instructions to American minister to Mexico. Polk rebukes House for its unconditional request.

1850   *Fleming v. Page:* Supreme Court clarifies and circumscribes the duties of the president when acting as commander in chief, asserting that in war, the duties and powers of the president acting in that capacity "are purely military."

1852   President Fillmore sends Commodore Perry with six warships to Japan to demand that Japanese ports be opened to Americans and that shipwrecked sailors be treated well and released. Japan refuses. But Fillmore recognizes that only Congress can declare war.

1854   House demands copy of Ostend Manifesto from President Pierce. State Department blatantly deceives Congress by omitting inflammatory page.

Pierce sends Perry on a second mission to Japan with seven ships with same demands as before. Pierce, like Fillmore, recognizes that only Congress can declare war.

1859   President James Buchanan recognizes that Congress has the sole and exclusive power under the Constitution to authorize hostilities whether general or limited in nature.

1860   *Durand v. Hollins:* Court recognizes the president as the "only legitimate Organ of General Government, to open and carry on correspondence or negotiations with foreign nations" and acknowledges that it is the duty of the president to use those powers under certain circumstances in the defense of American citizens or property abroad.

1861	Confederate forces open fire on federal garrison at Fort Sumter. With Congress out of session, President Lincoln calls 75,000 militia to federal service, blockades Southern ports, calls more than 40,000 volunteers into the service of the infantry and cavalry, increases the size of the regular army and navy, spends public money, and authorizes the suspension of the privilege of the writ of habeas corpus. Recognizing he has exceeded his authority, he calls Congress into session three months later and seeks and receives congressional approval for all acts except the suspension of writs of habeas corpus.
1861–1865	Lincoln exercises unilateral power until the end of the Civil War.
1863	*Prize Cases:* Supreme Court supports presidential use of emergency powers, affirming the limited right of the president to respond to sudden attacks. Bureau of Military Intelligence created.
1866	*Ex-parte Milligan:* Supreme Court repudiates the idea that in times of emergency there might be higher law than the Constitution.
1868	House of Representatives impeaches President Johnson for failure to carry out the law. He is acquitted by the Senate by a one-vote margin.
1870	*Miller v. U.S.:* Supreme Court holds that while "presidential war powers derived from congressional authorization, those of Congress were limited only by the 'law of nations.'"
	President Grant submits treaty to annex Dominican Republic. Senate rejects and ratifies no important treaties from 1871 to 1898.
1882	Office of Naval Intelligence created.
1885	Military Intelligence Division created.
1886	President Cleveland rejects congressional request for papers relating to the removal of a federal attorney. Senate responds by censuring attorney general for not delivering papers.
1890	*In re Neagle:* Supreme Court rules that the president "is vested" with those powers that are "necessary and implied" in order to carry out his charge to protect and defend the Constitution and his duty is not "limited to the enforcement of acts of Congress or of treaties of the United States according to their *express terms*" [emphasis in original]. Rather it includes "the rights, duties and obligations growing out of the Constitution itself, our international relations, and all the protection implied by the nature of the government under the Constitution."
1898	An explosion sinks the battleship USS *Maine* in Havana Harbor. With competing views on the cause of the explosion, Congress allows itself to get caught up in war hysteria and declares war on Spain.
1900	President McKinley dispatches troops to China in the wake of the Boxer Rebellion without seeking congressional authorization. He

fails to seek congressional approval for an agreement that ends the conflict.

1901–1909   President T. Roosevelt issues 1,006 executive orders—more than all prior or subsequent presidents combined, except for Wilson and F. D. Roosevelt.

1903   In violation of a treaty with Colombia and without congressional approval, Roosevelt dispatches warship to Panama to interfere in a rebellion against Colombia. Few in Congress object.

1907   Member of Roosevelt administration instructed not to respond to a Senate request for papers. Senate threatens to imprison the official for contempt. Roosevelt then orders papers delivered to the White House, challenging the Senate to come and get them. Congress acquiesces.

                  Roosevelt sends all 16 U.S. battleships around the world in a display of American naval might, informs skeptical congressmen that he has enough funds to get them halfway, and the choice is theirs as to whether to provide funding for their return.

1909–1913   President Taft intervenes twice in Nicaragua and once each in Cuba and Honduras without seeking congressional approval.

                  Taft instructs department heads to refer congressional requests for information to the president when they believe them to be incompatible with the national interest.

1914–1918   Congress delegates an extraordinary amount of power to President Wilson during war years.

1917   First U.S. signals intelligence agency is formed within the army. Congress remains content to leave intelligence matters up to the executive branch.

1918   Signals intelligence agency is transferred to State Department and tasked to focus on diplomatic rather than military communications.

1920   Senate rejects Versailles Treaty.

1924   President Coolidge refuses a Senate request for information. Senate takes no action.

1927   Coolidge sends marines back to Nicaragua without seeking congressional authorization. Few in Congress object. Coolidge introduces idea that troops aren't engaged in hostilities; they are more like policemen.

1933–1939   Congress grants F. D. Roosevelt extraordinary power to deal with the Depression.

1935–1939   Roosevelt kept on tight leash by Congress in foreign affairs. Even after war breaks out in Europe, Roosevelt feels need to go to Congress to seek repeal of arms embargo provisions of Neutrality Acts.

1935   *Schechter Poultry Corporation v. United States:* Supreme Court rules that Congress cannot delegate its authority to the president in the domestic arena.

1936   *United States v. Curtiss-Wright Export Corporation:* Supreme Court rules that the president has not only the power vested in him by Congress, but also "the very delicate, plenary, and exclusive power...as the sole organ of federal government in the field of international relations."

            United States v. Belmont: Supreme Court reiterates "sole organ" ruling and validates the right of the president to conclude executive agreements with foreign governments without Senate approval, which for all intents and purposes have the same effect as a treaty.

1939   Roosevelt declares limited national emergency.

1940   Roosevelt withholds aviation fuel and all scrap metals from Japan.

1941   Roosevelt appoints William Donovan coordinator of information and tasks him to form a nonmilitary intelligence organization.

            Roosevelt, without prior consultation or congressional approval, orders U.S. warships to patrol for German submarines, enters into an executive agreement with Denmark to send U.S. troops to Greenland, declares "unlimited national emergency," and informs Congress that he has dispatched naval forces to Iceland to protect that country from attack. Senator Taft protests that the president has no legal right to send troops to Iceland. Senate acquiesces.

            After U.S. destroyer *Greer* is attacked by German submarine, Roosevelt, without congressional authority, orders naval convoys to "shoot on sight" German submarines.

            Roosevelt freezes Japanese funds and stops all trade with Japan.

1942   Office of Strategic Services created under Joint Chiefs of Staff.

            Ex parte Quirin: Supreme Court upholds the authority of the president to convene military commissions to try unlawful combatants for attempts to commit sabotage.

1943   Bureau of Budget director refuses House subpoena to testify.

            Director of Office of Censorship refuses Senate committee request for information. No subpoena is issued.

1947   Congress passes National Security Act of 1947 and creates Central Intelligence Agency to correlate, evaluate, and disseminate intelligence obtained by intelligence elements of other departments and agencies and to be the focal point for national-level intelligence. Shortly afterward CIA is given additional responsibility for covert actions. Congress given role to oversee CIA activities. Few in Congress are involved. Congress is to leave intelligence matters in the hands of executive branch.

As internal and external security issues proliferate, President Truman clamps down on data flow to Congress, issuing sweeping orders blocking congressional efforts to acquire information.

1950   Immediately following the North Korean invasion of South Korea, Truman, without consulting Congress, deploys U.S. forces to assist South Korea. Four days after the attack, Truman orders U.S. ground forces into action. Truman does not seek congressional approval, calls engagement of U.S military forces a "police action."

Truman announces he intends to send four more divisions to Europe; declares he does not need congressional approval to do so; does not seek congressional approval.

1952   Truman becomes first president to claim "inherent powers" in both domestic and foreign affairs to meet great national emergencies.

Youngstown Sheet & Tube Co. et al. v. Sawyer: Supreme Court rules Truman's seizure of the steel mills is unconstitutional.

1953   President Eisenhower follows Truman's restrictive practice on information flow to Congress.

United States v. Reynolds: Supreme Court rules that the military may refuse to divulge requested information when national security is at stake.

1953–1961   Throughout this period, beyond seeing to intelligence agency appropriations, congressional involvement in U.S. foreign intelligence activities remains minimal.

Congress plays greater role than during Truman years on issues involving the movement of forces and their possible deployment into harm's way, as Eisenhower seeks congressional approval when deploying forces that might face hostilities.

Eisenhower does not seek congressional approval for covert actions.

1954   Eisenhower makes the most absolute assertion of presidential right to withhold information from Congress ever uttered to that day, when he asserts: "It is not in the public interest that any...conversations or communications [concerning advice of members of the executive branch], or any documents or reproductions, concerning such advice be disclosed." Congress acquiesces.

1958   *Kaiser Aluminum & Chemical Corp. v. United States:* Court rules that there is no absolute privilege to refuse to disclose information and it is ultimately up to the courts to determine the extent of privilege in litigations, but the assertion of "privilege by the Executive vis-à-vis Congress is a judicially undecided issue."

1961   President Kennedy authorizes the ill-fated attempt to invade Cuba and overthrow the government of Fidel Castro. Congress is neither consulted nor informed beforehand.

Kennedy more readily provides information to Congress than previous postwar presidents.

1962   Soviet missiles discovered in Cuba. Kennedy does not inform Congress, convenes Executive Committee, and initiates a quarantine of ships headed for Cuba. Congress defers to the president's supposed power in foreign affairs and war powers.

1963–1969   President Johnson, like Kennedy, is more open to sharing information with Congress than Truman or Eisenhower.

Congress continues practice of deference to the president on foreign policy.

1964   Congress passes Gulf of Tonkin Resolution. Following supposed second attack by North Vietnam on U.S. military ships, Johnson calls for and receives blank check from Congress to "take all necessary steps to repel any armed attack against U.S forces." Debate is limited. Congress fails to demand additional confirming information.

1964–1969   With Tonkin Resolution in hand, Johnson greatly expands war in Vietnam.

1965   Johnson, without congressional authority, sends military forces into Dominican Republic, ultimately deploying 22,000 troops. Congress does not object to Johnson's failure to seek approval.

1969   Senate subcommittee examines use of executive agreements by presidents in lieu of treaties. Senators are astonished to find how often their constitutional prerogatives have been circumvented and how often they have been left in the dark.

1969–1974   President Nixon or officials in his administration often refuse to provide Congress with documents or testimony; claim uncontrolled discretion to withhold information. Secrecy a key feature in Nixon's policies in Southeast Asia.

1969–1970   Nixon bombs Cambodia without seeking congressional approval.

1971   Nixon approves South Vietnamese invasion of Cambodia.

Congress repeals Gulf of Tonkin Resolution.

1972   U.S. 1972 opening to China initiated in secrecy without congressional involvement.

Nixon, without seeking congressional approval, announces a naval blockade of North Vietnam and the mining of Haiphong Harbor.

1973   Nixon unilaterally resumes the bombing Cambodia.

Congress passes War Powers Resolution.

1974   Nixon chooses to ignore War Powers Resolution, orders military forces to evacuate American civilians from Cyprus.

United States v. Nixon: Supreme Court upholds president's right to withhold information to ensure "complete candor and objectivity from advisors." However, Court rules that there is no "absolute, unqualified Presidential privilege of immunity from *judicial process* under all circumstances."

Congress passes Hughes-Ryan Amendment.

1974–1977   President Ford generally complies with requirements of War Powers Resolution but does not concede its constitutionality. Nor does he concede the right of the legislature to be given sensitive executive branch information.

1975   Church (Senate) and Pike (House) committees established to investigate intelligence abuses and covert operations.

1976   Senate Select Committee on Intelligence and House Permanent Select Committee established to oversee intelligence efforts.

1977–1981   President Carter generally complies with requirements of War Powers Resolution but does not concede its constitutionality.

Carter is cautious in withholding information from Congress but accepts principle that under certain circumstances the president could exercise prerogative to do so.

1977   *Nixon v. Administrator of General Services:* Court reiterates that exercise of executive privilege is a qualified, not absolute, right of the president, noting that it is narrow in scope, limited to communications "in performance of [a President's] responsibilities...of his office...and made in the process of shaping policies and making decisions." Court, once again, recognizes "Congress's broad investigative power."

United States v. AT&T: U.S. Court of Appeals, D.C. Circuit, notes that since the Constitution assigns both Congress and the president powers relating to national security, the executive branch has no absolute claim of executive privilege against Congress, even in the area of national security.

1978   Carter announces he will terminate diplomatic relations with the Republic of China, thus abrogating the Mutual Defense Treaty with Taiwan. He does not seek the advice and consent of Congress.

1979   *Goldwater v. Carter:* Supreme Court dismisses case contending that Carter exceeded his constitutional authorities in abrogating the Taiwan Mutual Defense Treaty as a nonjusticiable political question.

1980   President Carter uses military force without congressional approval in attempted rescue of American hostages held in Iran.

Congress passes Intelligence Oversight Act of 1980.

1981–1989   President Reagan reasserts claims to unconditional executive privilege but never follows through with such claims.

War Powers Act fails to constrain Reagan from deploying U.S. military forces into harm's way. Congress seems singularly unable or unwilling to control the president in his use of military forces abroad.

1982   Congress passes Boland Amendment, prohibiting covert assistance to the Contras for the purpose of overthrowing the government of Nicaragua.

1983   *INS v. Chadha:* Supreme Court invalidates the legislative veto.

1984   Senate intelligence committee members learn that CIA operatives had covertly assisted the Contras in the mining of Nicaraguan harbors in violation of international law.

1986   Iran-Contra affair is revealed. Congress investigates.

1989–1993 President G.H.W. Bush uses multiple means to deprive Congress of requested information.

Bush, like Reagan, is little constrained by War Powers Resolution in use of military forces abroad.

1989   With Congress in recess, Bush orders invasion of Panama. Bush does notify members of Congress a few hours before the invasion but does not seek congressional approval. Congress passes resolution praising Bush.

1990   Following Iraq's invasion of Kuwait, Bush deploys 150,000 military personnel to the Gulf. He makes no effort to seek congressional approval to do so.

Bush repeatedly holds that he did not need congressional authorization to go to war.

U.N. Security Council passes Resolution 678, authorizing member states to use "all necessary means" to force Iraq's withdrawal from Kuwait.

1991   Bush asks for and receives Congress's authority to go to war but continues to contend he has "inherent power" to commit U.S. forces to combat.

1992–1993 Bush continues to act as if Congress has no role other than to affirm his decisions on troop deployments and continue to provide the necessary funds for their operations.

1993–2001 President Clinton deploys troops regularly to support humanitarian missions or to protect or evacuate American citizens and third-country nationals from troubled countries. Clinton also employs American military forces in four other conflicts: Bosnia-Herzegovina (1992–1999), Iraq (1993–2000), Haiti (1993–1996), and Kosovo (1999), in addition to ordering cruise missile strikes against Sudan and Afghanistan (1998) and providing support for the UN multinational force in East Timor. He neither seeks nor receives congressional authorization for his use of military forces abroad.

Congress seems ill equipped to deal with this continuing assault on its constitutional prerogatives, often settling for nonbinding resolutions in attempting to constrain presidential power.

President Clinton, like Bush before him, uses multiple means to deprive Congress-requested information.

2001–2009   The administration of President G. W. Bush claims plenary authority as commander-in-chief and the sole organ of the nation in its foreign relations, to use military force abroad and ascribes to the president absolute, unqualified, unfettered power in foreign affairs and in matters of war and peace.

2001   Following 9/11 attacks, President Bush declares a "state of national emergency." Congress quickly grants the president sweeping powers.

Bush goes to war in Afghanistan, creates military tribunals to try non–U.S. citizens who may have assisted in the 9/11 attacks.

2002   Bush declares willingness to act alone and preemptively attack those who threaten the United States.

Claiming Iraq is in noncompliance with UN resolutions, has weapons of mass destruction, and is prepared to use them, Bush requests authority to take any necessary military action. Congress, without thoroughly examining the evidence, acquiesces to the president's wishes, granting him broad authority.

2003   On questionable intelligence later to prove completely wrong, Bush invades Iraq.

Notes

CHAPTER 1. INTELLECTUAL ORIGINS
OF THE AMERICAN CONSTITUTION

1. Gordon S. Wood, *The Making of the Constitution* (Waco, Tex.: Baylor University, 1987), 24.

2. Gordon Wood notes that Americans, in their attempt to understand the moral and social basis of politics, had a compulsive interest in the ancient republics. Gordon S. Wood, *The Creation of the American Republic* (Chapel Hill: University of North Carolina Press, 1998), 50.

3. Wood, *Making of the Constitution*, 10.

4. Quoted in Thomas G. Paterson, J. Gerry Clifford, Shane J. Maddock, Deborah Kisatsky, and Kenneth J. Haggan, *American Foreign Relations: A History to 1920, Volume 1* (New York: Houghton Mifflin, 2005), 27; from Frederick W. Marks III, *Independence on Trial* (Baton Rouge: Louisiana State University Press, 1973), 35.

5. Gordon Wood concisely outlines four interest groups that propelled the nation towards a strengthening of the government of the Confederacy—the officer corps of the army, concerned over back pay and pensions, public creditors who held federal bonds and loan certificates, those interested in strengthening commerce through the granting to Congress the power to regulate international trade, and those concerned about America's inability to deal effectively in the field of foreign relations. See Wood, *Making of the Constitution*, 10–13. Wood further notes that leading statesmen such as James Madison were becoming increasingly concerned about state legislatures, which were often dominated by "small minded," "parochial," "illiberal" legislators and selfish interested majorities. See Wood, *Making of the Constitution*, 16–17.

6. Letter of George Washington to John Jay, August 15, 1786, http://gwpapers.virginia.edu/documents/constitution/1784/jay2.html.

7. For additional detail see Joseph Story, LLD, *Commentaries on the Constitution of the United States* (Boston: Hilliard, Gray, 1833), vol. 1, book 3, chap. 1, sec. 272–74.

8. James Madison, "Vices of the Political system of the U. States. Observations, by J.M.," April 1787, at http://www.ungardesign.com/websites/madison/main_pages/madison_archives/constit_confed/confederation/confederacy_notes.htm

9. Letter of Henry Knox to John Sullivan, Philadelphia, May 21, 1787 cited in James H. Hutson, ed., *Supplement to Max Farrand's The Records of the Federal Convention of 1787* (New Haven, CT: Yale University Press, 1987, 12–13).

10. Notes of James Henry of Maryland in Max Farrand, ed., *The Records of the Federal Convention of 1787*, vol. 1, rev. ed. (New Haven, CT: Yale University Press, 1966), 24.

11. *Records*, vol. 1, 18–19.

12. *Records*, vol. 1, 291.

13. Though Randolph presented the Virginia Plan, it was largely the work of 36-year-old James Madison, who headed the Virginia delegation. Madison had been educated at the College of New Jersey, which later become known as Princeton University. He completed his studies in two years and with the assistance of private tutors had mastered Greek and Latin. At the age of 29, Madison was the youngest member of the Continental Congress.

14. Wood, *Creation of the American Republic*, 7.

15. Matthew Strickland, "Enforcers of Magna Carta (act. 1215–1216)," Oxford Dictionary of National Biography, http://www.oxforddnb.com/public/themes/93/93691.html.

16. Since the early 15th century, Parliament had voted to give the king the authority for life to collect taxes on every cask of wine and on imports.

17. 'Habeas Corpus" at http://www.uslaw.com/us_law_dictionary/h/Habeas+Corpus

18. The following draws heavily on the ideas presented by Bernard Bailyn in his *The Ideological Origins of the American Revolution* (Cambridge, Mass.: Belknap Press of Harvard University, 1992), especially 160–229.

19. James A. Donald, *Natural Law and Natural Rights*, http://jim.com/rights.html.

20. Sir William Blackstone, *Commentaries on the Laws of England*, bk. 1, chap. 2, 149. Yale Law School, the Avalon Project at http://avalon.law.yale.edu/subject_menus/blackstone.asp

21. Zubly also was in favor of reconciliation with Great Britain, opposed the break with England, and was accused of disloyalty by Congress. He was ordered arrested by the Council of Safety, escaped, sought refuge among loyalists in South Carolina, and died in 1781 while the outcome of the Revolutionary War remained very much in doubt. See "John J. Zubly," History and Archeology, *The New Georgia Encyclopedia*, http://www.georgiaencyclopedia.org/nge/Article.jsp?path=/HistoryArchaeology/ColonialEraTrusteePeriod/People-4&id=h-662

22. Quoted in Bailyn, *Ideological Origins*, 181.

23. Bailyn, *Ideological Origins*, 182.

24. For a more detailed discussion, see Bailyn, *Ideological Origins*, 182–84.

25. Ibid., 198–99.

26. Ibid., 199.

27. J. P. Sommerville, *1625–1629: The First Crisis of Charles I's Reign*, http://history.wisc.edu/sommerville/361/361-24.htm.

28. Margaret A. Judson, "Henry Parker and the Theory of Parliamentary Sovereignty," *Essays [to] McIlwain*, 152, 144, 150, 151, cited in Bailyn, *Ideological Origins*, 200.

29. Bailyn, *Ideological Origins*, 200.

30. The term "English Civil War" is used to refer to the civil wars that took place in England and Scotland. The first took place from 1642 to 1646, the second in 1648–1649, and the third from 1649 to 1651.

31. Bailyn, *Ideological Origins*, 201.

32. *The Declaratory Act*, http://www.constitution.org/bcp/decl_act.htm.

33. See Bailyn, *Ideological Origins*, 202–4, for a more extensive treatment of this subject.

34. Bailyn, *Ideological Origins*, 209–10.

35. Bailyn, *Ideological Origins*, 211–16.

36. [John Dickenson], *Letters from a Framer in Pennsylvania...* (Philadelphia, 1768: JHL Pamphlet 23), 20, 24 cited in Bailyn, *Ideological Origins*, 216.

37. Quoted in Bailyn, *Ideological Origins*, 221. Somewhat later Thomas Paine echoed a similar sentiment in his 1776 pamphlet *Common Sense*. He wrote: "But where say some is the King of America? I'll tell you Friend, he reigns above."

38. Bailyn, *Ideological Origins*, 224.

39. Bailyn, *Ideological Origins*, 225–26.

40. Bailyn, *Ideological Origins*, 214.

41. Quoted in Bailyn, *Ideological Origins*, 163.

42. See Bailyn, *Ideological Origins*, 164.

43. Bailyn, *Ideological Origins*, 173–74.

44. John Adams, "The Rule of Law and the Rule of Men," *Massachusetts Gazette*, February 6, 1775, reprinted in *The Annals of America* (Chicago: Encyclopaedia Britannica, Inc., 1976), vol. 2: 1755–1783, 310.

45. For a description of the various assemblies and the composition of the executive branch, see *The Roman Republican Constitution*, http://www.unrv.com/empire/roman-republican-constitution.php. Also see Frank Frost Abbott, *A History and Description of Roman Political Institutions* (Boston: Adamant Media, Elibron Classics series, 2006), 20–33.

46. Consuls were the highest civil and military magistrates, serving as the heads of government. Praetors were either commanders of the army or elected magistrates who were assigned duties that varied depending on the historical period. Censors were magistrates of high rank who bore the responsibility for maintaining the census, supervising public morality, and overseeing certain aspects of governmental finances. See http://en.wikipedia.org/wiki/Roman_consul, http://en.wikipedia.org/wiki/Praetors, http://en.wikipedia.org/wiki/Roman_censor, respectively.

47. Abbott, *Roman Political Institutions*, 257.

48. Marshall Davies Lloyd, "Polybius and the Founding Fathers: The Separation of Powers," St. Margaret's School, September 22, 1998, 3, http:/mlloyd.org/mdl-indx/polybius/into.htm.

49. Lloyd, "Polybius," 5.

50. For a brief but informative trace of the evolution of Enlightenment thinking see Paul Brians, "The Enlightenment," http://www.wsu.edu/~brians/hum_303/enlightenment.html.

51. Richard Hooker, "The European Enlightenment: The Philosophes," http://www.wsu.edu/~dee/ENLIGHT/PHIL.HTM.

52. For a discussion of British Whig thought and its influence on the American Revolution, see Bailyn, *Ideological Origins*, 33–54. Also see Wood, *Creation of the American Republic*, 3–45.

53. Thomas Hobbes, *Leviathan* in *Great Books of the Western World* (New York: Encyclopedia Britannica, Inc., 1952), bk 23., chap. 13, 85.

54. Adam Smith, *An Inquiry Into the Nature and Causes of the Wealth of Nations*, in *Great Books of the Western World* (New York: Encyclopedia Britannica, 1952), bk. 4, chap. 2, 194.

55. Smith, *An Inquiry*, bk. 1, chap. 11, 110.

56. Farrand, ed., *Records*, vol. 1, 82.

57. Brutus, "To the Citizens of the State of New York," *New York Journal*, October 18, 1787, reprinted in Ralph Ketcham, ed., *The Anti-Federalist Papers and the Constitutional Convention Debates* (New York: Penguin Putnam, 2003), 274.

58. For example, John Adams had read Thucydides and Plato in the original Greek and Cicero, Tacitus, and other Roman writers in Latin. See David McCullough, *John Adams* (Simon & Schuster: New York, 2001), 19. Thomas Jefferson "had numerous editions of Polybius' *Histories* in his personal library," had written "to Philip Mazzei for an Italian translation of Polybius," and had apparently sent a copy of Polybius's work to George Washington. See Lloyd, "Polybius," 6. Hamilton, in his notes made for his presentation to the delegates at the 1787 federal convention, mentions Aristotle and Cicero, as well as Montesquieu and Neckar (presumably Jacques Neckar, French statesman and foreign minister under Louis XVI). See Farrand, ed., *Records*, vol. 1, 308. Franklin, Jefferson, Madison, and Paine are among the many American writers frequently associated with the Age of Enlightenment.

CHAPTER 2. THE CONSTITUTIONAL CONVENTION: FORGING A NATION

1. Eight days after the signing of the Declaration of Independence, the first draft of the Articles of Confederation was presented to the Second Continental Congress. It took more than a year of debate before Congress adopted the articles.

2. A Committee of States, consisting of one delegate from each state, was to sit in recess of Congress and manage the affairs of the United States.

3. Letters of marque and reprisal, often referred to simply as letters of marque, are official commissions or warrants issued by a government that authorize an agent of that authority to undertake an action that might otherwise be considered an act of piracy. The letter of marque authorized the agent to proceed beyond the marque, or frontier, of the nation and search, seize, or destroy the assets (during this time, usually ships) or citizens of a foreign power. This was generally done as reprisal for some act committed by the foreign power that was viewed as an offense under the laws of nations against the assets or citizens of the issuing government.

4. Farrand, ed., *Records*, vol. 1, 34.

5. For a complete description of the New Jersey Plan as captured in the notes of James Madison, see Farrand, ed., *Records*, vol. 1, 242–45.

6. Farrand, ed., *Records*, vol. 1, 255.

7. Ibid., 262.

8. Ibid., 262–63.

9. Ibid., 284.

10. Ibid., 315.

11. Ibid., 317–19.

12. Ibid., 341. Even antifederalists such Robert Yates of New York acknowledged the weaknesses of the Confederation. During the debates over ratification of the Constitution that followed the convention, writing as "Brutus" in the *New York Journal*, Yates acknowledged, "Perhaps this country never saw so critical a period in their political concerns. We have felt the feebleness of the ties by which these United States are held together, and the want of sufficient energy in our present confederation, to manage, in some instances, our general concerns." Brutus, "To the Citizens of the State of New York," *New York Journal*, October 18, 1787, reprinted in Ketcham, ed., *The Anti-Federalist Papers*, 270.

13. Farrand, ed., *Records*, vol. 1, 347.

14. Hutson, ed., *Supplement to Max Farrand's The Records*, 16.

15. Farrand, ed., *Records*, vol. 2, 181–82.

16. Ibid., 319.

17. Ibid., 323.

18. See Bailyn, *Ideological Origins*, 340.

19. Thomas Hutchinson (1711–1780) was a Harvard-educated son of a wealthy merchant and loyalist. In 1737, he began his public life serving on the Boston Board of Selectmen, the city's governing board. Later he was chosen as a representative to the Massachusetts General Court (legislative assembly), serving almost continuously until 1749. He then served as a member of the state council (1749–1766), as chief justice of the Massachusetts Superior Court (1760–1769), and as lieutenant governor (1758–1771). In 1771 he was commissioned governor of the British North American Province of Massachusetts Bay, serving in that capacity until 1774. For greater detail, see Barnard Bailyn, *The Ordeal of Thomas Hutchinson* (Cambridge, Mass.: Belnap Press of Harvard University Press, 1974).

20. See Bailyn, *Ideological Origins*, 109.

21. The Society of Cincinnati was conceived by Major General Henry Knox, supported by General George Washington and founded in 1787. The society was created to preserve the ideals of the Revolutionary War and to continue the fellowship of the officers who fought for American independence. With branches in the United States and France, the society got its name from the story of a Roman farmer, Lucius Quintus Cincinnatus, who in the fifth century B.C. reportedly was called upon to leave his fields and lead Rome into battle. Turner had moved to Philadelphia and served as the society's secretary during its second general meeting in May 1787. For additional information on the Society of Cincinnati see "History of the Society of Cincinnati" at http://www.hereditary.us/cin_history.htm.

22. Hutson, ed., *Supplement to Max Farrand's Records*, 9.

23. Wood, *Making of the Constitution*, 17–18.

24. Farrand, ed., *Records*, vol. 1, 65.

25. Ibid., 66.

26. Ibid., 96–97.

27. Ibid., 113.

28. Richard M. Pious, *The American Presidency* (New York: Basic Books, 1979), 21–22, quoted in Gene Healy, *The Cult of the Presidency* (Washington, D.C.: CATO Institute, 2008), 15.

29. Farrand, ed., *Records*, Vol. I, 65.

30. Ibid., 68.

31. Ibid., 91.

32. Ibid., 69.

33. Ibid., 91.

34. Ibid., 69.

35. Ibid.

36. Ibid., 80.

37. Ibid., 77.

38. Farrand, ed., *Records*, vol. 2, 29.

39. Ibid., 34.

40. Ibid., 35.

41. Ibid., 56.

42. Ibid., 50–51.

43. Ibid., 97.

44. Ibid., 185.

45. Ibid., 397.

46. Ibid., 31.

47. Max Farrand, *The Framing of the Constitution of the United States* (New Haven, Conn.: Yale University Press, 1913), 116.

48. Farrand., ed., *Records*, vol. 2, 403.

49. Ibid., 500.

50. Ibid., 501.

51. Ibid., 511.

52. Ibid., 513.

53. Ibid., 23.

54. Farrand, ed., *Records*, vol. 1, 21.

55. Ibid., 67.

56. Ibid.

57. The New Jersey Plan as recorded by Madison, in Farrand, ed., *Records*, vol. 1, 244.

58. The New Jersey Plan made the executive(s) ineligible for a second term and removable by Congress on application of the executives of the several states.

59. Farrand, ed., *Records*, vol. 1, 66. The words in parentheses were added on the recommendation of General Pinckney.

60. This view was presented as part of the Hamilton Plan that had been suggested by Alexander Hamilton as an alternative to the Virginia and New Jersey Plans. See Farrand, ed., *Records*, vol. 1, 292.

61. Farrand, ed., *Records*, vol. 2, 23.

62. Ibid., 183, 185.

63. Ibid., 405.

64. Ibid., 183.

65. Ibid., 297.

66. Ibid., 392.

67. Ibid., 392–94.

68. Ibid., 495.

69. Ibid., 540–41.

70. See Farrand, ed., *Records*, vol. 1, 292.

71. Bailyn, *Ideological Origins*, 339.

72. Ibid., 61.

73. Ibid., 340. For example, also see "'Centinel,' Number 1" (October 5, 1787), reprinted in Ketcham, ed., *Anti-Federalist Papers*, 232; "Amendments Proposed by the Rhode Island Convention, March 6, 1790," in Ketcham, ed., 226; "The Address and Reasons of Dissent of the Minority of the Convention of Pennsylvania to their Constituents (December 18, 1787)," in Ketcham, ed., 254–55, and Brutus, "To the Citizens of the State of New York" (January 24, 1788), in Ketcham, ed., 287–92.

74. Farrand, ed., *Records*, vol. 2, 326.

75. Ibid., 329.

76. Ibid., 332.

77. See Ibid., 330–32.

78. Ibid., 331.

79. Ibid., 326.

80. Ibid., 331.

81. Ibid., 252.

82. Ibid., 513.

83. Farrand, ed., *Records*, vol. 1, 465.

84. *Constitution of the United States*, Art. 2, sec. 2.

85. See Ibid., 65.

86. See Ibid., 65.

87. Ibid., 73–74.

88. Ibid., 70.

89. Ibid., 292.

90. Farrand, ed., *Records*, vol. 2, 318.

91. Ibid.

92. Ibid., 319.

93. James Kent, *Commentaries on American Law* (New York: O. Halsted, 1826), part 1, lecture 3, sec. 2, at http://www.constitution.org/jk/jk_000.htm.

94. "Pacificus Number 1," *Gazette of the United States*, Philadelphia, June 29, 1793, reprinted in Morton J. Frisch, ed., *The Pacificus-Helvidius Debates of 1792–1794: Toward the Completion of the American Founding* (Indianapolis: Liberty Fund, 2007), 13. *Gazette of the United States* was a partisan newspaper friendly to the administration of President Washington.

95. "Helvidius Number 1," *Gazette of the United States*, Philadelphia, August 24, 1793, reprinted in Frisch, ed., *The Pacificus-Helvidius Debates*, 59, 62.

96. John Locke, "An Essay Concerning the True Original Extent and End of Civil Government," *Two Treatises on Civil Government*, 1690, section 159 in *Great Books of the Western World* (Chicago: Encyclopaedia Britannica, 1952), 58–59.

97. See Federalist 75 in Clinton Rossiter, ed., *The Federalist Papers* (New York: The New American Library, 2003), 451.

98. David Gray Adler and Larry N. George, eds., *The Constitution and the Conduct of American Foreign Policy* (Lawrence: University Press of Kansas, 1996), 3.

99. Arthur M. Schlesinger, Jr., foreword to Ibid., x.

100. Bailyn, *Ideological Origins*, 379.

CHAPTER 3. LAYING THE FOUNDATION

1. James Madison, letter to Thomas Jefferson, May 13, 1798, in Saul K. Padover, *The Complete Madison: His Basic Writings* (New York: Harper and Brothers, 1953), 257–58.

2. See Christopher Andrew, *For the President's Eyes Only* (New York: Harper Collins, 1995), 1.

3. Lawrence R. Houston, "Executive Privilege in the Field of Intelligence," Central Intelligence Agency Historical Release Program, released September 22, 1993, 1.

4. Hoffman, "Secrecy and Constitutional Controls" in Adler and George, *Constitution and Conduct*, 292. For the original statute see *United States Statutes at Large*, 1st Cong. 2nd sess.,129, at http://memory.loc.gov/ammem/amlaw/lwsl.html.

5. In the past, the president had forwarded information to Congress with the warning that it not be publicized for fear that its release might be injurious to the public interest. Houston, "Executive Privilege," 2.

6. Albert Ellery Bergh, ed., *The Writings of Thomas Jefferson*, vol. 1, 304–5, at http://www.constitution.org/tj/jeff.htm.

7. Louis Fisher, "Congressional Access to the Executive Branch Information: Legislative Tools," *CRS Report for Congress (RL30966)*, May 17, 2001, 4.

8. I draw heavily on the account of events by Walter Dellinger and H. Jefferson Powell, "The Attorney General's First Separation of Powers Opinion," *Constitutional Commentary* 13–3 (Winter 1996): 309–10.

9. Dellinger and Powell, "Attorney General's," 310.

10. James D. Richardson, ed., *A Compilation of the Messages and Papers of the Presidents* (a project of Gutenberg EBook, published by the Authority of Congress, 1902), vol. 1, pt. 1, Special Messages, February 26, 1794.

11. See Hoffman, "Secrecy and Constitutional Controls," 293.

12. I. Naamani Tarkow, "The Significance of the Act of Settlement in the Evolution of English Democracy," *Political Science Quarterly* 58, no. 4. (1943): 547.

13. For greater detail see Fisher, "Congressional Access," 5–9.

14. *Annals of Congress*, 4th Cong., 1st sess., 400–401, 759.

15. *Annals of Congress*, 4th Cong., 1st sess., 760–61.

16. Fisher, "Congressional Access," 6.

17. For more detail see Thomas G. Paterson, J. Gary Clifford, Shane J. Maddock, Deborah Kisatsky, and Kenneth J. Haggan, *American Foreign Relations: A History* (Boston: Wadsworth, Centgage Learning, 2010), vol. 1, 53–57.

18. *Annals of Congress*, 9th Cong., 2nd sess., 336.

19. Abraham D. Sofaer, *War, Foreign Affairs, and Constitutional Powers: The Origins* (Cambridge, Mass.: Ballinger, 1976), 190–92.

20. Arthur M. Schlesinger, *The Imperial Presidency* (Boston: Houghton Mifflin, 2004), 31–32.

21. See Schlesinger, *Imperial Presidency*, 44.

22. Ibid., 45.

23. Ibid., 46.

24. Schlesinger, *Imperial Presidency*, 47, quoting from Raoul Berger, "Executive Privilege v. Congressional Inquiry," *UCLA Law Review* 12 (1965): 1077.

25. Schlesinger, *Imperial Presidency*, 47.

26. Christopher Andrew, *For the President's Eyes Only* (New York: Harper Perennial, 1995), 11.

27. Cited in Schlesinger, *Imperial Presidency*, 48.

28. Ibid., 49. Also see Richardson, ed., *Compilation*, vol. 4, pt. 3, Special Messages, January 12, 1848.

29. Paterson et al., *American Foreign Relations*, vol. 1, 143–44.

30. Schlesinger, *Imperial Presidency*, 50.

31. Ibid., 77.

32. Joseph Story, *Commentaries on the Constitution of the United States* (Boston: Hilliard, Gray, 1833), vol. 3, ch. 37, para. 1555.

33. For Hamilton's and Madison's views on this issue see, respectively, "Pacificus Number 1," *Gazette of the United States*, Philadelphia, June 29; and "Helvidius Number 1," *Gazette of the United States*, Philadelphia, August 24, 1793.

34. For a fuller discussion see "Neutrality Controversy of 1793" at http://home.sandiego.edu/~miker/PacHel.pdf.

35. For a further exploration of this issue see Louis Fisher, *Presidential War Power* (Lawrence: University Press of Kansas, 2004), 26–30.

36. I Stat. 372 (1794). See *Statutes at Large*, 3rd Cong., 1st sess., at http://memory.loc.gov/ammem/amlaw/lwsl.html.

37. For example, see *United States v. Curtiss-Wright Export Corp.*, 299 U.S. 304.

38. I Stat. 264–265 (1792). See *Statutes at Large*, 2d Cong., 1st sess.

39. Louis Fisher, "The Barbary Wars: Legal Precedent for Invading Haiti?" in Adler and George, *Constitution and Conduct*, 313.

40. For a thoughtful and well documented discussion of this issue see Dean Alfange Jr., "The Quasi-War and Presidential Warmaking," in Adler and George, *Constitution and Conduct*, 274–90.

41. Alfange, "Quasi-War," 276.

42. Paterson et al., *American Foreign Relations*, vol. 1, 51.

43. Alfange, "Quasi-War," 277.

44. Ibid., 275, citing Francis D. Wormuth, "The Vietnam War: The President versus the Constitution," in Richard A. Falk, ed., *The Vietnam War and International Law* (Princeton, N.J.: Princeton University Press, 1969), 718–723.

45. Alfange, "Quasi-War," 279.

46. See *Bas v. Tingy*, 4 U.S. 4 Dall. 37 (1800).

47. *Talbot v. Seeman*, 5 U.S. 1 Cranch 11 (1801).

48. *Little v. Barreme*, 6 U.S. 2 Cranch 170 (1804)

49. Fisher, "The Barbary Wars," 313.

50. See Schlesinger, *Imperial Presidency*, 22–23; Fisher, "The Barbary Wars," 315; and Thomas Jefferson, "First Annual Message," December 8, 1801, in Richardson, ed., *Compilation*, vol. 1, pt. 3.

51. Schlesinger, *Imperial Presidency*, 23; and Richardson, ed., *Compilation*, vol. 1, pt. 3, "Special Messages," December 6, 1805.

52. For a brief but informative account of the events of the attack, see Paterson et al., *American Foreign Relations*, vol. 1, 39–42.

53. See Thomas Jefferson, "Seventh Annual Message," Richardson, ed., *Compilation*, vol. 1, pt. 3, October 27, 1807.

54. Paterson et al., *American Foreign Relations*, vol. 1, 41.

55. See Jefferson, "Seventh Annual Message."

56. Schlesinger, *Imperial Presidency*, 24–25.

57. James Monroe, "Seventh Annual Message," December 2, 1823, in Richardson, ed., *Compilations*, vol. 2, pt. 1.

58. Schlesinger, *Imperial Presidency*, 27.

59. R. J. Bartlett, ed., *The Record of American Diplomacy: Document and Readings in the History of American Foreign Relations* (New York: Knopf,1947), 185–86, cited in Schlesinger, *Imperial Presidency*, 27–28.

60. Schlesinger, *Imperial Presidency*, 26 and James Monroe, special message "To the Senate and House of Representative," March 25, 1818 in Richardson, *Compilations*, vol. 2. pt. 1.

61. Schlesinger, *Imperial Presidency*, 26–27; Paterson et al., *American Foreign Relations*, vol. 1, 96; and "Noteworthy Publications from the 15th Congress" at http://www.bunsei.co.jp/webbase/con15.htm.

62. Healy, *The Cult*, 37; and James Monroe, "Views of the President of the United States on the Subject of Internal Improvements," May 4, 1822, in Richardson, ed., *Compilation*, vol. 2, pt. 1.

63. Schlesinger, *Imperial Presidency*, 26, 28.

64. See Samuel Flagg Bemis, *The Latin American Policy of the United States* (New York: Harcourt, Brace, 1943), 70, partially cited in Schlesinger, *Imperial Presidency*, 28.

65. *Martin v. Mott*, 25 U.S. at 30 (1827).

66. Andrew Jackson, "Sixth Annual Message," December 1, 1834, in Richardson, ed., *Compilation*, vol. 3, pt. 1.

67. See Schlesinger, *Imperial Presidency*, 28.

68. Quoted by Irving Brant to Jacob K. Javits, April 2, 1972, in *Congressional Record*, April 10, 1972, S5756–5760, cited in Schlesinger, *Imperial Presidency*, 29.

69. Paterson et al., *American Foreign Relations*, vol. 1, 111.

70. See Schlesinger, *Imperial Presidency*, 39.

71. John Tyler, message "To the Senate of the United States," May 15, 1844, in Richardson, ed., *Compilation*, vol. 4, pt. 2.

72. Schlesinger, *Imperial Presidency*, 41.

73. James K. Polk, special message, "To the Senate and House of Representatives," May 11, 1846, in Richardson, ed., *Compilation*, vol. 4, pt. 3.

74. *Congressional Globe*, House of Representatives, 29th Cong., 1st sess., 791–95.

75. Paterson et al., *American Foreign Relations*, vol. 1, 84–86, 114–16. For an account of the Federalist opposition to the War of 1812 and its impact, see John B. Hovey, "Federalist Opposition to the War Of 1812," *Archiving Early America*, Winter 2000, at http://www.earlyamerica.com/review/winter2000/federalist.html.

76. *Congressional Globe*, House of Representatives, 29th Cong., 1st sess., 793.

77. Ibid., 30th Cong., 1st sess., 95.

78. Cited in Schlesinger, *Imperial Presidency*, 42–43.

79. Ibid., 43.

80. *Fleming v. Page*, 50 U.S. 603, 615(1850).

81. For example, see James Buchanan, "Third Annual Message," December 19, 1859, in Richardson, ed., *Compilation*, vol. 5, pt. 4.

82. James Buchanan, "Second Annual Message," December 6, 1858, in Richardson, ed., *Compilation*, vol. 5, pt. 4.

83. James Buchanan, "Special Messages," February 18, 1859, in Richardson, ed., *Compilation*, vol. 5, pt. 4.

84. See, for example, Buchanan's message to both Houses of Congress, February 18, 1859, in Richardson, ed., *Compilation*, vol. 5, pt. 4.

85. See *Durand v. Hollins*, 8 Fed. Cas. 111 (CCSDNY 1860).

86. Ibid., 112.

87. Schlesinger, *Imperial Presidency*, 58.

88. See Abraham Lincoln, Proclamations from April 15 to May 10, 1861, and "Special Session Message," July 4, 1861, in Richardson, ed., *Compilation*, vol. 6, pt. 1; also Schlesinger, *Imperial Presidency*, 58.

89. Lincoln, "Special Session Message," July 4, 1861, in Richardson, ed., *Compilation*, vol. 6, pt. 1.

90. 12 Stat. 326 (1861). See *Statutes at Large*, 37th Cong., 1st sess.

91. Lincoln, "Special Session Message," July 4, 1861, in Richardson, ed., *Compilation*, vol. 6, pt. 1.

92. *Prize Cases*, 67 U.S. at 668 (1863). Also see David Gray Alder, "Court, Constitution, and Foreign Affairs," in Alder and George, *Constitution and Conduct*, 23.

93. Schlesinger, *Imperial Presidency*, 58.

94. Ibid., 59.

95. Lincoln, "Fourth Annual Message," December 6, 1864, in Richardson, ed., *Compilation*, vol. 6, pt. 1.

96. Quoted in Schlesinger, *Imperial Presidency*, 63.

97. *Ex Parte Milligan*, 71 U.S. at 2, 30 (1866).

98. Matthew Crenson and Benjamin Ginsberg, *Presidential Power: Unchecked and Unbalanced* (New York: Norton, 2007), 328. Also see *Miller v. United States*, 78 U.S. 11 Wall. 296–308 (1870).

99. Schlesinger, *Imperial Presidency*, 51. Also see Ellen C. Collier, *Instances of Use of United States Forces Abroad, 1798–1993* (Washington, D.C.: Department of the Navy—Naval Historical Center, October 7, 1993).

100. Schlesinger, *Imperial Presidency*, 80.

101. W. S. Holt, *Treaties Defeated in the Senate: A Study of the Struggle Between President and Senate over the Conduct of Foreign Relations* (Baltimore: Johns Hopkins, 1933), 123–65, cited in Schlesinger, *Imperial Presidency*, 80.

102. See Andrew, *For the President's Eyes Only*, 13.

CHAPTER 4. GATHERING CLOUDS

1. *In re Neagle*, 135 U.S. at 81.

2. Ibid. at 64.

3. The Spanish board of inquiry concluded that the explosion most likely was caused by a spontaneous combustion of the ship's coal bunker. A U.S. court of inquiry, without establishing who was responsible for the explosion, concluded that the explosion "could have been produced only by the explosion of a mine situated under the bottom of the ship." In 1976 a private investigation initiated by Admiral Hyman Rickover seemed to reaffirm the conclusions of the Spanish board of inquiry, concluding that "the cause of the explosion originated within the ship."

4. Farrand, ed., *Records*, vol. 2, 540–41.

5. Paterson et al., *American Foreign Relations*, vol. 1, 175.

6. See Crenson and Ginsberg, *Presidential Power*, 31; and Schlesinger, *Imperial Presidency*, 88.

7. Schlesinger, *Imperial Presidency*, 89.

8. Healy, *The Cult*, 59.

9. Ibid.

10. Ibid., 58.

11. "Roosevelt Resents Senate Usurpation," *New York Times*, January 7, 1909.

12. Schlesinger, *Imperial Presidency*, 84, citing Archibald Butt, *Letters* (New York, 1924), 305–6. Major Butt was Roosevelt's personal aide.

13. William Michael Treanor, "Fame, the Founding, and the Power to Declare War," *Cornell Law Review* 82 (May 1997): 764, cited in Healy, *The Cult*, 60.

14. "America to Send Warships; Official News of the Revolution on the Isthmus Received—Hurried Conferences at the White House," *New York Times*, November 4, 1903.

15. Benjamin S. Dean, "The Treaty With New Granada," *New York Times*, January 17, 1904.

16. Henry F. Pringle, *Theodore Roosevelt: A Biography* (New York: Harcourt Brace, 1931), 330, cited in Fisher, *Presidential War Power*, 60.

17. Edward S. Corwin, *The President: Office and Powers, 1787–1984*, ed. Randall W. Bland, Theodore T. Hindson, and Jack W. Peltason 5th rev. ed. (New York: New York University, 1984) n. 94, 484.

18. Schlesinger, *Imperial Presidency*, 89.

19. Healy, *The Cult*, 60.

20. Fisher, *Presidential War Power*, 59.

21. Ibid., 59–60.

22. "Theodore Roosevelt and the Dominican Republic," *Oregon Coast Magazine Online*, at http://www.u-s-history.com/pages/h946.html.

23. See Corwin, *The President*, 242, n. 124, 488–89.

24. Fisher, *Presidential War Power*, 61.

25. Schlesinger, *Imperial Presidency*, 91.

26. Ibid., 84.

27. Woodrow Wilson, *Constitutional Government in the United States* (New York: Columbia University Press, 1908), 77.

28. For the following I have drawn heavily on Corwin, *The President*, 269–70.

29. *The Evolution of the U.S. Intelligence Community—An Historical Overview* at http://www.fas.org/irp/offdocs/int022.html.

30. Ibid.

31. Corwin, *The President*, 270.

32. See, for example, Corwin, *The President*, 270.

33. Mark J. Rozell, *Executive Privilege*, 2nd rev. (Lawrence: University Press of Kansas, 2002), 38, citing 65 *Cong. Rec.* 6087 (1924).

34. Schlesinger, *Imperial Presidency*, 94–95.

35. Fisher, *Presidential War Power*, 65–66.

36. Schlesinger, *Imperial Presidency*, 95.

37. Franklin D. Roosevelt, "Inaugural Address," March 4, 1933, The American Presidency Project at http://www.presidency.ucsb.edu/ws/index.php?pid=14473&st=&st1=

38. Ibid., 117.

39. Rozell, *Executive Privilege*, 38.

40. Corwin, *The President*, 130.

41. *Evolution of the U.S. Intelligence Community.*

42. For greater detail on this period see Walter LaFeber, *The American Age: U.S. Foreign Policy at Home and Abroad, 1750 to the Present* (New York: Norton, 1994), 375–84.

43. LaFeber, *American Age*, 388.

44. Robert A. Divine, *Roosevelt and World War II* (Baltimore: Johns Hopkins, 1968), ch. 2, cited in LaFeber, *American Age*, 392.

45. Ibid., 394.

46. Ibid., 396.

47. Schlesinger, *Imperial Presidency*, 110.

48. U.S. Department of State, *Peace and War: United States Foreign Policy, 1931–1941,* Publication 1983 (Washington, D.C.: U.S. Government Printing Office, 1943), 686–87.

49. R. A. Taft, *A Foreign Policy for Americans* (Garden City, N.Y.: 1951), 31, cited in Schlesinger, *Imperial Presidency,* 111–12.

50. Paterson et al., *American Foreign Relations,* vol. 2, 185.

51. Ibid.

52. Ibid., 187.

53. See *A.L.A. Schechter Poultry Corporation v. United States,* 295 U.S. 495.

54. *United States v. Curtiss-Wright Export Corp.,* 299 U.S. 304 (1936).

55. Locke, *Two Treatises,* sec. 141 in *Great Books,* 58.

56. See, for example, Fisher, *Presidential War Power,* 69–73; David Gray Adler, "Court, Constitution, and Foreign Affairs," in Adler and George, *Constitution and Conduct,* 25–27; and Schlesinger, *Imperial Presidency,* 100–103.

57. *U.S. v. Curtiss-Wright* at 320.

58. *United States v. Belmont,* 301 U.S. 324 at 330, 336 (1937).

59. Crenson and Ginsberg, *Presidential Power,* 321.

60. Schlesinger, *Imperial Presidency,* 115–19.

61. Healy, *The Cult,* 74.

62. *U.S. v. Curtiss-Wright* at 320.

63. For example, see Fisher, *Presidential War Power,* 206–7.

64. Ex Parte Quirin, 317 U.S. at 26 (1942).

CHAPTER 5. A RISE AND FALL IN PRESIDENTIAL POWER

1. Alexis de Tocqueville, *Democracy in America,* ed. by J. P. Mayer, trans. by George Lawrence (Garden City, N.Y.: Anchor Books, 1969), 123–26.

2. "National Security Council Intelligence Directive No. 5," dated December 12, 1947. National Archives and Records Administration, RG 59, Records of the Department of State, Records of the Executive Secretariat, NSC Files, Lot 66 D 95, NSCIDs.

3. *Legislative Oversight of Intelligence Activities: The U.S. Experience,* report prepared by the United States Senate Select Committee on Intelligence (Washington, D.C.: GPO, October 1994), 3.

4. M. Stanton Evans, *Blacklisted by History: The Untold Story of Senator Joe McCarthy and His Fight Against America's Enemies* (New York: Crown Forum, 2007), 23.

5. Frank, J. Smist Jr., *Congress Oversees the United States Intelligence Community* 2nd. ed. (Knoxville: University of Tennessee Press, 1994), 4.

6. Ibid., 5, quoting an interview with Walter Pforzheimer, January 18, 1983.

7. Ibid., quoting an interview with Clifford, May 27, 1983.

8. Ibid.

9. "The President's News Conference," April 24, 1952, in *Public Papers of Presidents: Harry S. Truman,* at http://www.presidency.ucsb.edu/ws/index.php?pid=14092&st=&st1=.

10. "Statement by the President on the Situation in Korea," April 27, 1950, *Public Papers: Truman.*

11. Schlesinger, *Imperial Presidency,* 132.

12. Ibid., 132–34.

13. For a critique of this argument see Louis Fisher, "Truman in Korea," in Adler and George, *Constitution and Conduct*, 326.

14. Schlesinger, *Imperial Presidency*, 134.

15. "The President's News Conference," January 4, 1951, in *Public Papers: Truman*.

16. "The President's News Conference," January 11, 1951, in *Public Papers: Truman*.

17. "The Congress: Decision in the Great Debate," *Time*, April 16, 1951, at http://www.time.com/time/magazine/article/0,9171,814662,00.html.

18. *Youngstown Co. v. Sawyer*, 343 U.S. at 587 (1952).

19. Schlesinger, *Imperial Presidency*, 156.

20. Ibid., quoting from the full text published in *U.S. News & World Report*, May 28, 1954.

21. Schlesinger, *Imperial Presidency*, 157.

22. David Greenberg, *What Is Executive Privilege and Why Do Presidents Like to Invoke It?* History News Network, December 25, 2001 at http://www.hnn.us/articles/470.html.

23. *United States v. Reynolds*, et al., 73 S. Ct. 528, 345 U.S. 1 at 10 (1953).

24. Raoul Berger, *Executive Privilege: A Constitutional Myth* (Cambridge, Mass., 1974), 355. Also see *Kaiser Aluminum & Chemical Corp. v. United States*, 157 F. Supp. 939, 141 Ct. Cl. 38 (Cl. Ct. 1958).

25. L. Britt Snider, "Congress as a User of Intelligence: Sharing Secrets with Lawmakers," at https://www.cia.gov/library/center-for-the-study-of-intelligence/csi-publications/csi-studies/studies/spring98/Congress.html.

26. *Legislative Oversight of Intelligence*, 3.

27. For a more detailed discussion of Senate and House approaches to oversight see Smist, *Congress Oversees*, 4–9.

28. Fisher, "Truman in Korea," 329.

29. Fisher, *Presidential War Power*, 118.

30. John F. Kennedy, Press Club speech, January 14, 1960, quoted in Schlesinger, *Imperial Presidency*, 169.

31. Schlesinger, *Imperial Presidency*, 172.

32. Morton Rosenberg, "Presidential Claims of Executive Privilege: History, Law, Practice and Recent Developments," *CRS Report for Congress RL 30319*, updated August 21, 2008, 37.

33. Schlesinger, *Imperial Presidency*, 172,

34. Ibid., 173.

35. 78 Stat. 697 (1962), quoted in Fisher, *Presidential War Power*, 126.

36. See Fisher, *Presidential War Power*, 126.

37. Ibid.

38. Professor Mark J. Rozell has identified only three instances in which executive branch officials refused to comply with congressional requests for information or testimony involving presidential actions. They did not, however, claim that the president had so directed them. See Mark J. Rozell, *Executive Privilege: Presidential Power, Secrecy and Accountability*, 2nd rev. ed. (Lawrence: University Press of Kansas, 2002), 41–42.

39. LaFeber, *American Age*, 549.

40. Stanley Karnow, *Vietnam: A History* (New York: The Viking Press, 1983), 370–74.

41. Schlesinger, *Imperial Presidency*, 179.

42. Quoted in Karnow, *Vietnam*, 374.

43. 110 *Cong. Rec.* 18543 (1964), quoted in Fisher, *Presidential War Power*, 131.

44. Karnow, *Vietnam*, 375.

45. Schlesinger, *Imperial Presidency*, 180–81.

46. See Karnow, *Vietnam*, 345, 358-62.

47. Fisher, *Presidential War Power*, 134.

48. "Statement by the President Upon Ordering Troops Into the Dominican Republic," April 28, 1965, *Public Papers of Presidents: Lyndon B. Johnson*, at http://www.presidency.ucsb.edu/ws/index.php?pid=26922&st=&st1=.

49. Schlesinger, *Imperial Presidency*, 178.

50. Ibid., 169.

51. Ibid., 169–70.

52. Richard Nixon, "Statement about Executive Privilege," March 12, 1973, at http://www.presidency.ucsb.edu/ws/index.php?pid=4137&st=&st1=.

53. Schlesinger, *Imperial Presidency*, 247, citing "The Present Limits of 'Executive Privilege,'" *Congressional Record*, March 28, 1973, H2242–46.

54. Schlesinger, *Imperial Presidency*, 247, citing the statement of Deputy Comptroller General R. F. Keller, *Congressional Record*, May 18, 1972, E-5506-8.

55. Schlesinger, *Imperial Presidency*, 201–2.

56. Ibid., 248.

57. Ibid., 250–51.

58. Nixon, "Statement about Executive Privilege," March 12, 1973.

59. "Watergate Scandal," *1973 Year in Review*, UPI.com at http://www.upi.com/Audio/Year_in_Review/Events-of-1973/Watergate-Scandal/12305770297723–4/.

60. *United States v. Nixon*, 418 U.S. at 706 (1974).

61. Ibid. at 684.

62. Ibid.

63. Ibid. at 712, n. 36.

64. See *Nixon v. Administrator of General Services*, 433 U.S. at 447 *passim*, 450, 454 (1977).

65. For an expanded list and greater detail see Harold C. Relyea, "Presidential Directives: Background and Overview," *CRS Report for Congress (98)*, updated November 26, 2008.

66. Schlesinger, *Imperial Presidency*, 377.

67. Subcommittee on the Separation of Powers of the Senate Committee of the Judiciary, *Congressional Oversight of Executive Agreements*: Hearings on S. 3475, 92nd Cong., 2nd sess., June 3, 1975, 1.

68. Ibid., 137.

69. Rudalevige, *New Imperial Presidency: Renewing Presidential Power after Watergate* (Ann Arbor: University of Michigan, 2006), 80.

70. Ibid., 81.

71. "Address to the Nation on the Situation in Southeast Asia," April 30, 1970, *Public Papers: Nixon*, at http://www.presidency.ucsb.edu/ws/index.php?pid=2490&st=&st1=.

72. Quoted in Schlesinger, *Imperial Presidency*, 189.

73. Rudalevige, *New Imperial Presidency*, 83.

74. Schlesinger, *Imperial Presidency*, xxvii.

75. See Public Law 93–148, 93rd Cong. H. J. Res. 542, November 7, 1973.

76. For additional commentary on questions that remain unanswered by the War Powers Resolution see Rudalevige, *New Imperial Presidency*, 193.

77. See, for example, Louis Fisher and David Gray Adler, "The War Powers Resolution: Time to Say Goodbye," *Political Science Quarterly* 113, no. 1 (1998): 1–20.

78. *INS v. Chadha*, 462 U.S. 919 (1983).

79. Rudalevige, *New Imperial Presidency*, 193.

80. See *Foreign Assistance Act of 1974*, Public Law No. 93–559, 88 stat, 1804.

81. Senate Resolution 400, 94th Congress (1976), Sec. 11(a).

82. For details see Fisher, *Presidential War Power*, 154–55.

83. "Letter to the Speaker of the House and the President Pro Tempore of the Senate Reporting on United States Actions in the Recovery of the SS Mayaguez, May 15, 1975, *Public Papers: Ford* at http://www.presidency.ucsb.edu/ws/index. php?pid=4913&st=&st1=.

84. Fisher, *Presidential War Power*, 157.

85. *Rappenecker v. United States* (1976), cited in Fisher, *Presidential War Power*, 158.

86. The use of the words "consistent with," without citing the operative Section 4(a)(1) of the War Powers Resolution, instead of the words "subject to" in that section served two purposes. First, it underscored the president's determination not to recognize that he considered the presidency subject to the provisions of the resolution. Second, it left open the question of whether the mandated 60-day clock had actually started.

87. "Rescue Attempt for American Hostages in Iran Letter to the Speaker of the House and the President Pro Tempore of the Senate Reporting on the Operation," April 26, 1980, *Public Papers: Carter* at http://www.presidency.ucsb.edu/ ws/index.php?pid=33328&st=&st1=.

88. Quoted in Fisher, *Presidential War Power*, 159.

89. *Goldwater v. Carter*, 444 U.S. at 996 (1979).

90. Mark J. Rozell, "Executive Privilege and Modern Presidents: In Nixon's Shadow," *Minnesota Law Review* 83 (May 1999): 1072; and Rudalevige, *New Imperial Presidency*, 106.

91. Rozell, "Executive Privilege," 1078–79.

92. Ibid., 1078.

93. Ibid., 1087–88.

94. Rosenberg, "Presidential Claims," 37.

95. *United States v. AT&T*, 567 F.2d 121. Also see Rosenberg, "Presidential Claims," 9.

96. Though significant majorities in both houses voted to establish the intelligence committees, debate on their establishment was fraught with disagreements over such issues as jurisdiction, committee size, membership selection and length of terms, partisan composition, ability to disclose classified material, and leadership structure. See Frederick M. Kaiser, "Congress and the Intelligence Community: Taking the Road Less Traveled," in *The Postreform Congress*, ed. Roger H. Davidson (New York: St. Martin's, 1991), 279.

97. Britt Snider, *Congressional Oversight of Intelligence: Some Reflections on the Last 25 Years* (Durham, N.C.: Center on Law, Ethics and National Security, 2003), 7.

98. See *Intelligence Authorization Act for Fiscal Year 1981*, Public Law 96–450, 96th Cong. (October 14, 1980), Title V, sec. 501.

99. Schlesinger, *Imperial Presidency*, 446.

100. See Rosenberg, "Presidential Claims," 38; and Rozell, "Executive Privilege," 1095–1102.

101. Snider, *Congressional Oversight*, 7.

102. Ibid., 7–8.

103. Snider, "Congress as a User."

104. For additional details see Richard F. Grimmett, *The War Powers Resolution: After Thirty Years*, CRS Report for Congress: RL32267, March 11, 2004.

105. James A. Baker III and Warren Christopher, co-chairs, *National War Powers Commission Report* (Charlottesville, Va.: Miller Center of Public Affairs, July 2008), 7–12.

106. See in turn *Crockett v. Reagan*, 558 F. Supp. 893 (D.D.C. 1982); *Conyers v. Reagan*, 578 F. Supp. 324 (D.D.C. 1984); *Lowry v. Reagan*, 676 F. Supp. 333 (D.D.C. 1987).

107. *Legislative Oversight of Intelligence*, 21–22.

108. The Boland amendments were named after Congressmen Edward Boland, chairman of the House Permanent Select Committee on Intelligence.

109. See Excerpt from Senate Select Committee on Intelligence Report, 98–665, October 10, 1984, at http://140.147.249.9/cgi-bin/query/z?r102:S05NO1-125.

110. *Legislative Oversight of Intelligence*, 22.

111. Smist, *Congress Oversees*, 123.

112. Ibid., 257.

113. *Legislative Oversight of Intelligence*, 22.

114. For an extensive discussion of these events, see Lawrence E. Walsh, *Final Report of the Independent Counsel for Iran/Contra Matters: Volume1, Investigations and Prosecutions*, Washington: D.C., August 4, 1993 at http://www.fas.org/irp/offdocs/walsh/.

115. Smist, *Congress Oversees*, 259.

116. *The Tower Commission* (New York: Random House, 1987), 78. Noted in Smist, *Congress Oversees*, 263.

117. Smist, *Congress Oversees*, 264.

118. Ibid., 265.

CHAPTER 6. A SEASON FOR ABDICATION

1. Schlesinger, *Imperial Presidency*, xvi.

2. Rosenberg, "Presidential Claims," 12.

3. See Rozell, "Executive Privilege and Modern Presidents," 1110–17. Also see Rudalevige, *New Imperial Presidency*, 183.

4. Rozell, *Executive Privilege*, 107.

5. See Lock K. Johnson, "Monitoring America's Secret Foreign Policy: Congress and the Intelligence Agencies After the Cold War," *Extensions* at http://www.ou.edu/special/albertctr/extensions/spring2001/Johnson.html.

6. *Legislative Oversight of Intelligence*, 24.

7. *Title V, National Security Act of 1947* (1991), sec. 503(e).

8. Ibid., sec. 502–3.

9. *Legislative Oversight of Intelligence*, 25.

10. See Grimmett, *War Powers Resolution*, 59; and Baker and Christopher, *National War Powers*, 15.

11. Grimmett, *War Powers Resolution,* 21–22; and Baker and Christopher, *National War Powers,* 13.

12. 136 *Cong. Rec.* 1511 (1990), cited in Fisher, *Presidential War Power,* 167.

13. Grimmett, *War Powers Resolution,* 24.

14. "Statement on Signing the Resolution Authorizing the Use of Military Force Against Iraq," January 14, 1991, *Public Papers: Bush* at http://www.presidency.ucsb.edu/ws/index.php?pid=19217&st=&st1=.

15. "Remarks at Dedication Ceremony of the Social Sciences Complex at Princeton University in Princeton, New Jersey, May 10, 1991," *Public Papers: Bush.*

16. 16 Op. O.L.C. 6 (1992), citing 40 Op. Att'y Gen. 58, 62 (1991), cited by Fisher, *Presidential War Power,* 177–78.

17. For example, see Michael Kranish, "Bush Assails Clinton's Draft Record Again," *Boston Globe,* November 2, 1992.

18. Fisher, *Presidential War Power,* 175.

19. Grimmett, *War Powers Resolution,* 30–31.

20. See Ibid., 61–70.

21. "Interview with Radio Reporters," October 18, 1993, *Public Papers: Clinton* at http://www.presidency.ucsb.edu/ws/index.php?pid=47217&st=&st1=.

22. "Address to the Nation on the Strike on Iraqi Intelligence Headquarters," June 26, 1993, in *Public Papers: Clinton.*

23. Letter to Congressional Leaders on the Strike on Iraqi Intelligence Headquarters, June 28, 1993, in *Public Papers: Clinton.*

24. Cited in Fisher, *Presidential War Power,* 181–82.

25. Ibid., 185.

26. Ibid.

27. Ibid., 178.

28. Ibid., 180.

29. Ibid., 184.

30. Ibid., 190–91.

31. Rozell, "Executive Privilege," 1118.

32. Rosenberg, "Presidential Claims," 12.

33. Rozell, "Executive Privilege," 1118.

34. Rosenberg, "Presidential Claims," 4, n. 21.

35. See, for example, *Watkins v. United States,* 354 U.S. 173, 187 (1957); *McGrain v. Daugherty,* 272 U.S. 135, 177 (1926); *Eastland v. U.S. Servicemen's Fund,* 421 U.S. 491, 504 n.15 (1975), cited in Rosenberg, "Presidential Claims," 6, n. 28.

36. Rosenberg, "Presidential Claims," 38–39.

37. Ibid., 17.

38. See Ibid., 17–18.

39. See Ibid., 19–20.

40. Snider, "Congress as a User."

41. Blackstone, *Commentaries,* bk. 1, chap. 7, 245–63.

42. See, for example, comments made at the Constitutional Convention by Hamilton (Farrand, ed., vol. 1, 292); Gerry (Farrand, ed., vol. 2, 318); Madison (Farrand, ed., vol. 1, 70); Pinckney (Farrand, ed., vol. 1, 65); and Wilson (Farrand, ed., vol. 1, 65, 73–74).

43. John C. Yoo, "The President's Constitutional Authority to Conduct Military Operations against Terrorist and Nations Supporting Them," September 25, 2001, at http://www.justice.gov/olc/warpowers925.htm.

44. Farrand, vol. 1, 465.

45. Healy, *The Cult*, 2.

46. Public Law 107–40 (S.J. Res. 23), Authorization for Use of Military Force, September 18, 2001.

47. See Richard F. Grimmitt, "Authorization for Use of Military Force in Response to the 9/11 Attacks (P.L. 107–40): Legislative History," CRS Report to Congress, RS 22357, January 16, 2007, 2, 5-6.

48. Rudalevige, *New Imperial Presidency*, 215–16.

49. "Address to the Nation Announcing Strikes against Al Qaida Training Camps and Taliban Military Installations in Afghanistan," October 7, 2001, *Public Papers: Bush* at http://www.presidency.ucsb.edu/ws/index.php?pid=65088&st=&st1=.

50. For details see Fisher, *Presidential War Power*, 206–8.

51. Ibid., 208.

52. The president outlined this doctrine in his commencement address at the United States Military Academy in West Point, New York, June 1, 2002, *Public Papers: Bush*, and enshrined it in *The National Security Strategy of the United States of America*, September 2002, 6, on-line at http://www.globalsecurity.org/military/library/policy/national/nss-020920.pdf.

53. Quoted in Rudalevige, *New Imperial Presidency*, 220, from Ron Suskind, "Without a Doubt," *New York Times Magazine*, October 17, 2004.

54. *Authorization for the Use of Military Force Against Iraq Resolution 2002*, 107–243, 107th Cong., 2nd sess. (October 16, 2002, 116).

55. "Transcript: David Kay at Senate Hearing," January 28, 2004, at http://www.cnn.com/2004/US/01/28/kay.transcript/.

56. "President Bush Outlines Iraqi Threat," remarks by the President on Iraq, Cincinnati Museum Center, Cincinnati Union Terminal, Cincinnati, Ohio, October 7, 2002, at http://merln.ndu.edu/MERLN/PFIraq/archive/wh/20021007-8.pdf.

57. Ibid.

58. Ambassador Joseph Wilson, *The Politics of Truth* (New York: Carroll & Graf, 2004), 28.

59. Wolf Blitzer, "Did the Bush Administration Exaggerate the Threat from Iraq?" CNN.com/inside politics, July 8, 2003 at www.cnn.com/2003/ALLPOLI TICS/07/08/wbr.iraq.claims/.

60. Blix, *Disarming Iraq*, 211.

61. Ibid., 9.

62. For a further discussion of this issue see Robert Kennedy, *Of Knowledge and Power: The Complexities of National Intelligence* (Westport, Conn: Praeger Security International, 2008), 84–85.

63. "President Delivers 'State of the Union.'" January 28, 2003, at http://merln.ndu.edu/MERLN/PFIraq/archive/wh/20030328-19.pdf.

64. Rudalevige, *New Imperial Presidency*, 185.

65. See Rosenberg, "Presidential Claims," 39–40.

66. *Rules of Procedure for the Select Committee on Intelligence United States Senate*, 110th Congress, 1st Session, March 2007, Rule 7.

67. *Rules of Procedure for the Permanent Select Committee on Intelligence United States House of Representatives*, 110th Congress, January 18, 2007, para. 10(a).

68. Transcript of Panel 1: *What Is Good Congressional Oversight?* Congressional Oversight Conference, Center for Congressional and Presidential Studies, School of Public Affairs, American University, August 22, 2006.

69. Ibid.

70. *A Resolution Establishing a Select Committee on Intelligence*, 94th Cong. 2nd sess. 1976, S.Res. 400.

71. Dana Priest, "Congressional Oversight of Intelligence Criticized," *Washington Post*, April 27, 2004.

72. Anonymous interview with a member of the Senate Select Committee on Intelligence, March 2005.

CONCLUSIONS

1. Fisher and Adler, "The War Powers Resolution."

2. Federalist 8 in Rossiter, *Federalist Papers*, 62.

3. Schlesinger, *Imperial Presidency*, xi.

4. Polk, special message, "To the Senate and House of Representatives," May 11, 1846, in Richardson, ed., *Compilation*, vol. 4, pt. 3.

5. Federalist 48 in Rossiter, *Federalist Papers*, 305.

6. *Records*, vol. 3, 85. This anecdote is from the notes taken at the Constitutional Convention by James McHenry, delegate from the state of Maryland. His notes were first published in *The American Historical Review*. When they were included in Max Farrand's *Records of the Federal Convention* a footnote stated that the date the anecdote was written was uncertain.

7. Schlesinger, *Imperial President*, 150.

8. John Stuart Mill, *Representative Government in Great Books of the Western World* (New York: Encyclopedia Britannica, 1952), chap. 10, 393.

Index

Acheson, Dean, 90

Act of Settlement, 4–5, 8, 46

Adams, John: fear of despotism, 25; French relations and, 54–55, 56; on government, 15; "X, Y, Z" Affair, 47–48

Adams, John Quincy, 60–61, 64

Afghanistan, 119, 125

Age of Enlightenment, 15–19, 41–42

Alfange, Dean, Jr., 55

al-Qaeda, 126, 127

American Civil War, 44, 68, 70, 71, 72, 96

American colonies (colonial experience): Age of Enlightenment and, 17; concept of sovereignty, 10–13; concepts of representation, 13–15; grand American experiment, 1, 19; rights of individuals, 9–10; Shay's Rebellion, 2; sovereignty/autonomy in, 9–10, 13–15, 35

American common law, 12, 25

American constitution: Age of Enlightenment, 15–19, 41–42; colonial experience, 8–15; vs. English constitutional traditions, 4–8. *See also* Articles of Confederation; Constitutional Convention; Executive branch powers; Powers of Congress; Supreme Court

Annapolis Convention, 3

Articles of Confederation: amending, 3, 19; delegates and, 1–2, 4; failings of, 2–4; powers of Congress under, 20–23, 24, 31, 35. *See also* Constitutional Convention

Ashmun, George, 64

Atomic Energy Committee, 98

"Attorney-client privilege," 116

Bailyn, Bernard, 10, 11, 12, 34, 41

Barbary Pirates, 57, 58

Bas v. Tingy (1800), 56

"Bay of Pigs," 94

Biddle, Francis, 80

Bill of Rights, 7–8

Bingham, Hiram, 79

Blackstone, William, 9, 25, 40, 67, 123

Bonaparte, Joseph, 75

Bosch, Juan, 96

Bosnia-Herzegovina, 119, 121

Boston Massacre, 34, 35

Boutros-Ghali, Boutros, 120

Boxer Rebellion, 74

About the Author

ROBERT KENNEDY, Professor, Sam Nunn School of International Affairs, Georgia Institute of Technology, Atlanta, Georgia, previously served as director of the joint German-American George C. Marshall European Center for Security Studies in Germany. In nearly 35 years of government service, he also has served as Civilian Deputy Commandant, NATO Defense College in Rome, Italy; Dwight D. Eisenhower Professor of National Security Studies and research analyst at the U.S. Army War College; Foreign Affairs Officer, U.S. Arms Control and Disarmament Agency; and a command pilot on active duty with the U.S. Air Force and later with the reserve forces. His most recent previous publication is *Of Knowledge and Power: The Complexities of National Intelligence.*